Script and Glyph

STUDIES IN PRE-COLUMBIAN ART & ARCHAEOLOGY
NUMBER THIRTY-SIX

Script and Glyph

Pre-Hispanic History, Colonial Bookmaking and the *Historia Tolteca-Chichimeca*

Dana Leibsohn

Published *by* Dumbarton Oaks Research Library and Collection, Washington, D.C.
Distributed *by* Harvard University Press, 2009

General editor Joanne Pillsbury
Managing editor Grace Morsberger
Art director Denise Arnot
Proofreader Hilary Parkinson

ISBN 978-0-88402-361-6 (cloth)
ISBN 978-0-88402-342-5 (paper)

Library of Congress Cataloging-in-Publication Data

Leibsohn, Dana.
    Script and glyph : pre-hispanic history, colonial bookmaking and the
    historia tolteca-chichimeca / Dana Leibsohn ; Joanne Pillsbury, general editor.
    p. cm.—(Studies in pre-Columbian art & archaeology ; no. 36)
    Includes bibliographical references.
    ISBN 978-0-88402-361-6 — ISBN 978-0-88402-342-5 (pbk.)
    1. Chichimecs—History. 2. Toltecs—History. 3. Manuscripts,
Nahuatl—Mexico—Cuauhtinchan—History. 4. Bibliothèque nationale de France.
Manuscript. Mexicain 46-58. 5. Cuauhtinchan (Mexico)—History. 6. Cuauhtinchan
(Mexico)—Maps. I. Pillsbury, Joanne. II. Dumbarton Oaks. III. Title.
F1219.8.C55L45 2009
972'.01—dc22   2008039499

Printed in China by Oceanic Graphics Printing, Ltd.

*To Marian and Gene, who first taught me that
our own past is not the only one that matters.*

TABLE OF CONTENTS

ILLUSTRATIONS

FOREWORD

A NUMBER OF REMARKABLE sixteenth-century manuscripts and paintings from the town of Cuauhtinchan, in the state of Puebla, Mexico, have survived to the present day. Several of these are prose documents on European paper, such as the *Libro de los Guardianes*, and others are finely painted maps on *amatl*, a bark paper favored in Pre-Hispanic times. Perhaps the best known of the Cuauhtinchan documents, however, is a manuscript composed in alphabetic script and on European paper, but with exquisite paintings recording ancestral migrations and sacred landscapes in a composite style that draws from both Pre-Hispanic and European models. Known as the *Historia Tolteca-Chichimeca*, it was created in the mid-sixteenth century, a time of particular fluidity when social relations, questions of territorial control, and political authority were in flux. The *Historia* addresses the presentation of the past and its legacy of ancestral time and place in the concerns of the present.

The *Historia Tolteca-Chichimeca* was created at a pivotal transitional moment in central Mexico, bridging an era when pictorial manuscripts dominated, and witnessing the rising hegemony of alphabetic texts. The *Historia* was composed using both systems, yet, as Dana Leibsohn notes, neither was fully trusted. Leibsohn analyzes the choices made by the patron, don Alonso de Castañeda, and *tlacuilos* enlisted to create the manuscript. How does one create a history? Which narratives are included and which are strikingly absent? Which modes of representation are called upon to convey certain types of information? Leibsohn argues how the very practice of history-keeping itself sustains or challenges a current reality.

Central to the *Historia Tolteca-Chichimeca* is the creation, representation, and understanding of landscape. In the recording of ancestral migrations the *Historia* painters and writers delineate territory, noting boundaries and their histories, but also revealing relationships with a sacred landscape, detailing how relationships with territory were constantly re-inscribed, both on the landscape itself and in the documents that were created to record these relationships. In this sense, *Script and Glyph: Pre-Hispanic History, Colonial Bookmaking and the* Historia Tolteca-Chichimeca is a particularly appropriate volume for Dumbarton Oaks, as it crosses the boundaries of two of the three traditional areas of study here, Pre-Columbian and Landscape.

I would like to thank Dana Leibsohn for illuminating both the complexities of the creation of this particular sixteenth-century history, and the broader challenges inherent in recording landscape and memory. I would also like to thank Elizabeth Boone, Jeffrey Quilter, Grace Morsberger, Hilary Parkinson, and Emily Gulick for their kind help in bringing about this publication.

Joanne Pillsbury
Director of Studies, Pre-Columbian Program

THIS IS AN ACCOUNT of a 500-year-old book that contains narratives that are older yet by centuries. Known today as the *Historia Tolteca-Chichimeca*, this work contains a remarkable convergence of histories—some colonial, others Pre-Hispanic; most have been scripted in Nahuatl, others have been sketched in earthy chromatic hues. Beyond its written words, the *Historia* is filled with maps and glyphs, songs and prayers, landscape scenes and ancestral portraits. What comes together in its pages are not merely disparate accounts of the past, but highly distinct and sometimes dueling modes of representation. The *Historia* is thus a work deeply engaged with the burden of making history.

How to lend the past visual and material meaning? That was the *Historia's* charge. The answer it offered must have been acceptable, for the man who commissioned it, don Alonso de Castañeda, was a patron of noble status and standards. Not just any history would do—not for him, nor for his ancestors, or for that matter, posterity. And this was a man who knew about history.

In the summer of 1546, perhaps at just about the time he commissioned his book, don Alonso found himself in Mexico City. In the company of other indigenous notables he had traveled to the capital to press for the restitution of Pre-Hispanic boundaries. Documents tell us that don Alonso and his compatriots found the road to Mexico City from Cuauhtinchan, their home near Cholula in what is today the state of Puebla, long and wearying, and their stay in the capital expensive. Yet they must have seen in this expedition a fitting venture. In exchange for their time and money, the persuasive words of lawyers and interpreters could return to these nobles what had once been rightfully theirs: land holdings of considerable antiquity.

Ventures of this sort, in which indigenous people sought territorial and legal justice from the authorities of New Spain, were not uncommon in the sixteenth century. Nor was it exceptional for such cases, as did this one, to turn on the testimony of elders who could recite how, under Mexica rulership, custom and land were distributed. No sense of colonial nostalgia is betrayed in this; such appeals represented no particular affection for the former regime. Rather, those who had prospered under the rule of Pre-Hispanic lords quickly learned that Spaniards would listen to—and oft times respect—how affairs and properties had been arranged and claimed in centuries past. When they petitioned the Royal Audiencia, the men from Cuauhtinchan played a favored yet effective card: the boundaries set by the Mexica, the boundaries with historical antiquity, were the ones that still mattered most, even as times changed.

There is some poignancy in the role don Alonso fulfilled that summer. Cuauhtinchan had just weathered the worst epidemic in living memory and a series of debilitating agricultural failures wreaked havoc on the survivors. Yet what animated the costly excursion to the capital was the need to apply history. There is, as well, some irony here. When the Mexica conquered the people of Cuauhtinchan in the fifteenth century and redistributed the estates and boundaries, they broke the prestige of local potentates. Among those who suffered the greatest dishonor were the male leaders of don Alonso's lineage. They had to forfeit the rulership of Cuauhtinchan, and watch others ascend in their place. By the mid-sixteenth century, however, newer indignities and greater obstacles required redress. And the territorial array set out at the bitter end of the 1460s by Axayacatzin, the ruler in Tenochtitlan, became the accepted, ancestral order of things.

To modern readers of Latin American history, the dilemma faced by don Alonso seems familiar, yet the implications of his plight remain compelling, particularly to those of us who care about the Pre-Hispanic past. This is because don Alonso's grasp of what constituted—indeed, what could constitute—a proper, ancient history had no canonical form. The issue stretches beyond colonial rupture (although that surely plays some role), for the Pre-Hispanic past was always contentious. It had never been polished like a jewel to be handed down from generation to generation as if an heirloom. Put simply, there was no one in sixteenth-century New Spain who could tell don Alonso precisely what he could or could not say about the Pre-Hispanic past. This was as true when he proffered his report in the courtroom in Mexico City as it was when he pored over his manuscript at home. The shape of the past had to be negotiated, time and again, by each community and its elders. No one would have started from scratch, but neither did any local leader enjoy the luxury of truths set in stone.

Such historical negotiations leave too few traces. This is one reason why the *Historia*, with its ambitions to anchor the Pre-Hispanic past via word and image, is no incidental object. If we read this book carefully, we sense how finely tuned are its ancient passions. The *Historia* summons, for instance, far more enthusiasm and exuberance for deeds that unfolded deep in antiquity than it does for the "recent Pre-Hispanic past," the years just antecedent to, and including don Alonso's own birth. How ancestral warriors centuries before prepared for battle, what colors they painted their shields, how carefully stitched were their uniforms—this is the kind of history upon which the *Historia* lingers. Given all that transpired in indigenous towns in the first generations after the Spanish conquest, setting such narratives of antiquity down in alphabetic script, on sheet after sheet of imported European paper, could hardly have been don Alonso's only alternative.

In the book *The Mestizo Mind*, Serge Gruzinski turns his keen eye to early colonial visual culture, developing the metaphor of the attractor in which, magnetlike, elements once foreign to one another converge on painted surfaces (2002: 128–129). This magnet metaphor is useful, opening as it does the possibility of repulsion as well as of affinity. It reminds us that not just anything (or even everything) from the Pre-Hispanic past could be brought into alignment with the colonial present. To understand the antique ambitions of both don Alonso and the *Historia* requires a reckoning with the conceptual horizons of possibility, not just the material facts of their existence. Of course don Alonso would not have thought of things precisely this way. But therein lies my point. His history was not really a

Pre-Hispanic history; it was a history built of the possibility that the Pre-Hispanic and the colonial could successfully engage, and hold the attention of one another. If nothing else, we should learn this lesson from the convergence of don Alonso and the *Historia*.

Ultimately, we do not know if don Alonso was proud of his book. In time, it would become a family treasure. Passed down from generation to generation, it would have garnered a certain authority. Later yet it would be collected, with other local documents, and sent to Europe, its value in no small part set by its rarity and its ability to spark curiosity. To modern sensibilities, a bittersweet caché clings to the *Historia*. It is not the most famous book of indigenous history now known from central Mexico, nor does it shed much direct light on colonial realities. All manner of things that would help us understand don Alonso's sense of the world—how he and his compatriots thought of local Spanish officials, how they managed their fields and collected their tribute, what they hoped for when they prayed on Sundays, or how they raised their daughters—these rituals barely register in the annals' account. What this 500-year-old book can tell us, however, is no small verity: how palpable the desire was to keep the ancestors close by, even at the exclusion of so much. The language of don Alonso's manuscript may seem today digressive, and its paintings as challenging as they are handsome. The *Historia* remains an extraordinary testament, however, to what it meant be alive in the sixteenth century, yet think in terms of other times.

Dana Leibsohn

ACKNOWLEDGMENTS

WE ALL OWE MORE intellectual debts than we can pay. In my case, the debts seem particularly long-standing, as I first began work on Cuauhtinchan as a graduate student in the 1990s. While they would not endorse all that appears here, nor necessarily have suggested that I take the approach I have, Elizabeth Hill Boone, Doris Heyden, James Lockhart, Cecelia F. Klein, and Mary Elizabeth Smith have been extraordinary mentors and teachers. They were the first to convince me that Mexican manuscripts could be interesting documents, and they played no small role in helping me develop the skills to comprehend this. From them I learned to read Nahuatl and fine points of manuscript history, and to take seriously the most vexing issue about these documents, which is why anyone should care. Keiko Yoneda was both gracious and generous when I first visited Mexico to begin my study of sixteenth-century Cuauhtinchan, so too were colleagues at Dumbarton Oaks and the Center for Advanced Study in the Visual Arts at the National Gallery of Art— both institutions that supported my early research on the *Historia* and *Mapas de Cuauhtinchan* with predoctoral fellowships. More recently, David Carrasco's project on *Mapa 2 de Cuauhtinchan* and the colleagues I have met in that context have been generous in sharing work and debating ideas. My sharpest interlocutors—who have patiently admonished me to think ever harder about what can actually be known (and said) about the Pre-Hispanic past—include Daniel Bridgman, Carolyn Dean, Tom Cummins, Byron Hamann, Barbara Mundy, and Joanne Rappaport. Some of them have heard more about the *Historia* than they ever imagined possible. Jeffrey Quilter, María Bernal-García, and two anonymous reviewers have made many helpful suggestions. This manuscript was written while I was teaching at Smith College and I gratefully acknowledge the College's support, from its exceptional interlibrary loan program to its help in making newly photographed images of the *Historia* a possibility. I owe Monique Cohen, at the Bibliothèque Nationale de France, much gratitude for allowing me to study the original *Historia* and other manuscripts held there, and to Georgette Ballez for assisting me with photographs of the *Historia*. Joanne Pillsbury has been unstinting in her encouragement and her willingness to usher this manuscript into a publishable form. Thank you, all. And thank you, especially, Dan.

D.L.

PRE·HISPANIC LEGACIES,
CONIAL BOOKS

PRE·HISPANIC LEGACIES, COLONIAL BOOKS

THIS PROJECT OPENS in the colonial past, travels back in time toward
Pre-Hispanic antiquity and then forward again, drawing to a close in the present.
In crossing this temporal span, the argument I make concerns the practice of keeping
history: to understand the Pre-Hispanic past in nuanced and sophisticated ways, the
predilections of colonial and modern history-writing cannot be incidental. While the
three epochs seem to form a continuous chronology—flowing, in principle, from the
Pre-Hispanic to the colonial era and into the modern moment—the relationship is
in actuality more reciprocal. In conceptual terms, this study explores the texture and
contours of this reciprocity. In the material and visual realm, this project focuses on
a hand-painted manuscript from the sixteenth century; and geographically speaking,
my study is grounded in central Mexico, in a town called Cuauhtinchan. It was
here, between 1530 and 1560, that local Nahuas produced a wealth of Pre-Hispanic
histories. What those histories came to mean, how they came to be regarded,
we first sense from the documents belonging to a dying colonial woman.

In July of 1652, in her last will and testament, doña María Ruiz de Castañeda
parsed her belongings, leaving what she had of value to her progeny and associates.
A Nahua, Christian woman, doña María traced her descent from the nobility of
Cuauhtinchan (whose name translates as "Home of the Eagle"). It was there, in the
cemetery of the Franciscan *convento*, that she asked to be buried. Although doña
María was a woman of illustrious indigenous ancestry, her possessions were unlikely
to impress contemporaries of Spanish descent, the truly affluent of Mexico City, or
even Puebla—the nearest major city to Cuauhtinchan. Yet by local standards she was
a woman of substantial wealth; the majority in Cuauhtinchan were far poorer than
she. Topping the list of objects doña María offered her kin were various plots of land.
Territorial holdings comprised the lion's share of material riches, and this was typical
for a woman of her social position in a town such as Cuauhtinchan. Other bequests
were familiar and preeminently practical ones: metates and doors, a marble statue.

Doña María's testament never lingers unduly on any particular object, and this,
too, was common in that time and place. It does, however, single out an unusual
instrument and its legacy: doña María leaves to Miguel Ruiz, a man who may well
have been a relative (although he figures in her will as merely an "yndio del dicho
pueblo"), a collection of family papers proffered as testimony to the noble ancestry
of her lineage and conquests of its land (Reyes García 1988: 173). Precisely what
Miguel Ruiz did with these papers, precisely how he might have wielded them, we do

not know, although he must have invested some labor and care in their preservation. Almost a century later they were culled from his hometown by a European collector; today they still survive, under the modern name *Historia Tolteca-Chichimeca*.

In formal terms, these testimonial documents intermix pages of Nahuatl script and vividly colored paintings set out upon European paper (pl. 4) with some leaves left only partially painted or nearly blank. The narrative focus rests upon the Pre-Hispanic past, with alphabet and glyphs keeping a count of indigenous years—Reed, Flint Knife, House, and Rabbit—in the form of annals. It is this compilation, this hybrid collection of history papers, which forms the seminal object of my study. As a work deeply entangled with events and cultural practices from long ago, the *Historia* prompts a seemingly simple question: what can these papers reveal to us about shifting ambitions to know the ancient past? The answer, it turns out, implicates not only doña María, but also her ancestral kin and their aspirations for a prosperous future. As it does us.

Today the *Historia* resides in Paris, in the Bibliothèque Nationale de France (see Appendix 1 for a thorough description and plates 1–18). Known as the Manuscript Mexicain #46–50, #51–53, and #54–58, the gently decomposing folios have been imprinted with the stamp of their French collectors, two gentlemen named J. M. A. Aubin and Eugène Goupil. No doubt, this arrangement would have astonished don Alonso. His sense of record keeping was local to a fault: the *Historia* works mightily to thrust his ancestors into the limelight, to foreground his *altepetl*.[1] Across its pages is manifest a partiality of view contrived to the considerable advantage of both the *Historia's* birthplace, Cuauhtinchan, and its patrons, the Castañeda lineage. Yet the practice of conserving archaic documents, of curating them as patrimony to be passed from one generation to the next, might have struck a reassuring chord with don Alonso. For as Luis Reyes García has convincingly argued, don Alonso's book became the very papers mentioned in doña María's mid-seventeenth-century will (Reyes García 1977: 6, 10; 1988: 172–174). As it happens, doña María was the granddaughter of don Alonso, and her passing of the manuscript seems to conform to family custom. Created a century before her death, the *Historia* had been owned by two generations of relations who, through acts of conservation and prescient bequest, turned these annals into a family heirloom.

Although it is the tendency of archivists to label and sort documents, making order out of the untidiness of the past, for the *Historia's* European collectors, order did not come easily. In Paris, they inventoried the manuscript pages as three separate items, with nineteenth-century facsimiles of its paintings interspersed among those of the sixteenth-century. Other pictorial documents from Cuauhtinchan not original to the manuscript also have been folded into the current collection of papers, and on many a page there appear miniscule glosses in French, and sometimes Spanish. These scripted accessories, which are modern in date, seek to anchor the slippage of Nahuatl text and painted scene, sometimes to little effect. All this makes it difficult to grasp how the *Historia* once looked, how the visual narrative of the whole coalesced for don Alonso and his constituency—be they members of his lineage or other local leaders with histories of their own. Yet the practice of copying records, and of salting new works inspired by old among the leaves of an original, such that the pages and stories of one run into the other, is something don Alonso would have understood well. For even in the 1540s and 1550s, at the time of its creation, the *Historia* was a mélange of Pre-Hispanic (and perhaps other, earlier colonial-era) scraps and fragments, fashioned ceremoniously into a European-looking book. To craft such a history required not only the sorting of old documents but also their copying, redaction, and re-assembly. There may not be many points upon which don Alonso's life or project impinges upon those we undertake today, but his commitment to objects sutured from, and then back into, other histories offers a significant beginning.

Questions of Interpretation

Of all the manuscripts to survive from sixteenth-century Mexico, the *Historia* is extraordinarily complex visually. Heroes and warriors, ancestral landscapes and sacred cities tumble across its pages; the paintings tempt our iconographic impulses and this in turn encourages us to marvel at their chromatic dexterity and intricacy. When, as a graduate student, I first set eyes upon the *Historia*, it struck me as a curiously intimidating object. Its scripted words coursed riverlike one into the other, its pictures seemed foreign, unmanageable, and immanently untranslatable; no less stymieing was the fact that my Nahuatl was, at best, nascent and the field of art history still harbored considerable indifference to the kind of "derivativeness" associated with colonial manuscript painting. It was James Lockhart who first convinced me to sit vigil with the manuscript, to see what it might reveal to a contemporary interlocutor. It was good advice. Getting to know the *Historia* was not wasted energy.

The queries one might put to this manuscript are many in number and diverse in kind. Given my intellectual leanings, I am most compelled to inquire about the relationships the *Historia* constructs between an ancient, Pre-Hispanic past and the colonial "present" in which the manuscript first circulated. Simply put, the *Historia* raises the question of how, in the first generations after the Spanish conquest, Pre-Hispanic history was structured by Nahuas, the descendents of the central Mexicans often known today as the Aztecs or Mexica. The temporal issue is critical here, for in the mid-sixteenth century people with direct experiences and memories of Pre-Hispanic life were still alive. Fewer than twenty manuscripts of Pre-Hispanic manufacture have survived to the present, even though before the Spanish conquest, nobles, priests, and elders possessed significant collections of pictorial histories and prognosticatory books. Knowledge of the Pre-Hispanic period today must be gleaned from artifacts and post-conquest accounts which, due to the nature of conquest, come to us multiply mediated.

Of course the past always takes form via translation of one type into another—image, language, gesture, memory. What concerns me here, in particular, are the material and symbolic forms of the *Historia*'s Pre-Hispanic past. For this manuscript, while hardly a record of memory pure and simple, can reveal much about the ways in which Pre-Hispanic history was retold, and ultimately remembered. Underlying what follows is my conviction that only by understanding how indigenous people organized and registered their histories can we begin to know the limits of our own modes of explanation, our own historical designs.[2] And so the story I tell does not focus upon what "really happened" in Pre-Hispanic, or even colonial times; rather, I seek to tease from the *Historia* what passed as influential history in an influential family in the first decades after the founding of New Spain.

It is perhaps obvious but nonetheless important that the *Historia* was created during a time of cultural and economic upheaval in central Mexico. In the mid-sixteenth century, for instance, people in Cuauhtinchan were forcibly relocated to a newly designated site under the Spanish policy of congregation; hundreds had been lost to the catastrophic power of recently introduced disease; and harsh lessons were passed down as Christianity struggled to make itself at home in this region (Medina Lima 1995; Ruiz Medrano 2007). Yet this manuscript was not a tragedy written by an indigenous nobleman watching his life evaporate into thin air; it is not an attempt to gather up all that existed just as it faded from view. The *Historia* was, to the contrary, a cagey enterprise in which the past that it deserves is the past that it retrieves. Indeed, this pluck is part of its charm.

To be clear, don Alonso's history book does not, in the end, cohere into a treatise on "Pre-Hispanicity." Others have asked how true (and, inversely, how false) is the *Historia*, but such queries miss the point. Pre-Hispanic history never had just one, authoritative configuration that history-keepers could, if up to the challenge, describe with accuracy. As with so many others' antiquity, certain facts may have been widely accepted, but their structure and scope demanded persistent reconsideration in order to sustain their significance. Ultimately, it is the morpho-genesis of Pre-Hispanic history that my study explores. To extract this from colonial records, I ask the documents two questions: 1) for high-status Nahuas, what limits and conditions of possibility are discernable in sixteenth-century accounts of pre-conquest times; and 2) how were memories of the past re-cast and lent material substance at a time when neither alphabetic writing nor pictorial imagery was fully trusted by indigenous writers?

The path I pursue below is that of a case study. In more innovative corners of the humanities, the extended study of isolated objects—i.e., a particular manuscript in lieu of comparative projects or thematizations—retains a musty smell. Yet I relish this opportunity to unpack the *Historia*: as a self-referential entity, a convergence of contradictory forces and processes, an object with a social life. In part, this is propelled by the predelictions of my discipline. Apart from its devotion to iconographic decryption, twenty-first-century manuscript-studies remain riveted to "close reading" techniques; iconographic decoding persists as the sine qua non of art-historically driven investigations, with semiotic analysis coming close on its heels. Indeed, even a cursory scan of works published recently suggests the vibrant affinity for colonial manuscript painting, especially among accomplished iconographers and those with semiotic leanings (e.g., Asselbergs 2004; Boone 2000, 2005; Carrasco and Sessions 2007b; Diel 2005; Douglas 2003; Magaloni 2003; Navarrete 1999, 2000; Russo 2005; Schwaller 2003; Stone 2004; and Yoneda 2001, 2003, 2005).

Beyond this I have taken up the close reading of a single object in order to examine a question often overlooked in the field: the relationship of the part to the whole. There are two levels to this. First, in the case of the *Historia*, scholars have fixated on oft-quoted scenes and passages that relate to broad patterns of belief in Mesoamerica, particularly those featuring the sacred caves and cities of Chicomoztoc and Cholula, ignoring the broader scope and meaning of the document's internal machinations, many of which bear directly on the selfsame scenes. The question is whether we learn something new or grander by looking at the complexities of the ensemble. Second, there exist an embarrassingly small number of indigenous manuscripts that scholars outside our field can name or, even more tellingly, engage in a sustained way—perhaps the *Florentine Codex* and *Codex Mendoza*, perhaps Felipe Guaman Poma de Ayala's *Nueva crónica y buen gobierno*—but the list quickly collapses. What I wonder is this: if one takes seriously the structures and facts embedded in indigenous accounts, would there be reason enough to render the canon of history more inclusive? Perhaps more sophisticated readings of the *Historia* or its contemporaries are by definition irrelevant to work transpiring in other arenas of the humanities and social sciences, but I remain unconvinced this need be the case.

Of the hundreds of manuscripts that exist, why turn to the *Historia*? As one of the most extensive histories known today that was penned in Nahuatl and created to serve local, indigenous ends, the *Historia*—which is our name for this document, not don Alonso's—is as unusual as it is representative of a peculiar historical moment. As a set of painted annals, it stood apart from other forms of pictorial and historical record keeping in Cuauhtinchan. Yet the narrative it retells and the anxieties it sets into motion are hardly unique. What can emerge from the study of this kind of manuscript is a sense of the particularities of one historical enterprise, but also a broader purchase on the fashioning of Pre-Hispanic history, especially by those who directly witnessed their tales being absorbed into grander narratives and events as the arrival of Europeans reverberated through their social fabric.[3]

In 1521, when the Spaniards subjugated the people of Cuauhtinchan, most of the vanquished were Nahuatl speakers, although Popoloca was also spoken (Gerhard 1972; Swanton 2001). The primary language of the Mexica empire, Nahuatl emerged as the indigenous lingua franca of New Spain. Yet language was not the only cultural trait Cuauhtinchan shared with other altepetl in central Mexico on the eve of conquest. The Cuauhtinchantlaca (people of Cuauhtinchan) also owed tribute to the Mexica, worshipped deities venerated elsewhere in the region, and kept records in oral and pictorial form. Although local differences separated the people of Cuauhtinchan from those of adjacent altepetl, in the eyes of administrators—first Mexica, then Spanish—this community was an inscribed atoll in a vast cultural sea. Indeed, evidence suggests that the sixteenth-century experiences of the Cuauhtinchantlaca were echoed by those of hundreds of other Nahuas. In part, then, it is the unexceptional quality of don Alonso's hometown and daily life that leads me to his history.

There are other factors to consider, however. Elizabeth Brumfiel has recently noted that certain aspects of Aztec imperial ideology did "not play well in the provinces" (2006: 174). One reason to look at Cuauhtinchan, which had been subjugated by the Mexica but did not share in all of the practices of the capital, lies in attempting to understand how patterns of history-keeping sustained or challenged broader patterns of imperial dominance. The altepetl of Cuauhtinchan spawned one of the most coherent corpora of autonomous Nahua histories from early New Spain known today. These materials include two sets of annals: the *Historia* and the *Libro de los Guardianes*, and four historical paintings: *Mapas de Cuauhtinchan* 1, 2, and 3, and the *Mapa Pintado en papel Europeo y aforrado en el Indiano* (see discussion, Appendix 2). All but the *Libro de los Guardianes* were created between 1530 and 1570, and assembled together, this collection represents an exceptional catalog of indigenous histories produced at the edges of Spanish purview. Neither commissioned by, nor executed for Spanish officials, these histories constitute a discourse that served local designs and ambitions. The *Historia* therefore takes on meaning as part of a larger, but profoundly local indigenous historical enterprise. In addition, although don Alonso's manuscript finds parallels in the other sixteenth-century histories from Cuauhtinchan, it is decidedly unlike them. For only the *Libro de los Guardianes* also relies upon the format of a European-style book to register past events, and while it too presents an annalistic account, its commonalities with the *Historia*, especially in presentation of events and visual appearance, are few and far between. The singularity of the *Historia* thus constitutes the other part of my story.

In the last two decades, those who study how history is fashioned, how it relates to memory or present-day preoccupations have become a force of no small concern to the fields of indigenous visual culture, ethnohistory, and anthropology. The writings of several students of indigenous Andean and Mesoamerican histories, in particular, have simultaneously inspired and vexed me.[4] Indeed, I have tried to build my own study so that it will contribute to, but also run against the grain of, those projects that pore over the fabricated nature of the Latin American past. And yet, without being too presumptuous, I have also tried to approach the *Historia*'s history-project in a way that stretches the terms of debate rather than merely confirms then. That is, I have tried to design this study to consider issues too often left out of the mix.

Among those who study Mesoamerica, the first questions posed about post-conquest accounts of pre-conquest life are what can this work reveal about what happened in Central Mexico before the arrival of Europeans and how much can we trust what such documents say? Our conclusions on both fronts have, overall, been intriguing, if not also unsatisfying. I can think of few studies of Nahua historical manuscripts that do not, when all is said and done, note that these documents fail to provide—at least under our contemporary spotlight of historical inquiry—a fully reliable perspective onto the Pre-Hispanic past. For some, this kind of viewing through a glass darkly is doomed to remain an aporia, for others it is nothing more than a modest snag in the interpretive road.[5] In either case, however, the realists are hard to ignore. It seems nearly unimaginable that indigenous histories cannot gain a purchase on the facts of Pre-Hispanic existence.

The approach that I take with the *Historia* does not resolve this dilemma. I start from the premise that the production of history hinged neither on some remote

Pre-Hispanic dreamtime, nor on a harsh and relentless colonial "high noon" of reckoning. That is, the past did not, by its very nature, demand or requisition records; nor did people in Cuauhtinchan create for themselves a cynical history that served craven material or instrumental ends. While the propagandistic aspect of Mexica history has been well aired, my position renders mute that perspective. So, too, I remain skeptical of certain strains of structural reading of post-conquest histories.[6]

To summarize, then, my claim is that history does not already exist elsewhere, in an "ancient time" awaiting recollection, rather history comes into being in no small part through the tropes and contraptions that record it. Thus the Pre-Hispanic past was neither simply represented by, nor recollected in, the *Historia*. Instead, the cracks and joins of the manuscript—the patterning of its irregularities and smooth passages—constitute one thread of that history.

Beyond this, I find that the visual materials of don Alonso's book were instrumental to its vocation, and thus implicated in its historical fate. Although much sound scholarship has focused on the glyphs and iconography of post-conquest histories, too few readings of documents like the *Historia* regard them as vehicles of significant and complex visual ambition. Yet there can be little doubt that for don Alonso and others of his social sphere, how the past looked—in both material and pictorial detail—was not a small matter. And so, in each of the following chapters, I take up and pursue the visual and lexical strands of his story, holding them up against the annals' scene-setting, textual plots, and rhetorical ruses.

Overall, then, this study tries to balance the art of the close reading against what it might mean, for scholars today, to write history more broadly. In this latter regard, I owe much to those who have studied the meaning and production of history in other parts of the world, including Luisa Passerini (1987, 2007), Donna Merwick (1997, 1999), Tom Conley (1996), and Michel de Certeau (1984). My interpretation of the *Historia* therefore takes as a given the possibility that significant histories can be read from, and made in, acts as mundane as putting alphabetic script or colored pigment to a page of European-made paper. This suggests that don Alonso's Pre-Hispanic history was no waxy impression of a prior world, nor was it a manipulative take on ancient truths. I have attempted to regard it as an object that perpetually recreated him even as he commissioned and reviewed its lineaments. He knew more and different things about the past each time he read from his book. And likewise, upon each rereading, his book coalesced into a different account of things Pre-Hispanic. This reciprocation means that his history was neither contained by the book nor produced apart from it. The field in between—this is where both people and their histories reside and fashion each other.

Don Alonso's Wager

By the time the *Historia*'s scribe set his pen to paper, indigenous people in Cuauhtinchan would have absorbed a visceral education in the daily rituals that followed Spanish settlement in New Spain. There would have been little news, in fact very few surprises, when legal documents were read aloud in local churches;

diseases raced through families pocking those they did not decimate; horses tromped through town bearing men upon their backs; and *encomenderos* collected their tribute in coin, goods, and service. A few in Cuauhtinchan learned how to read and write in Nahuatl, if not also in Spanish; more could have recited the catechism, and most would have heard of Christ's coming. The implications of all this—that is, what the Spanish conquest meant for indigenous residents of central Mexico—was not so much explicitly articulated as lived. In the mid-sixteenth century, in towns like Cuauhtinchan, men and women were still alive who could recall Pre-Hispanic events as well as the early brutality unleashed upon pre-conquest remnants of belief and ritual and the bearing of ancient witness. Don Alonso was certainly one such player in this game of life-after-conquest. What precisely he experienced or remembered of the Pre-Hispanic past remains elusive, but some of his recollections would have been writ upon his body and inscribed in visual memory, not strictly inherited as stories from others.

This point is worth underscoring because the relationship among don Alonso, the *Historia*, and Pre-Hispanic antiquity is a tangled one with some formidable knots. The *Historia* is not signed—at least none of the pages that have come down to us bear the signature of a sixteenth-century writer, painter, or reader. Reyes García's argument that the document was don Alonso's, I find wholly plausible and worthy of exploration. And so, I bind don Alonso's name to the *Historia* throughout this study more insistently than others have in the past. On one hand, this merely reiterates a historical fact, but it is also a strategy to encourage us, as modern inter-preters, to consider how forcefully Pre-Hispanic histories might condense individual ambitions, not merely those dispersed across an entire lineage, community, or ethnic enclave. To be sure, calling attention to don Alonso's ownership of the *Historia* elevates his historical status and, more to the point, his ambitions. Some readers may find my commitment to his aspirations superfluous and prefer the material splendor of the book. I see no reason, however, to shortchange the man. Moreover, there are too few indigenous dossiers we can even begin to approach—much less know—in conjunction with a significant pictorial compendium. This dilemma is particularly acute when we seek to reconstruct the perspectives of Nahuas born before the wave of Spanish settlers curled across the Atlantic. In 2009, it may be intellectually unfashionable to fix our eyes too keenly on patrons and intentions, but in the case of colonial manuscripts too many still circulate as iconographic reservoirs and signifiers of indigeneity cut loose from local aspirations.

From here, however, the interpretive ground grows slipperier. To tie a book to a man's name is not to say the two formed one seamless project. Nothing survives to reveal, in any direct or precise way, what don Alonso imagined or sought when he commissioned the *Historia*, and so I do not wish to argue that the *Historia* was wholly of his design, or that its execution fully satisfied his aims. In fact, unlike the *Codex Selden*, which couched its antiquity to accommodate presentation in a legal setting (Smith 1994), it is uncertain whether don Alonso ever sought readers outside of Cuauhtinchan, any eyes apart from those of family and peers. Beyond this, no documents have surfaced to illuminate how, on any given day, don Alonso might have handled his papers—where he stored them, when he consulted them, whether any of the paintings or revisions represented his handiwork. There is so much that cannot be known.

Yet if we attend diligently to the manuscript's formal cues, and compare the *Historia* with other local histories, this 500-year-old book requires understanding, not merely as a history of the ancestors but as a sizeable investment of material and symbolic capital. And with investment, we know, there is an attendant risk. In commissioning the *Historia*, don Alonso shouldered considerable anxiety and ambition that, although not explicitly articulated in the document, surely framed its production. For unlike other sixteenth-century histories from Cuauhtinchan, the *Historia* is not a programmatic pictorial narrative painted on bark paper or cloth. Nor is it a screenfold, the other main variety of pictorial record known to predate the Spanish conquest. Neither is it a solely alphabetic text of the kind that often circulated through New Spain at mid-century.

Rather don Alonso's book has the whiff and the look and feel of a newfangled type of history: it resembles a European-style codex, replete with alphabetic calligraphy, yet it displays glyphs and paintings of a style anchored in Pre-Hispanic customs. Certainly within a book of pre-conquest events it would have been possible—perhaps even desirable—to eschew, or at the very least, to bracket European record-keeping conventions. Just a few years earlier in Cuauhtinchan a painting of ancestral boundaries on European paper accomplished precisely this (fig. 17, see chapter 3, page 72). It is therefore neither incidental nor insignificant that the *Historia* takes another route. Don Alonso's book makes it clear that while his commitment to the past was profound, he had little interest in accounting for ancient events in any ancestral media of the day. Instead, he seemed to want a book that was both old and new, that simultaneously preserved and updated the past.

What this book may have wanted in return is a question that must be set to the margins (Mitchell 1996). As it is, it is difficult to say precisely *why* don Alonso's book differs so profoundly from other local records. It was not mere happenstance: the *Historia*'s form was too complex, its internal logic too consistent, and the labor and effort of its construction too dear. Moreover there exist logical visual and structural parallels with European books of the era which suggest the scribe(s) knew well the mechanics and meanings of imported models (Fiering and Mathes 1990). James Lockhart has taught us much about Nahua history-keeping, but when he calls the *Historia* a hodgepodge, his judgment is too hasty (1992: 350). This is no catch-as-catch-can kind of history. Indeed, if we are to understand not only the material and visual conditions of the *Historia* but also their implications, the heuristic metaphor that seems most apt is the creative wager. I thus have come to see the *Historia* as a kind of nervy gamble: this invented form of record-keeping, unlike others known and used nearby, is the one most befitting Pre-Hispanic history; this new way is the one worth entrusting with the virtues of ancient knowledge. What was at stake for don Alonso in this venture, I am reluctant to put too fine a point on. This unsettles my positivist and authorial impulses, yet we would be mistaken to presume don Alonso wanted just one thing from his history. No one ever does.

By many measures, don Alonso and his kin were faring well enough in the first years after the Spanish conquest. Their lot, however, was not beyond improvement; nor did local conditions seem to offer any particularly safe harbors. The shifting tides of local life in Cuauhtinchan at mid-century were registered both in that town (Medina Lima 1995; *Historia* 1976; Reyes García 1988), and since by modern scholars (Gerhard 1972; Leibsohn n.d.; Olivera 1976, 1978; and Ruiz Medrano 2007). What is clear from both kinds of accounts is that don Alonso's life must have been far from tragic, but his moorings had once seemed considerably more secure. Seen in this light, the *Historia* becomes a way to think anew about the predicament of indigenous leaders in the early years of colonial enterprise in Mexico. The relationship it struck between inheritance and invention was its gamble. Like many a bet, the outcomes were less than predictable, and whether don Alonso would have considered his game a draw or a win is impossible to say. It could not have been a catastrophic loss, for the *Historia* became a family heirloom and Nahuas did not treat objects of insignificant value in this way.

To modern historians, it is this question of value—of what dividends the *Historia* could have returned—that seems most confounding. What a gambler values in any wager, however, rests on the power of the imaginary as much as any promise of material gain. We learn this from Las Vegas. When people borrow money against a usurious credit card to keep themselves in play at the gaming tables, more is at stake than the sheer monetary value pegged to any dice. To wager is to risk, but also to imagine and hope. No gambler willfully spends his chits without some anticipated chance of success, some hope for a perceptible change of destiny. Today, given what we know of Latin American and colonial history, the prospects of an indigenous nobleman pinning his aspirations to history may seem a desperate gesture. Yet in the mid-sixteenth century, for a man like don Alonso, the *Historia* represented a genuine investment. And we should trust he was no fool. The recasting of history that his book accomplishes was a gamble with memory, but also an optimistic projection into an unknowable future.

We are told that the act of remembering, like the act of forgetting, is fraught with strategic expediencies. Thus don Alonso's preoccupation with times Pre-Hispanic, no less than his aspirations for the future, were played close to the vest. If he had made his thoughts public at all, he would have spoken of them quite differently than I shall in the following pages. Even so, his story would also have drawn together fortuitous fragments; it would have gleaned meanings from written passages, painted images, and memories. The intensity of his account of Pre-Hispanic times would also have cast certain affairs into shadow, and through those absences brought others to light. This does not render his history deliberately tendentious or tainted, although it does remind us that his pre-conquest past, like any coherent past, requires fabrication and not passive remembrance.

This is no less true today. And so my account of the *Historia* proposes a wager of its own. Although I do my level best to grasp the stakes, if not the lessons, that don Alonso's history was designed to cover, my view of the Pre-Hispanic cannot but diverge from his. I therefore aspire to his model of history-keeping—betting that any Pre-Hispanic past worth knowing is one worth updating.

A Game Plan

My explication of the *Historia* and its interest in things Pre-Hispanic unfolds across four chapters and two appendices. In Chapter 1, I begin with the colonial history of don Alonso and the *Historia* and end by tracing the narrative sweep of the manuscript. Chapter 2 turns from the colonial period to antiquity, and specifically to the ways in which ancestral figures were cast into history; the main issue is how Pre-Hispanic alliances and enmities lent the past its texture. Chapter 3 covers the land, and assesses the mutual construction of territory and history. In the final chapter of this study, Chapter 4, I attempt to stand back from the manuscript and don Alonso's aspirations. Here, I assess the qualities of the Pre-Hispanic past that the *Historia* creates and ask why, today, this history might still matter. Appendix 1 examines the main pictorial images of the *Historia*, attending to their visual compositions, iconographies, and narrative implications. Appendix 2 discusses the provenance of the sixteenth-century pictorial histories from Cuauhtinchan.

When conducting my research on the *Historia*, I opted to work from the images and texts in the manuscript, rather than redraw those scenes or re-script those pages. This was less out of any sense of purity, than the conviction that this working method could sharpen my sense of the distance between there and here, then and now. Because this theme, the tension between past legacies and present histories, anchors the whole project, I have been fortunate that Dumbarton Oaks was willing to publish photographs of the indigenous images discussed here rather than insist upon modern drawings.

A Note About Nahuatl

I have retained the original spelling of the *Historia* scribe when I quote his works directly. For other spellings, I have omitted diacritic marks and, in several places, for clarity, chosen modern over sixteenth-century spelling. Thus Quauhtinchan has become Cuauhtinchan, and Tepeyacac has become Tepeaca. A few Nahuatl words, such as altepetl, teccalli and tlatoani, appear frequently as part of my English text; in these instances, I ask readers to rely upon the context of their use to discern when one altepetl (or teccalli) is at issue, when many.

Notes

1. The basic unit of self-definition and affiliation in post-conquest central Mexico was the altepetl, a Nahuatl word that combines terms for water (*atl*) and mountain (*tepetl*). In some ways similar to contemporary, Western notions of community, the altepetl was a corporate group that possessed and managed specific territory. Each had its own leader: before the conquest and a few years thereafter rulership was dynastic, but over time elected councils became more common. Beyond this, a tradition of ethnic distinctness was put into place; every altepetl fostered and nourished its own, and sometimes competing, historical narratives, its own symbols of identity (Lockhart 1992: 14–58).

2. Joanne Rappaport has recently argued against reifying the boundaries between indigenous and Spanish societies in our constructions of colonial history (2002). While her point is well taken, the histories produced in New Spain in the mid-sixteenth century by indigenous people—even those people such as don Alonso, highly fluent with alphabetic script, Christianity, and the nuances of colonial social practice—differ substantively from other modes of colonial history-keeping; moreover, the particularities of these indigenous documents have the potential to challenge modern modes of writing history in substantive ways. See discussion, Chapter 4.

3. This tension, between representative exempla and the unique object, has long been at play in art historical approaches to Mesoamerica. It is a point to which I return at the end of my study, but for recent, and provocative engagements with the theme and its implications, see Quilter (2001, 2006) and Boone (2006).

4. Among those that have been most helpful, both for specific insights and for the theoretical questions they raise are the studies by Adorno (2000), Boone (1991, 1998, 2000), Florescano (1985), Gruzinski (1993), Lockhart (1992), López-Austin (1985), Mignolo (1995, 2000), Rappaport (1990, 1994), Russo (2005), Salomon (1982, 1998), and Urton (1990).

5. See Cecelia Klein (1995) for a provocative discussion of what can be gleaned about the Pre-Hispanic past from post-conquest manuscripts, and, moreover, our responsibilities to tease what we can from these works.

6. This is not to say that I have not learned much of value from the strengths and limits of such approaches. Indeed, my own teasing of patterns from the *Historia* at times owes much to the writings of Joyce Marcus (1992), Susan Gillespie (1989, 1998), and others who have followed their lead. At the end of the intellectual day, however, I do not find the implications of either propaganda-centered or structuralist arguments fully satisfying. See discussion, Chapter 4.

CHAPTER 1

SUBJECTS OF HISTORY

TO BEGIN AT THE BEGINNING: The *Historia* is of course a book of prospects—a collection of written words and pictures on paper—executed according to material and cultural constraints in a corner of New Spain. In hindsight, we read this as one more document set forth outside an urban center, at just about the time that historical paradigms were dragging Europe and the Americas, Africa and East Asia into the condition of "early modernity." Compared to the grand narratives of the Americas penned in the courts and metropolitan cities of Europe, don Alonso's tropes seem fraught with dubious claims, over-proud of sketchy associations with Pre-Hispanic luminaries, indifferent to historical peccadilloes. This judgment may seem callous: don Alonso and his annals-makers were not looking to write court history. Nor did Europeans have the market cornered on good history-keeping; their records were but one manner of getting to history from memory and back again. Yet we know, as don Alonso certainly knew, more than one kind of history existed. And so his document raises the question of which historical projects shall, or should, or can, figure in the binding of any verifiable past.

To adjudicate historical claims made in the *Historia* is not to blindly accept that all primary documents are equal reserves for exegetical or redemptive labor. It is true that don Alonso's book is a work of unusual visual and rhetorical ambition, and given the uneven reception that early colonial documents have suffered among modern scholars, an effort to reclaim the cultural significance of the *Historia* does not seem misguided. My interest in the hand-painted manuscript, however, extends beyond historical revision. As far as I am able to discern, the *Historia*, although commissioned by a wealthy Nahua man, was penned and painted independently of Spanish authority, and as such represents a core instance in Latin American history-keeping that is distinct from those records crafted for, or in collusion with, Spanish authorities. Whether the *Historia* represents a kind of subaltern history, whether it carves out a niche, or even occupies a middle ground of the sort Richard White (1991) has described, remains an open question. Ultimately I will return to the theme of modern reception, and ask whether deeper knowledge of indigenous accounts such as the *Historia*—and others of its time and place, such as the *Codex Mendoza*, the *Codex Xolotl*, or *Lienzo de Quauhquechollan*—might be used to complicate debates in the fields of American history or early modern visual culture. Perhaps such designs are too grand to be sustained by these documents alone, but if so, we should pursue why this is the case. First, though, it is the colonial and Pre-Hispanic histories of the *Historia* that require unpacking.

Pre-Hispanic Tenochtitlan, Cholula, and Cuauhtinchan became part of New Spain in the sixteenth century through both violent usurpation and more subtle means. The *Historia* narrative, which covers over four hundred years of deed and event, remains obdurately mute about most of this. It would seem that however harsh and unforgiving institutions of colonial rule were, don Alonso's narrative had other concerns. This outward indifference to colonial events, and this privileging of antiquity strikes the modern eye hard, almost begs for explanation. Recent scholarship on colonialism and its legacies has taught us to expect local histories, especially those that bypass metropolitan conventions, to be diffuse in aim and unruly in form (Chakrabarty 2000; Mignolo 2000). In the terms of his day, however, don Alonso harbored the skills, affluence, and wherewithal to write his ancestors into history in any number of ways. His options bore their own limits—some of which were pragmatically driven, some conceptually so. At issue in this chapter, then, are the relationships among these conditions.

The second theme I explore is how, via the narrative of the *Historia*, don Alonso and his kin became the subjects of history. This is not quite the same as reconstructing the colonial mise-en-scène of this manuscript and its patron. If we accept as given the reciprocity of history-writing, then the Pre-Hispanic past cannot (indeed, does not) occupy one epistemological ground, and sixteenth-century existence under Spanish rule another. The two came into being together. It is thus impossible to read the surviving traces of indigenous life in Cuauhtinchan—be they a convento painting, records of a boundary dispute, a set of legal strictures, or excavated urban structures—as simple, static, contextual frames for the Pre-Hispanic ambitions that crisscross don Alonso's book. Rather, all this "evidence" begs the question of historical causality: did the Pre-Hispanic past of the *Historia* exhibit its distinctive material and visual forms because of don Alonso's colonial circumstances, or were those circumstances instead perceived and shaped by the past that was registered in the *Historia*'s pages? What, in other words, was the real, what the representation? As Gabrielle Spiegel has suggested, when writers look back in time, they do not save the past or return it to what once existed; rather they transform that past into something it never was: history (2002). Once written, or recited aloud, such histories participate in the real, they circulate and perform work in the world. This is a lesson in which don Alonso seems to have placed considerable trust. And so, to conclude this chapter, I turn to the narrative strategies through which the ancestors took form, and claimed their meaning, in his history-book.

A Sense of Local Landscapes

In 1548, a colonial inspector (*visitador*) surveying the region south and east of Mexico City passed through Cuauhtinchan. By the time of his visit, don Alonso had been standing at the head of his lineage for nearly thirty years, and knew the social and physical scaffolding of Cuauhtinchan in intimate detail. One way Nahuas described

Fig. 1 View of Cuauhtinchan, Mexico, from San Juan Bautista
(Franciscan convento). *Photograph courtesy of the author.*

an altepetl was by reciting sites and boundary markers, and don Alonso would have
certainly memorized more than one run or two of itineraries along local boundaries.
Indigenous men and women could also have conveyed their sense of place via
Christian similes for gardens and cities as well as via the somatic rites and metaphors
based on treks along roadways, the grooming of fields, and the labor of building new
towns (Burkhart 1989, 1998). The visitador relays none of this, yet had he surveyed
the region beside don Alonso both would have recognized the valley's common
landmarks. Without doubt their descriptions would have diverged, or contested the
valley's finer points from a metaphysical or realtor's perspective, but both parties
would have intuitively grasped the scope (and limits) of the administrative influence
that radiated from Mexico City. Given the nature of colonial politics, neither could
have afforded to undervalue the other's knowledge of the local landscape (fig. 1).

We know from the visitador's census that he counted just over fifteen hundred
households in Cuauhtinchan, each headed by a male occupant overseeing an
extended *familia*. While the survey gives short shrift to the physical distribution
of the community's residents, it does proffer remarks on the local agronomy. Crops
of European origin—wheat and *frutas de Castilla*—stood under cultivation, as did
products indigenous to the region—cochineal, beans, corn, chili, chia, and squashes.
Compared with its neighbors, Cuauhtinchan was a modestly successful town,
neither the largest nor wealthiest in the region, but respectable nonetheless.
In nearby Tepeaca, for instance, Nahuas of social consequence impressed the
visitador with their well-fed sheep; yet, he mentions no livestock in Cuauhtinchan
and so we presume he saw none grazing there. With time, this would change, and
ganado menor would pasture on hillocks owned by the wealthy. At mid-century,
however, no one in Cuauhtinchan had the material resources to purchase or consume
all of the local goods or imports (Paso y Troncoso 1905: 109–111; Reyes García 1988).

Don Alonso's journey to the capital provides further
evidence that the people of Cuauhtinchan were becoming
seasoned survivors of life in New Spain. By 1560, they paid
tribute in material items and services to both the Spanish
crown and an *encomendero*; locally, a *cabildo* governed the
community and notaries kept records in alphabetic Nahuatl.
Within forty years of the Spanish conquest, more than
one ravenous epidemic had consumed the community, a
congregación had been imposed, the construction of a local
church had begun, and the souls of Cuauhtinchan's residents

had fallen prey to a vociferous contest between Dominican and Franciscan friars. People had also witnessed the foundation of Puebla de los Angeles and felt the yoke of its material needs tighten, as the goods and services necessary to sustain the Spanish city bore down upon indigenous communities nearby.[1] There was also the question of land tenure. Between 1532 and 1560, don Alonso's acquaintances and clients found themselves testifying before numerous authorities invested with the power to arbitrate their boundary and territorial disputes. Some officials handed down judgments in favor of Cuauhtinchantlaca, although others did not.[2]

It is also clear from hand-written records and images applied to the walls of public buildings that expressive means of European heritage, not strictly material goods and policies, were reshaping the lives of Cuauhtinchantlaca. The process was not merely an absorptive one: as local builders coursed the stones of their church, and painted its freshly plastered walls, they re-made the imported imagery and architectural models introduced by friars. The Franciscan convento built and reveted not long after 1550 offers a case in point. The church of San Juan Bautista, with its continuous nave and choir above (figs. 2, 3), is an example of the stripped down, spare aesthetic that George Kubler christened the "fortress church" (1948). Two towers flank the western façade, and massive walls enclose the plaza, which stretches away from the building's main entry. While much of the original decoration has been lost or covered over, some of the early murals remain, revealing glimpses of an interior once richly arrayed in color. The ceiling of the apse was painted in trompe l'oeil stonework, and beneath layers of chipping whitewash hints of the church painters' brilliant palette can still be seen. The color scheme ranges across the warm tones—red, pink, orange, and gold—but does not stint on the cool ones, the blues and greens. While some murals appear only in tones of black and gray today, the original painted program betrays a taste for bold contrast: red and blue vibrated against orange backgrounds; orange and green images jostled for attention against red grounds. This fondness for vivid color was fueled at least in part by European graphic conventions, which also inspired, although did not define, much of the convento's visual vocabulary. Putti and griffin-like dragons, ribbons, and urns festoon the chapel walls and side altars (fig. 4). Sometimes these elements decorate large mural planes, achieving a wallpaper-like effect; in other instances they create deliberate frames for Christian paintings.

Today, the restored murals of Juan Gerson in Tecamachalco, which stand not far removed either temporally or geographically, beckon even more pointedly to European prototypes and codified Christian iconography (Camelo Arredondo et al. 1964; Gruzinski 1994). Yet the painted murals of Cuauhtinchan confirm that European visual models were not shunned here. As was the case in other monastic decorative programs, painters in Cuauhtinchan modulated Christian scenes, adding image components of Pre-Hispanic origin, rather than blindly copying imported scenery. For example, fray Geronimo de Mendieta reports that an indigenous calendar wheel had been painted on the plaza façade. And on one wall of the cloister a painted jaguar and eagle stand guard over the Annunciation (fig. 5). This image represents a startling admixture of elements, at least to modern eyes: a quintessential Christian scene, worked up from a woodblock source, framed by the

Fig. 5 Annunciation flanked by eagle and jaguar (mural detail), San Juan Bautista, Cuauhtinchan. *Photograph courtesy of the author.*

avatars of the two primary Mexica warrior societies and a Franciscan knotted cord (Reyes Valerio 1976).

In a tour de force of iconographic analysis, Pablo Escalante Gonzalbo has read the cloister in San Juan Bautista, where this image resides, as an evocation of Christian ideal space and as the Nahua sacred cave of emergence. The painting itself, through an uncanny exchange of iconographic elements, summons the narrative of Christ's conception and Christian associations with felines and raptors, no more and no less than it does the ancestral histories of Cuauhtinchan's noble lineages—including that of don Alonso (1997: 215–236). These concatenations of meaning, while unique in their details, align Cuauhtinchan with other mendicant projects in sixteenth-century Mexico (Edgerton 2001; Peterson 1993; Reyes Valerio 1989). They also call to mind the mélanges Serge Gruzinski describes, as not merely juxtapositions or transpositions; but combinations of "motifs and forms that, whatever their origin—local or European—had already been the object of one or several indigenous reinterpretations" (2002: 128–129). Indeed, the porousness of the graphic conventions here should not be underestimated.

Although the depiction of the Virgin attended by Mexica animals functions as visual marginalia in the broader decorative program of San Juan Bautista, it retains a poignant bearing on the kind of significance both sought and summoned by the *Historia*. Indeed, hovering near the bottom of one folio (f. 19v, ms. 54–58; fig. 6) are a painted eagle and jaguar that enjamb an architectural edifice. Notwithstanding differences in iconographic detail, the cloister mural and the manuscript illustration are strikingly parallel in certain respects. In the annals painting, a building that combines curving, horn-shaped elements with architectural forms derived from European prototypes takes the place of the Annunciation vignette. In the cloister, as in the manuscript, to the right and left the propitious animals stand as sentries to Mary's chamber.

And in both the annals and the mural the eagle and jaguar appear at a scale that supercedes the architectural elements they flank. The dating and stylistic details of these images make a single painter unlikely, with the *Historia* image being the earlier of the two.[3] Nevertheless these two scenes were certainly bound together in an aesthetic conversation across media and time. This fact reveals how deeply and mutually engaged were the *Historia*'s painters and readers with the visual (and spiritual) idioms of their community. The sacred Pre-Hispanic cities painted into this book were, to no small degree, sites that resonated with colonial sacrality as well.

Economies of Lineage and Privilege

Beyond the complexion of Cuauhtinchan at mid-century, we need to consider don Alonso's biography, for the *Historia* conjures a historical stage upon which the Castañeda lineage plays a leading role. We know that don Alonso did not make the expedition to Mexico City in 1546 on his own. He was one of several leaders who spoke in the capital about the Pre-Hispanic past, one of various high-status men deemed qualified to defend the territorial rights of the Cuauhtinchantlaca. Furthermore this was not the only instance in which don Alonso played this kind of role. Five years later, in August of 1553, a dispute between competing factions in Cuauhtinchan summoned to the altepetl a *juez de comisión*

Fig. 6 Eagle and jaguar flanking an elaborate building, *Historia Tolteca-Chichimeca.* Pigment on European paper. Bibliothèque Nationale, Paris, f. 19v, ms. 54–58 (detail). *Photograph courtesy of the Bibliothèque Nationale, Paris.*

from Mexico City. At that hearing, not unlike the other senior men interviewed, don Alonso re-articulated his claim to high status and rightful property and in so doing lodged a conservative plea: the shape of Cuauhtinchan should resemble that of the altepetl his ancestors built in Pre-Hispanic times.[4]

In the 1450s, a locally based apparatus of resource management and administration had become deeply woven into the fabric of daily life in central Mexico. This was no less true in the 1550s. So it is hardly surprising to find indigenous leaders maintaining a stake in the conservatism of community affairs. Moreover, arrangements developed by the Mexica—which opened the most influential roles in the community to a small group of men—had nourished the economic and social interests of individuals like don Alonso. And throughout the sixteenth century, Spanish officials were often willing to recognize and uphold elements of this system. Thus, perpetuity of the Pre-Hispanic past was often fostered by those people with the greatest symbolic and material stakes in the old regime. In this, of course, parallels with other indigenous societies stretch across the history of colonialism.

In the specifically colonial context of New Spain, don Alonso's prestige as a spokesman had many sources. Born before the Spanish conquest into a family of exceptional local prestige, he inherited the position of *tlatoani* (dynastic ruler of an altepetl) in the same year that Cortés forged his alliance with the Tlaxcalans, 1519–1520 (*Historia*, f. 50v, ms. 54–58). In the mid-sixteenth century, the Castañedas dominated one of at least seven powerful groups in Cuauhtinchan. Called *teccalli* (lordly houses), each of these had its own hereditary leaders, genealogical history, and claims to landed estate.[5] In the mid-sixteenth century, then, one of don Alonso's preferred identities was that of lineage leader who exerted influence in the altepetl as the descendant of Pre-Hispanic nobility. So too, in 1553, when he recounted Cuauhtinchan's history before the juez de comisión, don Alonso proffered information as an elder who had living memory of the world that existed before the arrival of Spaniards. In the mid-sixteenth century, his word—both among Cuauhtinchantlaca and colonial officials—carried significant weight.

Records substantiate that, like a Nahua lord in the pre-conquest era, don Alonso's benefits accrued as both tribute payment and territory. In 1564, for instance, he received a weekly tribute of one hen, eighty cacao beans, and the services of four commoners (two men and their wives).[6] In addition, prominent men like don Alonso controlled extensive tracts of territory. In the 1550s, and probably throughout the 1500s, access to land and the right to manage territory was a fundamental prerogative of hereditary standing. Apart from their land holdings, Nahuas retained few opportunities to acquire wealth, much less influence.[7] Although descendants of Pre-Hispanic nobles were not the only Nahuas who sought the material benefits of land management, a comparison of the wills of male leaders with those of humbler people indicates that a definitive gap existed: the amount of territory controlled by a few influential families vastly dwarfed the holdings of others. Yet the actual amount of land dominated by people like don Alonso represents only a slice of the larger picture. Of paramount importance was the tight bond between land ownership and social privilege. Under the Mexica, and under Spanish rule as well, local decisions formed the crux of land tenuring. Thus altepetl leaders kept records of land ownership and updated them as required; they also intervened in daily affairs. For example, land census data from the Cuernavaca region indicates that altepetl officers and local nobles—who in the sixteenth century were often one and the same—wielded the power to assign parcels to individuals (Lockhart 1992: 143). Hence, in communities like Cuauhtinchan, local leaders were not only wealthy landowners, they also acted as de facto curators of community resources.

Yet when the *Historia* was drafted—less than thirty years after the Spanish conquest—all was not running in don Alonso's favor. Although he numbered among Cuauhtinchan's most privileged residents, he was still less fortunate than some. Luis Reyes García has convincingly demonstrated that the teccalli of Cuauhtinchan owed their prestige to Pre-Hispanic origins, and that, within the altepetl, there was a significant differential of power that pitted ambitious men against others. If we follow his analysis, which remains one of the most compelling yet offered for Pre-Hispanic and early colonial Cuauhtinchan (Reyes García 1977: 81–88), the picture that emerges looks somewhat like this. In the post-conquest period, seven teccalli leaders marshaled whatever they possessed in internecine contests to best each other in terms of influence and political advantage. What caught don Alonso was a political situation that had crystallized before the Spanish conquest: the teccalli of Cuauhtinchan were distributed into two rival *parcialidades* (factions)— four teccalli comprised the Nahua parcialidad, three the Pinome. Don Alonso belonged to one of the Nahua groups, yet it was the Pinome that held the more distinguished position in the mid-sixteenth century. The ascent of the Pinome was relatively recent. In fact, the *Historia* goes to some pains to demonstrate that, in ancient times, when Cuauhtinchan was a nascent altepetl, the renown of the Nahua parcialidad went unchallenged. The Nahua faction distinguished itself by fighting valiantly alongside the Tolteca at Cholula. Nahuas also married the daughters of these prestigious allies, and were first to lay claim to the altepetl of Cuauhtinchan. The Pinome, by contrast, were of foreign, as in Mixteca, extraction. Immigrants who arrived in Cuauhtinchan post-altepetl formation, the newcomers prospered and intermarried with people well settled in the region but, in the eyes of the *Historia* writer, they lacked the ancestral luster of the Nahua teccalli. For they could never claim direct descent from the founders of the altepetl and the daughters of the Tolteca. Then, too, from the time of Cuauhtinchan's founding in the twelfth century, Nahua leaders, rather than Pinome, reigned ascendant in the altepetl political structure. It was not until the Tlatelolcans conquered Cuauhtinchan in the fifteenth century that the balance of power shifted to favor the Pinome. When the Spanish subjugated Cuauhtinchan, the descendants of the Pinome were still enjoying hegemony, and they continued to assert their social prerogatives throughout the sixteenth century.

In the 1550s, don Alonso found himself entangled in both fortuitous and lamentable circumstances. By the measure of the average Cuauhtinchan resident, his affluence and social standing were enviable. Yet as a descendant of a Nahua tlatoani, don Alonso belonged to the now-subordinate parcialidad. Although the nobles of the Nahua and Pinome teccalli often struck temporary alliances, evidence suggests that the enmity between them was not inconsequential. For instance, several sixteenth-century records from Cuauhtinchan register the teccalli and/or parcialidad affiliations of local leaders, as well as the history of these divisions within the community. In their careful attention to these distinctions, the documents imply that such social and political divisions colored, and most likely shaped, the aspirations and sway of men like don Alonso. Throughout the 1550s, then, Cuauhtinchan emerges as a unified polity crisscrossed by internal factionalism. In this, the altepetl seems to have been much like others throughout central Mexico where internal diversity—often structured along ethnic and/or genealogical lines— prevailed. To be successful in sixteenth-century New Spain, Nahuas thus sought to optimize a variety of alliances: familial, ethnic, and altepetl (Lockhart 1982: 367–393, 1991: 2–65).

Seen in this light, the position that don Alonso occupied was not atypical of many Nahua leaders in the early colonial years. As the progeny of indigenous nobles, he enjoyed position and wealth that set him far above commoners. Don Alonso had also been baptized (early on in Cuauhtinchan's Christianization and thus by Franciscans) and would have been familiar with Christian teachings. He could most certainly read and write alphabetic letters—in Nahuatl, if not also Spanish and Latin—and he had developed into a skillful mediator, negotiating with both colonial and indigenous officials. Nevertheless, his status and station, especially on the local scene, were also subject to pre-conquest factional politics, politics that often set Nahua against Nahua and lineage against lineage.

When he commissioned the *Historia*, then, don Alonso was a man with considerable value to place on the table. Like many indigenous leaders he sought not only to conserve his privileges and economic security, but also to compound them through precedents established in the Pre-Hispanic past. Herein lies some of the irony in don Alonso's 1546 expedition to Mexico City. For the very boundaries he sought to have reinstated were those set into place not long after the Pinome dislodged the Nahua teccalli, and thus his ancestral fathers, from their position of dominance in Cuauhtinchan. Yet even as he made this case before the Audiencia, don Alonso kept his sights trained on a deeper antiquity, on those times before this ignominy befell his lineage. It is this point that the *Historia* makes so clear. For the *Historia* belongs to (and in fact interpolates) readers for whom multiple, competing versions of the Pre-Hispanic past could be accepted as proper and binding, even if those narratives could not be brought into alignment or wielded to produce but one outcome. In modern terms, what the *Historia* and don Alonso betray is a keen commitment to strategic history-keeping. This is not the same as lying or even keeping secrets about the past (White 2000), but neither is it a confusion or misrepresentation about what really happened a long time ago. Rather what we see at work in the annals and their owner's biography is the acknowledgment that in the mid-sixteenth century many strands of the Pre-Hispanic past still held enormous tensile strength, even if they could not be woven into a whole or beautiful cloth.

And so, if there existed for don Alonso any sense of a dilemma about antiquity, it might be cast in this way. In the pre-conquest past, the fate of the Castañeda lineage had become less fortunate, at least compared with earlier times. From our vantage, it is impossible to say precisely how welcome don Alonso would have found the transformation of this situation. We can be sure, however—as was he—that such a change in circumstances would not be easy to arrange. For it would require reviving in colonial times the most ancient of altepetl arrangements. Could an elaborate book of history facilitate such an endeavor? Perhaps. Even if don Alonso knew the chance of such change was slim, the very existence of the *Historia* implies much about the shape and sense of his optimism. It also hints at the kind of confidence don Alonso and his kin were willing to place in objects that, though wrought of written marks, paint, and paper, made manifest verities about the deep ground of history.

Metaphors of Connection, Metaphors of Transport

Over the last century, scholars of early colonial manuscripts have honed their analytic techniques and presumptions. One of the most dearly held convictions concerns the abilities of indigenous manuscripts of the sixteenth century to mediate or shed light on the Pre-Hispanic world. Much literature simultaneously presumes and argues that Nahua documents could—and indeed routinely did—convey Pre-Hispanic memories, images, and traditions to colonial viewers. How manuscripts did this, and how transparently their writing and painting performed this task continues to foment debate among academic writers.[8] Because so few documents of Pre-Hispanic manufacture survive, and because interpretive desires to know a world uncolored by the presence of Europeans run so deep, these issues are far from negligible.

Our conundrum is not simply whether particular authors or painters were competent, but rather the degree and manner of their dependence upon European precedents—be they alphabetic or pictorial. Early colonial images and graphic conventions are vexing, because if Pre-Hispanic antiquity is ever to be recovered from written and painted vehicles it must be disentangled from documents that are, by definition, heterogeneous and cross-purposed. And yet, despite extraordinary examination of sixteenth-century codices, we—and here I mean all who study and write about early colonial manuscripts—have yet to clarify how, precisely, objects such as the *Florentine Codex*, the *Codex Telleriano Remensis*, or even the *Historia* relate things Pre-Hispanic to things colonial. Our explanatory models, much less our notions of connection and separation are, I would argue, underdeveloped for the task at hand. Yet, as scholars as diverse as James Clifford (1997), Michael Taussig (1993, 2003), and Hayden White (1978, 1981) have argued, languages of analytical description, that is, our metaphors of analysis, are more than incidental.

It is the nature of metaphor to tap subtlety. That is why the "in-between" stature of works such as the *Historia* matter. One story line, then, might run like this. When the *Historia* was created, the epistemological ground of don Alonso's world was literally and figuratively shifting. Stable social and political foundations were quite frankly harder to come by. Although political affairs had been shaky in Pre-Hispanic times, the difficulties of 1550 were not the same, in kind or consequence, as those experienced in 1450. And so history-keeping, if it was to be at all useful, required re-fashioning. New varieties of visual and alphabetic narration appeared, and the *Historia* seems to function like an anchor, buried in a precarious present, meant to stabilize a shifting past. This tale is a thoroughly modern one, drawn from clues that don Alonso's book and biography provide. People in Cuauhtinchan would have enlisted other kinds of metaphor to describe the elaborate literary enterprise that is the *Historia*, and while I respect their positions, my account of their history cannot replicate it. My task, in other words, is not theirs. Consequently, I seek not to re-create the vision of don Alonso and his contemporaries but rather to transport it—from colonial times to the present. Their metaphors, then, must differ from ours.

In recent years, two paradigms can be discerned in discussions of works similar to the *Historia*. For some, sixteenth-century codices are bridges between pre- and post-conquest periods, implying, of course, the existence of a chasm with walls stable enough to permit the construction of a secure crossing for people, their traditions, and their memories. Guide rails of linear chronology direct traffic along this bridge in a single direction, from the Pre-Hispanic to the post-conquest. For other modern writers manuscripts are more like historical palimpsests. This analogy draws upon the spatial and sedimentary principle wherein pre-conquest features shine darkly through a semitranslucent colonial surface or skin. This results in loose constellations of Pre-Hispanic fact or shadowy pre-conquest presences that, although extant, are barely visible beneath the cover of European forms. Of these two models, the second implies greater cultural violence, for when one set of traditions nearly smothers another, the metaphor becomes both dark and complex.

Near the end of this study, I will return to these paradigms and parse their implications. Here, I want only to note that neither one quite captures the *Historia*. To my eye, the creators of this document struggled mightily to translate older visual and rhetorical practices into new, but meaningful, forms. There are signs that they were not always successful. And this implies that their burden was not a light one. The evidence suggests that their enterprise was driven by sincere ambition, yet, like many a colonial project, was troubled by contradictory objectives. Those who crafted the *Historia* accomplished what they did, not by merely recalling what had happened long ago, or faithfully copying older records. Don Alonso's book neither exactly bridges pre-conquest with post-conquest record-keeping, nor does it preserve Pre-Hispanic forms beneath a blanket of European introductions. Rather, the *Historia* is a highly interpretive enterprise—a re-working of the past in order to make it comprehensible and, I would add, responsive to the colonial present. This means that the writer and painters of the *Historia* painstakingly winnowed their sources, and in so doing built a history that would not pose as Pre-Hispanic, yet would possess an aura of the antique. Their strategies, as with all such projects, were sometimes more nimble than others but they worked along multiple formal and material paths. [9]

For instance, although alphabetic writing is a signpost of post-conquest expression, the *Historia* put Nahuatl script to work in non-European ways. The

[handwritten margin note: BUT ISN'T THIS TRUE OF ALL HISTORY?]

alphabetic Nahuatl of the *Historia* displays such consistency in vocabulary, phrasing, and visual appearance that it must have been transcribed by a single well-trained scribe. Whether or not this person served as a *tlacuilo* (formally trained scribe) in pre-conquest times, is unprovable; nonetheless a close reading of the *Historia* reveals that redactive practices were put into play. The writer of the *Historia* thus had both access to older works and a more-than-passing comprehension of them, for his references to other records include both omission and expansion, as well as an occasional "et cetera." Such telltale signs of redaction imply a scribe unafraid to betray his working method and acknowledge that his own document was built from other, perhaps more venerable, sources. These traces also implicate the annals' reader in a larger historical enterprise, one that extended beyond preservation to embrace renovation. In this case, the reinvented codex bespeaks the lineaments and character-istics of antiquity, as it sets innovation into dialogue with its documentary precursors.

Fifty years after the *Historia* had been composed, at the turn of the seventeenth century, the Nahua annals penned by Chimalpahin would turn resolutely to alpha-betic writing, eschewing all pictorial presentation (Anderson and Schroeder 1997; Lockhart et al. 2006). In the mid-sixteenth century, however, writing, painting, and oral recitation were mutually reinforcing strands of historical enunciation. Compared to Chimalpahin's endeavor, the *Historia* seems fugue-like in the way it braids three modes of exchange (writing, picturing, and reciting), but in so doing it references Pre-Hispanic histories that would have been strictly pictorial and oral. The scene of the annals, for instance, does not reiterate any single Homeric performance, yet the words of songs and conversations, and the cadence and phrasing of polite speech have been carefully transcribed. In addition, repetitions and parallel structures with their origins in mnemonic recitations further infuse the annals with oral pattern and meter. Because written words often garner significance in the *Historia* through visual disposition or juxtaposition, it is not only their denotative dimension that signifies. As a matter of fact, the writing in don Alonso's book is emphatically a mode of picturing (Leibsohn 1992, n.d.). This reciprocity would likewise have triggered visual memories for the annals' readers, aligning the newly assembled colonial codex with Pre-Hispanic modes of representation. Yet the manuscript worked along nuanced lines. The most explicit references to oral tradition in the annals appear early on, when events deep in the Pre-Hispanic past are recounted. More recent events, and certainly all of those that are colonial, do not partake in the same oral traditions of earlier actors and times. While this probably betrays the oral nature of the annalist's sources, it also creates a temporal drift in the manuscript wherein written speech signifies antiquity, its absence colonial "modernity."

The warp and woof of reference that bind don Alonso's book to ancient narrative and documentary practices enable multidirectional conversation among colonial affairs, Pre-Hispanic records, and past events. And this, I believe, was key to the *Historia*'s endeavor. No less crucial for shuttling between past and present was the pictorial interplay of the manuscript's various registers. In contrast to the written text, several hands executed the painted images in the *Historia*—all of them familiar with Pre-Hispanic–style and European-style graphic conventions. The greatest number of painted elements in the manuscript by far would be glyphs that identify dates, actors, and places (see, for instance, fig. 20). Full-page paintings also appear, all of which hint at, if not openly acknowledge, familiarity with European graphic conventions. Landscape elements, the muscular articulation of bodies, and the torsion of three-dimensional objects in virtual space provide the most obvious examples (pls. 1, 6). Yet no image in the annals draws strictly from either European or Pre-Hispanic sources; it is as if the painters felt a compulsive need to wind together elements from both traditions. Thus, toponymic glyphs may appear interspersed with landscape features from European pictorials, or warriors may wield pre-conquest weapons but hover over their enemies as quasi-Renaissance *putti* (pl. 17). Through their mixture of iconography and stylistic inventiveness, the *Historia* painters infused their project with a novel visual presence. At the same time, and perhaps more profoundly, they also demonstrated the flexibility of Pre-Hispanic representational conventions, which could be coaxed, as they were here, to intertwine with other (sometimes quite alien) forms of image- and history-making.

In its narrative ambition, the *Historia* also owes a substantial debt to Pre-Hispanic histories. The manuscript takes up events that unfolded across a span of over 400 years, from the mid-twelfth through the mid-sixteenth centuries. Yet for all its temporal reach, it skews its account toward antique recollection. It accomplishes this, in part, by devoting over forty-nine of its fifty-two folios to conversations, genealogies, rites, and other deeds of Pre-Hispanic date. Certainly don Alonso and others in Cuauhtinchan were acutely aware of changes wrought by the European conquest. Only occasionally, however, do European actors edge into the foreground of the *Historia*. Generally, their actions comprise a foil or scrim against which notable ancient Nahuas play out their legendary roles.[10] We experience this most viscerally, I believe, in the manuscript's gloss of the Spanish conquest. An event of considerable importance to modern historians, the *Historia* spins the Spanish conquest as only the most recent—not necessarily the most consequential—setback in a historical sequence of defeats. And it dispatches the affair in just two sentences. The implication of this taciturnity is intriguing. For the *Historia* is just one of several colonial documents that subvert what modern readers expect: an event of extraordinary significance given its due by the vanquished.

There are, in fact, a whole suite of post-conquest traumas the *Historia* fails to mention. Smallpox epidemics, for example—which repeatedly surface in the *Annals of Tecamachalco* and the *Libro de los Guardianes* from Cuauhtinchan—do not appear in the *Historia*, nor do the extraordinary demands for labor and material goods required by the newly founded Spanish city of Puebla de los Angeles. Tribulation associated with the inculcation of Christian practice is also suppressed. For instance, according to Spanish chroniclers, in 1529 elders in Cuauhtinchan killed two children who had been sent to the altepetl from Tlaxcala to flush out inappropriate (as in idolatrous) images. Of this, the *Historia* makes no mention. Indeed, the annals' makers found nothing worth reporting to have transpired that year: the date is given, but nothing more. Likewise, the execution of don Carlos Ometochtzin, the Texcocan ruler found guilty of criticizing mendicant activities in New Spain, and one of the most widely noted anti-indigenous events of the early colonial period in central Mexico, receives no mention (although see Ruiz Medrano 2007: 104–105).

James Lockhart has suggested that "Nahuas judged what they perceived by the criteria of their own culture, forcing the new into their own frameworks whether it fit well or not" (1994: 228). Interactions with other indigenous people—both kin and rival—truly did occupy people far more intensively than did exchanges with friars or other colonial authorities. Seen in this light, the quiet of the *Historia* is itself unremarkable. There is probably something to this: day-by-day, "the Spanish conquest" would not have been the most important thing on don Alonso's mind. Yet neither would its material and psychological legacies have been easy to ignore.

A spate of interpretive literature on memory and the representation of historical trauma has prompted scholarly speculation on why contemporary sources tend to "underplay" events like the Spanish conquest or the brutalities of war. For instance, scholars of the Holocaust tapping the psychoanalytic literature have shed considerable light on the obstinate relationship between truth and testimony, latency and history (Caruth 1995). Hence Dominick La Capra's claim that the representation of trauma can place identity into such doubt that it comes close to shattering, and only after a period of latency can tragic events be unrepressed and registered (1998). Another vein of scholarship views muteness as a strategy, enlisted to achieve particular social and ideological ends; in this context, *el pacto de olvido*— the implicit agreement among Spaniards to hold their tongues about the horrors of Franco's regime, undertaken less in the name of (further) historical repression than democratic optimism—is one example. Yet "strategies of forgetting" need not be explicit, although they are often essential to the creation, preservation, and advancement of personal and corporate selves.[11]

For modern readers with an expansive theoretical bent, there might be good reason to bring such modes of analysis to bear on sixteenth-century sources. The documentary record is spare, however, and our transmission theories—of ideas, cultural values, bodily practices—remain anemic, at least for sixteenth-century Mexico. Material evidence abounds, indicating that Pre-Hispanic practices and customs were passed from generation to generation, but the mechanics of this, if not the kinds of subject positions such passage necessitated, await sustained (and inventive) analysis.[12]

Working from presence rather than absence, then, it seems the *Historia* had little impetus to ascribe much relevance to the Spanish conquest. As far as don Alonso's manuscript was concerned, the consequences of Spanish rule were as yet acceptable. Much more pressing, at least according to the narrative force of the *Historia*—and other sixteenth-century records concerned with territory, such as the *Manuscript of 1546* and *Manuscript of 1553*—are details surrounding the fifteenth-century Tlatelolcan conquest of Cuauhtinchan and the subsequent reapportionment of boundaries by Axayacatzin. Both events had clear (and dire) consequences for certain factions in Cuauhtinchan—the Tlatelolcan victory ousted the ruling lineage, and the Mexica reapportioned the altepetl's territory, significantly reducing its holdings. In contrast, we might say that for these Nahua historians, traumas wrought by Spanish colonization had not yet become necessary to lament—at least not by pen set to paper. From this we sense it is not conquest, per se, that the *Historia* holds at bay, just the most recent one.[13]

One effect of underplaying the Spanish conquest is that continuity becomes the crucial subplot, deeply coloring the annals. Yet the *Historia* goes another step in cleaving to Pre-Hispanic perspectives. On the surface, the account of the Spanish conquest is profoundly reductive: the manuscript merely notes that Cuauhtinchan was conquered along with Tecali, Tecamachalco, Quecholac, and Tepeaca, all communities that had been subject to Cuauhtinchan in Pre-Hispanic times. In stating the case in this manner, the *Historia* and its implicit protagonist (Cuauhtinchan) take a cunning turn by reassembling entities that had remained estranged for over fifty years, and reconstituting on paper the Cuauhtinchan that had been a grander and more glorious entity. This representational strategy takes on even greater significance when we realize that the *Historia* writer has omitted from his account the altepetl of Totomihuacan, which was not only physically closer to Cuauhtinchan than either Tecamachalco or Quecholac, but was subjugated by the Spaniards in the same campaign. Moreover, because Totomihuacan plays a prominent role elsewhere in the annals, as the sister altepetl of Cuauhtinchan, its omission here speaks volumes. In evoking the Spanish conquest as he does, the writer reminds initiated readers that (and how) the "old" Cuauhtinchan should be remembered and thus invested with significance, even as it crumbled under the weight of foreign might.

What I am suggesting, then, is that the *Historia* did not so much manipulate the past as it did shift its scope and emphasis of memory. The past most clearly "remembered" is one wherein Pre-Hispanic figures and esteemed values loom largest. Why this was so, we will never know for certain. Even don Alonso and the *Historia*'s composers may not have been able to say. This is, in fact, how memory works: it may leave a profound trace upon the physical world, but offers little in the way of justification, and indulges none of our desire for self-reflection. Ambitions and intentions thus become difficult to anchor. It nevertheless seems certain that the *Historia* was designed to transmit ancestral deeds and their morals into the present, and onto the future. To accomplish this, don Alonso needed more than a story. His kin, both of days long gone and days yet to come, apparently required a book—an object that could describe the noble past even as it wrote the ancients into a history that was still unfolding.

The *Historia*'s Story

Although the *Historia* narrative opens with a "once upon a time" beginning, it does not unfold uninterrupted to any neat or pat ending. Rather, the manuscript has four sections, each of which highlights a distinct set of events and ancestral figures. Through an overlap of characters and circumstances the different chapters converge, yet the narrative never melds into a seamless tale. The history of Cuauhtinchan presented in this book is a history stitched together, not woven as one cloth.

True to the annals genre, the *Historia* stages its tale by compiling an accretion of narrative fragments. The book's reiteration of tropes, however, circumvents the fragmented surface of this tradition. Threading through the manuscript is, in fact, a suite of themes: legitimation of political rule, connections to ancestral leaders via genealogy and deed, rightful claims to territory, and interaction with neighboring altepetl. Migrations and ritual acts, appeals to deities, genealogical lines, and military conquests punctuate the annals, but these are usually subordinated to larger narrative themes; even eclipses, floods, and other climatic events reported in other Nahua annals fail to surface here. Other priorities prevail. We sense this, for instance, when we read at the closing of each chapter a description of newly established boundaries. Such recurrences underpin the moral lessons of the manuscript—lessons wherein the longevity and consistency of Nahua beliefs and practices emerge. The fabric of the *Historia* narrative may thus cover many heroic deeds, yet only rarely do individuals or events infringe upon the broader patterns of Nahua belief.

The first two sections of the *Historia* neither mention Cuauhtinchan, nor hint in any way at the altepetl's historical destiny.[14] Instead, the narrative begins in Tollan and proceeds to chronicle a fall from Edenic grace. The annals therefore open by listing the twenty groups who comprised the altepetl of Tollan; this roll call appears even before the first date in the manuscript. Thus the social organization of Tollan takes on meaning as the primordial arrangement, an arrangement that will be undone when regular time, the time of ancestral heroes, begins. As a good central Mexican history, the first date in the *Historia* is 1 Flint Knife, the year of significant beginnings (Umberger 1981). The narrative also singles out the two most important groups of residents of Tollan, the Nonoualca and the Tolteca-Chichimeca. From the very outset, then, the annals establish a crucial kind of relationship: a pair of similar, but not truly identical, groups.

In fact, while the narrative implies that the two groups are equals, the first pictorial image of the *Historia*, which appears on folio 2r (ms. 54–58; fig. 7), establishes a hierarchy. The painting depicts four culture heroes, Icxicoatl, Xelhuan, Quetzaltehueyac, and Huehuetzin, flanking an elaborate stand of reeds that evokes Tollan glyphically (Place of Reeds). Icxicoatl and Quetzaltehueyac, the Tolteca-Chichimeca leaders who come to play starring roles in the annals, are shown as full standing figures, while the other two, who are Nonoualca leaders and thus important early on but not across the *longue durée*, are shown only as small profile heads. The opening painting of the annals, then, situates the viewer in Tollan as it establishes those in this tale who will come to matter most. Beyond this, the relationship between the opening imagery and related text establishes a pattern that will continue throughout the annals: while the two media may focus upon identical moments in time, they convey distinct aspects of, and nuances about, actors and events. A savvy reader would be well served by devotion to both.

As in any Eden, all begins well in Tollan. Conflict arises in this paradise soon after an outsider, a child named Huemac, is taken in by the Tolteca-Chichimeca. Before long, Huemac is revealed to be an enfant terrible, whose demanding requests of the Nonoualca include not only service but also women. Indeed, the narrative

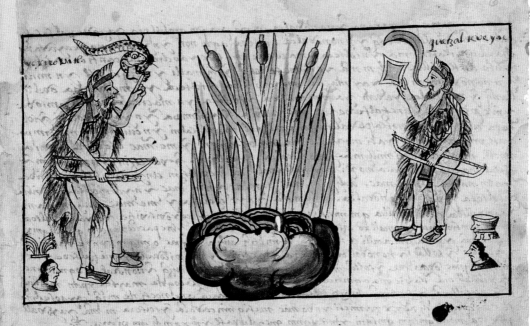

Cca. i. tecpatl. xiuitl. Jnicacico ytollan ynompavalle
vaque Jtcolhuacatepec ynitol tecadich meca. ymic picovall. J
gnetzalteveyac. Jtezcavitill. Jytololovitzin. avan yno novalca
dri chi meca. Jyelhua. ynovebetzin. Jgnauhtzin Jcaittal macue
tzin. ceyiuhtica ynoc pacticatca. ym maçica Jtoltera dri chi
meca.

C.2. Calli. xiuitl. ympa yyamonetecheva Jyamochalla
ma yyaqmi nex yna michia ynitoca me mac. ca qm mo tehq
Jtoltera ypil tzmtli. avh mi bua con mani liq Jedomtin qm3
calltiqne qm vapanhq Jtoltera. avh tlaia con yveyo Jtezca
tlepoca ca yeyitla. dri chival ymic picmgne ymicmoyavaz
yn toltera. dri chi meca yoon yno novalca dri chi meca ymic m
Jxna mi q̃q Jtoltera ymi maçica ynonovalca. Avh ym gnac
yatel pochtli J memac. mi ma yaqmi navatia ymicychom tlapi zzq yno novale
ca ynnemac. avh mi ma qmi lhm q̃ yno novalca. mavvi. nopiltzin maticdri
voeon Jttem toco monegmiltia. mi ma yayc ychom vallapi a ynonovallia
vemac. avh mi msa yaqmi mi tlamillia. cova qm millhm ia yno noval caa
negh momaqmilizg. cina. pamech nonavatillia yevatl ynavittetl ymchi
ta mal pattavac. ogmilhm q̃ yn no novalca mavvi. maocticte moca campa
ficanativi ynavittetl ymichim ta mal pa ttavac. avh mi ma qm mo nanaco
yncina navime ynaocavilli ymicvevey. a moyyegmih ym tlato ma chval
oqm millhm yn nonovalca a moyyegmih ymic negmi a moaci y navittetl y
rim tzmtamall cencavey ymic negmi. mi ma cenca oqnalla nsavaq J nonovalca

plays out Huemac's requirements in some detail. He asks the Nonoualca to guard his home and he requests from them four virgins whose buttocks measure four spans across. The Nonoualca are willing servants, but they cannot find women of the appropriate size, and instead they offer others whom Huemac finds unacceptable (f. 2r, ms. 54–58). When he refuses the women sent to him, the Nonoualca become enraged and denounce his supporters, the Tolteca-Chichimeca. This precipitates the first military altercation of the *Historia*. The Nonoualca turn on their former allies and brutally attack. Ultimately, the Nonoualca find Huemac, the source of their strife, hiding in a cave; they drag him by the hair from his shelter and dispatch his body (perhaps by arrow sacrifice). In spite of Huemac's demise, there is no victory celebration in Tollan, for the Nonoualca are too upset and ashamed. Michel Graulich captures the sense of the *Historia* well, describing how Huemac's desires left a stain on Tollan (1997: 203). And so, under the cloak of darkness, the Nonoualca abandoned their allies and their homeland.

This exodus sends the Nonoualca into terra incognita, and their journey frequently requires them to conquer the belligerent inhabitants of regions before settling. Occasionally they leave members of their group at these subject sites; in other instances they settle just long enough to regain strength before moving on to the next locale. The first chapter of the annals closes with a roster of the boundaries that limn the territory that the Nonoualca finally settle. In fact, this chapter both opens and concludes with descriptions of how people occupy particular lands. In the initial instance, the narrative charts the distribution of groups at Tollan, in the end, it adumbrates the territory claimed by the Nonoualca. While the annals do not follow these particular actors after they define their new boundaries, they do imply that upon these lands they will flourish, even if they cannot recapture the glory of their residence at Tollan.

The second portion of the *Historia* pursues the dissolution of Tollan, but shifts the locus of narration to the Tolteca-Chichimeca. This chapter is both longer and more detailed than the previous section, and it is pictorially more diverse.[15] The chapter opens with a treatment of the Tolteca-Chichimeca exodus from the ancestral site of Chicomoztoc (Place of Seven Caves) and their relocation at Tollan, where they reside for fifteen years. In contrast to the Nonoualca departure, no particular event prompts the Tolteca-Chichimeca decision to leave the fabled Tollan; the *Historia* simply implies the time for leave-taking had arrived. Indeed, the Tolteca-Chichimeca reside in Tollan for thirteen years without their Nonoualca allies—given that the number thirteen defines a Mesoamerican calendrical cycle, the timing of their departure was symbolically marked. And unlike the Nonoualca, who left in shame, the Tolteca-Chichimeca take great care to plot their migration by sending a priest to scout a place appropriate for their settlement; the priest winds his way to Cholula,

Fig. 7 Opening scene at Tollan, *Historia Tolteca-Chichimeca*.
Pigment on European paper, ca. 28.5 (height) × 20 cm (width).
Bibliothèque Nationale, Paris, f. 2r, ms. 54–58. *Photograph courtesy of the Bibliothèque Nationale, Paris.*

where his prayers are answered by a divine being (identified as the Giver of Life, Quetzalcoatl). The divinity tells the explorer that the Tolteca may claim Cholula as their new home; he assures the priestly guide that the people who already inhabit the site can be forced out and, when the time is right, he, as Giver of Life, will help make this possible.

With this news, the priest returns to Tollan and recounts his experiences to the Tolteca-Chichimeca leaders; almost immediately the people agree to desert Tollan. Crucial here is their assent to move under the guidance of Quetzalcoatl. For the narrative to continue, the leaders of the Tolteca-Chichimeca are obliged to embrace his words and embark upon a migration that has received divine sanction, yet their exodus must be humanly orchestrated. The Tolteca-Chichimeca travel for several years before they reach Cholula, and their journey takes on meaning as a propitious expedition that resonates with Mesoamerican number symbolism. For instance, the wandering band passes through fifty-one places before reaching their goal, Cholula, the fifty-second. And so their peregrination unfolds across the same span as a major calendrical cycle. The names of each site along the way are scrupulously identified, as are the durations of each sojourn. The narrative thus hinges upon both the territorial and temporal details of the Tolteca-Chichimeca migration. At only two sites is war waged against local inhabitants; by and large, the migration period is peaceful and, unlike the Nonoualca who splintered as they traveled, the Tolteca-Chichimeca remain united—no member of the group loiters along the path, no named player fails to arrive in Cholula.

Settling in Cholula, however, proves no simple matter. The local Olmeca Xicalanca rulers grant the newcomers permission to live among them, and at first the arrangement is acceptable. Before long, however, the Tolteca-Chichimeca grow dissatisfied. The current rulers of Cholula lord their power over the newcomers, humiliating them with abusive insults and demands for excessive tribute. The Tolteca become increasingly distraught, and one night, as they gather to commiserate, the Giver of Life (this time in the guise of Tezcatlipoca) overhears their remarks. Speaking directly to the two Tolteca-Chichimeca leaders who dominate the annals, Icxicoatl and Quetzaltehueyac, Tezcatlipoca outlines a plan for overthrowing the Olmeca Xicalanca by trickery. He tells them to put on a military performance wherein the Tolteca must borrow old, worn-out weapons and combat gear from the Olmeca Xicalanca. So attired, with their overlords lulled into defenseless expectation of dance and song, the Tolteca are advised to launch a surprise assault. With Icxicoatl and Quetzaltehueyac as the primary negotiators, the Olmeca Xicalanca rulers agree to their proposal and set a date. The Tolteca then spring into action. They go from house to house collecting the oldest, most decrepit weapons and military costumes. Late into the evenings they labor over this equipment, stitching, sewing, and transforming the borrowed relics into items suitable for deadly combat. On the fourth day they are ready. And, of course, their ruse is successful: the Tolteca rout the Olmeca Xicalanca.

Oddly, at least to modern readers, the narrative breaks off here, giving no account of the Tolteca performance or the ensuing battle. On the last page of this section, however, the text refers to Icxicoatl and Quetzaltehueyac as Cholteca, rather than Tolteca. With this, the *Historia* writer makes it clear that the Tolteca have been victorious and now claim the right to rule in Cholula (f. 13v, ms. 54–58). This section of the manuscript closes in a manner reminiscent of the first, with a recitation of the boundaries that define the territory that Icxicoatl and Quetzaltehueyac now command. What this section of the annals highlights that the first did not is a prime lesson of the *Historia*: the importance of a properly sanctioned homeland founded through the guidance of a pair of exceptionally skilled male leaders. Such an objective is momentous enough to enlist the advice of the gods. How the Tolteca-Chichimeca secured their divinely sanctioned realm—the details of their journey, their conversations with deities, and their military proficiency—this becomes the very stuff of history.

The third chapter of the manuscript, which stretches across folios 14r through 36v (ms. 46–50, 54–58), is the most detailed in the *Historia*. It is here that several pivotal events transpire: the Tolteca-Chichimeca permanently solidify their claims upon Cholula, the ancestral heroes who found Cuauhtinchan emerge onto the historical stage, and the altepetl of Cuauhtinchan—along with its sister community, Totomihuacan—is born. This section also contains an abundance of elaborate paintings, from the representation of Cholula, Chicomoztoc, and the two newly founded altepetl of Totomihuacan and Cuauhtinchan, to the depiction of Pre-Hispanic sacrificial rites (see Appendix 1). Yet this part of the narrative also adopts a more leisurely pace. Time decelerates and events receive day-by-day as well as year-by-year recollection. Lengthy conversations between individuals and transcriptions of songs sung by ancestral heroes are also registered in full. Taken together, these features imply that here, in the third section of the annals, the narrative has transitioned from its preamble to the core of significant action.

This portion of the narrative opens in Cholula, describing a political climate that is stable and calm. However, just as military conflict unraveled the idyllic Tollan, several local groups band together and attack the new rulers of Cholula, threatening their sovereignty over the site. In great distress, the Tolteca caucus to discuss their options. Once more the Giver of Life (here, Macochehe and Tepotzehe) appears and answers their pleas. He offers the following instructions: the Tolteca must travel to the cave of Chicomoztoc and solicit the aid of the great warriors who live there. Immediately and dutifully, Icxicoatl and Quetzaltehueyac set out on this mission.

After several days of travel, the two reach Chicomoztoc, where they prepare for their assignment through prayers and ritual deeds (pl. 5). The leaders approach the cave in turn—each performing some rite and then, in recompense, assuming a new name. Icxicoatl feels the cave one day and listens at its exterior wall another. After each incident he adopts an epithet that refers to the respective activity. In contrast to these contemplative acts, Quetzaltehueyac aggressively strikes the cave and breaks a hole in the side wall. The names he assumes thus relate to his intrusive deeds. Once the cave is broken open, Tezcatlipoca makes his final appearance in the annals, encouraging the leaders to press onward and make contact with those inside. In keeping with his role, Quetzaltehueyac thrusts a long staff into the cave. Shortly thereafter, a Chichimeca interpreter named Coatzin emerges from the cave. The activities of Icxicoatl and Quetzaltehueyac can be thus understood as "birth-giving." It is through the ritual actions of the two men that the cave is opened (Quetzaltehueyac actually thrusts his spear into Chicomoztoc). And, as a result, the Tolteca bear significant responsibility for "delivering" the Chichimeca warriors from the cave into this world.

There is no spilling out into the world, however. The Chichimeca—108 men and sixteen women—must be convinced to leave their mountain cave and travel to Cholula. It is Coatzin the interpreter (a moniker that underscores the distinction between the Tolteca, who speak one language, and the Chichimeca, who speak another) who plays the crucial diplomatic role in these negotiations. Ultimately, six Chichimeca warriors from the larger assembly are singled out—including the one who will become a founding father of both Cuauhtinchan and don Alonso's lineage—and after a ritual fast and septum-piercing rite (pls. 7, 8), they are invested with the authority to rule in this world, not only that of their cavern home.[16] The entourage then journeys to Cholula and upon arrival turns its attention to the military crisis at hand. In this story, the Giver of Life gives only sage advice. The Chichimeca triumph easily, in just a single day of battle. Unlike either the Nonoualca victory over Huemac or the Tolteca overthrow of the Olmeca Xicalanca, this triumph is celebrated with great fanfare. The defeated rulers are brought to Cholula and sacrificed. In gratitude, the Tolteca not only fete their defenders with music and song, they also give the Chichimeca rulers their daughters in marriage, thus cementing the union between the two groups through an exchange of women for military labor.

The Chichimeca warriors cannot, however, remain in Cholula, for that is the domain of Tolteca sovereignty. And so the warriors depart in search of a place of their own. Icxicoatl and Quetzaltehueyac travel with them, indicating sites that will serve as the boundaries of their allies' new settlements. Only now, in the wake of their victory at Cholula, does the story focus on Cuauhtinchan. In keeping with the pattern of pairs set forth early on with the Nonoualca and Tolteca, Cuauhtinchan is founded alongside another altepetl, Totomihuacan. One community is settled under the guidance of Icxicoatl, the other under the tutelage of Quetzaltehueyac. And in the year 8 Reed, the year of Cuauhtinchan's founding, boundaries between the two new altepetl are confirmed (pl. 16). This chapter closes, as do those that precede it, with a recital of boundaries. In this case it is the borders that define the region settled by the Totomihuaque and Cuauhtinchantlaca. Icxicoatl and Quetzaltehueyac, with their work accomplished, now fade from view and two Cuauhtinchantlaca leaders, Moquihuix and Teuhctlecozauhqui, take center stage. At the end of the annals' third section, then, the scene and actors shift, but the story reiterates its point: under the leadership of fine male warriors, a people can establish an altepetl where they will be independent and come to prosper.

The last section of the manuscript, folios 37r through 51v (ms. 46–50, 54–58), covers the most substantial span of time, from the settlement of Cuauhtinchan in the mid-twelfth century through the years following the Spanish conquest. Although this section represents the time closest to living memory, it is the most fragmented and perfunctory of any in the *Historia*. Considerable hiatuses mark the narrative, as conversations and lengthy descriptions are abandoned in favor of terse entries sprinkled throughout many years for which no event is recorded. In general, the final section of the annals fixes on conquests and military battles, the relocation of people in various communities, and the succession of rulers. The arrival of the Mixteca Popoloca in Cuauhtinchan is noted, as are numerous border wars against neighboring altepetl and the death of Moquihuix, one of the founders of Cuauhtinchan and an ancestor of don Alonso's.

Following these passages, the narrative recounts two major upheavals that permanently fracture the autonomy of Cuauhtinchan. The first is the conquest by Tlatelolcans under the leadership of Quauhtlatoa. This fifteenth-century battle terminates the political hegemony of the ruling Nahua dynasty in Cuauhtinchan, a dynasty that had led the altepetl for over two centuries. In its wake, people of Mixteca Popoloca descent rise to a position of dominance in Cuauhtinchan. This is a critical turning point in the community's history as it is the first time that Nahua political control falters. So significant is this loss, that it is the only event in the final section of the annals to receive detailed and extensive pictorial elaboration (pls. 17/18). In fact, the battle scene with opposing forces arrayed across two facing pages is the final extended painting in the *Historia*. Later in the annals, pages were set aside to accommodate large images, yet these remain unpainted. One set of blank sheets, for example, follows a discussion of new boundaries established by the Mexica (f. 45v–46r, ms. 54–58); the other appears immediately after the arrival of Spaniards on the coast of Veracruz (f. 50r, ms. 54–58). In spite of initial intentions, neither of these paintings was even sketched. By default, and then ultimately choice, the battle with Tlatelolco has become the last painting in the annals. This effectively reinforces the importance of the event (see discussion, Chapter 3 and Appendix 1). The second upheaval transpires sixty-nine years hence, when the Mexica divide the altepetl of Cuauhtinchan into five parts, further compromising its independence. It is the Mexica ruler Axayacatzin who sends emissaries to establish new borders in 1478. And so lands that had belonged to the altepetl of Cuauhtinchan are re-partitioned among Tepeaca, Quecholac, Tecali, and Tecamachalco, as well as Cuauhtinchan.[17]

The annals culminate with post-conquest events. The Spanish conquest follows the two central Mexican encroachments on local authority. Yet as we have seen, in contrast to these Pre-Hispanic losses, which radically affected the size and independence of Cuauhtinchan, the *Historia* intimates that Spaniards posed no significant challenge to the integrity of the altepetl. Over time the *Historia* records new tribute requirements, the arrival of a friar from Tepeaca who baptizes and marries people, and the establishment of a local cabildo. The final event in the *Historia* pertains to the 1546 territorial dispute that sent don Alonso to the capital of New Spain. To defend their position against the encroachments of another Nahua altepetl, the people of Cuauhtinchan record the boundaries that the Mexica established, and, although don Alonso is not mentioned by name, it is his delegation of which the annals speak. The manuscript breaks off in media res just after Cuauhtinchan wins its case before the Audiencia.

Although the remaining pages of the *Historia* are now lost, the final section of the annals ends as do all the others, with discussion of boundaries as fundamental to altepetl sovereignty. From this we recognize that the history set forth here accounts for, yet stretches well beyond, ancestral deeds and community foundation. The *Historia* is a book whose structure and story—from Tollan to Cuauhtinchan—concerns the legitimacy of territorial claims. Yet not all claims to territory become the substance of history. Rather the claims worthy of record, the *Historia* notes, are those articulated by the people of Cuauhtinchan and Totomihuacan, by the ancestral allies of both groups, the Tolteca, and by their allies from Tollan, the Nonoualca. The *Historia* is thus a narrative wherein the connections among these groups, as well as the propriety of their behavior, anchors their authority to rule over desired lands encircled by desired boundaries.

Notes

1. This sketch of the mid-sixteenth century draws upon a range of local sources, including the *Historia*, the *Libro de los Guardianes*, and the testaments of several Cuauhtinchan residents (Kirchhoff et al. 1976; Medina Lima 1995; Reyes García 1988). To fill out this picture, I have depended upon the wealth of scholarship focusing on Nahua communities in the sixteenth century and their early relationships with Puebla. See, for instance, Carrasco (1963), Cline (1986, 1993), Gerhard (1972), Gibson (1964), Haskett (1991), Himmerich y Valencia (1992), Hirshberg (n.d.), Horn (1997), Kellogg and Restall (1998), Lockhart (1992, 1994), Martínez (1984), Olivera (1976, 1978), Prem (1978), and, also Ruiz Medizano (2007).

2. The primary conflicts are recorded in the *Historia*, the *Manuscript of 1546*, and the *Manuscript of 1553*. Luis Reyes García also transcribes several documents related to disputes that pit Cuauhtinchan's residents against other indigenous petitioners or Spaniards, and particularly the city of Puebla (1988). The surviving documentation makes it clear that Europeans may have threatened Cuauhtinchan's autonomy and the status of its leaders, but significant threats also came from indigenous people—both outside of Cuauhtinchan and within. Throughout the sixteenth century, Cuauhtinchantlaca were required to defend their borders several times against encroachments by Nahuas from nearby altepetl, and indigenous nobles had to defend their claims to territory against competitors within Cuauhtinchan itself. In many instances it was these disputes among Nahuas that proved most challenging for Cuauhtinchan to withstand. This situation, wherein factionalism and internal disputes are as arduous as (if not more arduous than) any conflict between an indigenous community and the dominant political power, can manifest itself in a number of ways. Alan Sandstrom has documented some of the ways this has played out in Nahua villages in the Huasteca (1991). For a historical comparison with Europe, Ruth Behar's work on Spain is particularly insightful (1986).

3. The actual date of the building's construction is uncertain. According to Mendieta, the church was begun in 1569 (García Icazbalceta 1941: 83), but work on the rectory and other structures began earlier, perhaps between 1558 and 1560 (cited in Kubler 1948: 60, 120). If this is correct, then only the initial stages of the building project overlapped with the period in which the *Historia* was produced. Kirchhoff et al. assign the manuscript a date of 1545–1563 on the basis of paleography and watermarks (1976: 11–15), while Pablo Escalante Gonzalbo implies it may well have been finished as early as the 1540s (1997: 218, n. 19). In either case, it seems the mural painting postdates the scene in the annals.

4. This desire is implicit in don Alonso's testimony: see the *Manuscript of 1553*, especially paragraphs 172–187, but also paragraphs 88, 91, 106, 135, and 151 (Reyes García 1988: 80–100).

5. The *Historia* and the *Manuscript of 1553* clearly speak of the altepetl as a complex social and political entity, with seven teccalli, several *calpolli*, and two parcialidades. The most explicit discussion of the internal organization of Cuauhtinchan appears in Reyes García (1977), although see also Ruiz Medrano (2007). Summarizing Reyes García's account, James Lockhart claims that the number seven "may have represented an ideal based on group legend, but also appears to have been a way of accommodating two originally very distinct ethnicities, the Nahuas and the Pinome, since the rulerships [of the teccalli] were divided between them, with . . . four held by one group and the rest by the other"; moreover, the teccalli were ranked hierarchically with some holding more sway than the others, although the landholdings of each group were interspersed with those of the others (1992: 24).

6. See Scholes and Adams (1958: 120–122). For tribute paid to indigenous leaders throughout the region, see Carrasco (1963: 97–119), Olivera (1976: 181–206, 1978: 154–231), and Reyes García (1977: 109).

7. The testaments of several of Cuauhtinchan's sixteenth-century leaders reveal that their primary object of value was land, although some also bequeathed houses, livestock, jewelry, and feather objects to their kin: see transcriptions in Reyes García (1988: 109–122, 139–144, 145–149, 158–162). We sense the continued importance of this pattern in the seventeenth century, in the testament of doña María Ruiz de Castañeda (Introduction). On the basis of Robert Haskett's research in Cuernavaca, it seems that other markers of wealth in indigenous communities included Spanish-introduced items such as tables, chests, and horses as well as symbols of indigenous rank such as shields for dancing, feathered headdresses, and drums (1991: 163). See also the essays in Kellogg and Restall on the ways that wealth was measured, accrued, and lost throughout the colonial period in both Mesoamerica and the Andes (1998).

8. The literature on this topic is considerable. Among the more provocative contributions of the last two decades are those put forward by Gillespie (1989), Klein (1995), and Prem (1997), but see also Quiñones Keber (1995) and Boone (2000) for excellent explications of Pre-Hispanic narratives contained in post-conquest manuscripts, as well as the arguments by Russo (2005) on the persistence of certain conceptual traditions from the Pre-Hispanic past in indigenous cartographs.

9. My position here differs from that of Kirchhoff et al. who, in identifying the calendrical documents used as references for the *Historia*, assume a too-direct relationship between the annals and their sources, implying that the writer was primarily a copyist, transcribing whatever was available to him (1976: 16–18). While this may have been one mode of production in the sixteenth century, I am inclined to see more active editorial decision-making and innovation in the redaction of historical records; moreover the disjunctions in the *Historia* were not necessarily copying "errors," but rather moments wherein the most difficult translation and interpretive decisions were being made.

10. Almost equally insignificant to the historical drama are commoners (see discussion, Chapter 2).

11. The literature on theories of memory and the production of selves is extensive; for examples that have relevance for ethnohistoric sources see Cohen (1994), Fentriss and Wickham (1992), and the essays in Neisser and Fivush (1994). For yet a different position on the absence of elaborate accounts of the Spanish conquest, one which stresses the narrative tendencies and predispositions of Nahua annals, see Lockhart (1994: 229–235).

12. Forays into this arena can be found, although they are not yet common. See, for instance, Peterson on the scribe-painters of the *Florentine Codex* (2003), Adorno (2000) and Pratt (1994) on Guaman Poma, Gruzinski on the Otomí (1998), and Rappaport among the Cumbé (1990). Margaret Conkey addresses this broadly, particularly for the study of gender (2001).

13. The conquest does not surface in other sixteenth-century pictorials from the altepetl, although the *Libro de los Guardianes*, alphabetic annals from Cuauhtinchan that cover the period from 1519 to 1640 and, compared to the *Historia*, devote far more attention to European individuals and events, discusses the arrival of the Spaniards and the conquest of Mexico City in considerable detail, recording the roles of Malinche and Alvarado as well as Cortés, and giving yearly updates on the various battles. Yet even these annals gloss over Cuauhtinchan's conquest (Medina Lima 1995: 30–37). For contemporary Nahua accounts, which do address the Spanish conquest in more depth, see the analysis and translations in Lockhart (1993).

14. The first section runs from folios 1v through 4v (ms. 54–58); the second from folios 5r through 12r (ms. 51–53, 54–58). Cuauhtinchan and don Alonso's ancestors are mentioned for the first time, only toward the end of the manuscript's third section—relatively late in the book, but not in the chronology of the overall story, for the annals cover another several centuries after they appear on the scene.

15. This section includes the first of several full-page spreads with imagery centering on Chicomoztoc and Cholula, and it acquaints readers with a visual repertoire that will resonate throughout the annals. See Appendix 1 for analyses and descriptions of the images "First Exodus from Colhuacatepec" (pl. 1), "Arriving at Cholula" (pl. 2), and "Cholula Under the Olmeca-Xicalanca" (pl. 3).

16. The number of groups that leave Chicomoztoc is ambiguous, as is the number of Chichimeca leaders invested with the authority to rule. Although the text claims that seven groups emerge from the cave, it names eight (f. 19r, ms. 54–58). Moreover, four Chichimeca leaders are represented fasting in one painting (pl. 7), six are shown having their noses pierced in another image (pl. 8), and five names are given in the text (f. 21v, ms. 46–50).

17. Almost immediately, people in Cuauhtinchan defy the Mexica by ignoring the new borders. In some cases they return to lands they previously occupied. Nevertheless, by the mid-sixteenth century, the boundaries imposed by the Mexica represent the accepted Pre-Hispanic arrangement. And in post-conquest land disputes these borders are invoked as the appropriate "legal" divisions of territory, as in 1546 when don Alonso journeyed to Mexico City. See, for example, the *Manuscript of 1546* in Reyes García (1988: 1–78).

CHAPTER 2

OF ALLIES AND RIVALS

SET DOWN ON EUROPEAN PAPER between 1545 and 1563, the *Historia* reckons via the indigenous cycle of years—Reed, Flint Knife, House, and Rabbit—to both keep time and register events. We know that in a community like Cuauhtinchan this manuscript would have been a costly undertaking. European paper was dear throughout New Spain; transcribing such lengthy texts, no less than painting such extensive imagery, would also have been formidable tasks. It seems the challenge may indeed have been too great. For even now blank spaces stand in reserve on pages where date glyphs were to have been painted, song passages to have been registered. Traces of sketch marks also hint at planned paintings that never came to fruition. Such unrealized intentions aside, the formal armature of the *Historia* indicates that don Alonso and those who worked for him did not take their historic project lightly. What mattered most to the crafters of these annals is hard to say. They might have reserved the most precious parts of their history for ephemeral venues and media, perhaps to be chanted or performed in an evening or over a series of days and then carried in memory. It is nevertheless likely that the sections of the manuscript most carefully elaborated—those most beautifully adorned with paint, and fully explicated in script—were places in narrative, and in the past, that the annals' readers were meant to dwell.

We should be wary of the visual fallacy: what looks most exquisite to us, today, may well have registered differently to eyes born in the sixteenth century. Yet if we trace the investment of creative labor in the *Historia*, it is the scene of ancestral emergence from the primordial site of Colhuacatepec-Chicomoztoc (pl. 5) that beckons most insistently. Executed on a single sheet of European paper, this work barely exceeds the dimensions of a modern, 8 1/2 × 11-inch, sheet of paper. While not the largest painting in the manuscript, it is the most painstakingly executed and the grandest in narrative aspiration. Among Nahuas, exodus from a primordial cavern was an arch trope in the construction of prestigious identity, and sixteenth-century documents spin primordial caves into thick webs of temporal, religious, and political connotation. Caves play a seminal role in creation tales where wombs, fertility, and political legitimacy intersect. They are also a quintessential sign of originary moments and auspicious beginnings.[1] Moreover, emergence from a primeval cavern seems to have been a particularly potent symbol for those Nahuas in the early colonial—and we deduce, Pre-Hispanic—period seeking to establish a venerable antiquity for their lineage.

There is much to recommend this painting, which within the *Historia* narrative signals a new beginning, to the modern eye.[2] Men and their women, Chichimeca warriors and Tolteca priests, glyphic date signs and diplomatic negotiations are all portrayed at this dusky cavern arrayed in desert flora. Pictorial evocations of propitious events also infuse this scene. The man draped in a wolf's skin and hunched over a fire drill in the upper right, and the glyphs that float near the cave's floor are two of the more prominent examples. Indeed, this Chicomoztoc image sets the tone for much of the *Historia*, for it implicates don Alonso's designs to possess an auspicious beginning represented not in haste, but rather unfolded in luxurious detail. Moving from painting to manuscript, we sense this as well: even a cursory review of the *Historia* betrays a plot awash in specificity. From the very first page, readers are thrust into lists of proper names, soon followed by lengthy conversations, descriptions of battles and colloquies, accounts of marriage and genealogy.

Recent literature on memory and self-fashioning suggests that convincing accounts of the past are those that rhetorically and topically correspond with socially recognized narratives. Innovation can be both useful and tolerated, but the most compelling histories tend to merge with those recollective patterns in which a society invests most heavily and which it comes to trust.[3] This is certainly borne out in the *Historia*, for the document depends upon, and at times gives privilege to, narrative tropes that parallel other contemporary Nahua accounts. These patterns and templates, we must presume, represented compelling recollections of the past in sixteenth-century altepetl life.

To grasp what this means for the *Historia* requires a close read of the annals for both plot and semiotic execution. By attending to the manuscript's pictures and words—not only via what is shown or said, but in the ways ideas and concepts coalesce as visual and syntactic registers—two key features of don Alonso's project surface. First, although salient historical concepts and tropes are marked in both an alphabetic and pictorial register, the *Historia*'s creators seem wary about both systems of record-keeping. They prefer to record events in a manner that is syncopated, but doubled. Second, the annals are at once descriptive and prescriptive. What actually happened in the past, the *Historia* notes, is precisely—and only—what could have happened. This is not to say that don Alonso's book shaped memory in some cynical way. As is the case with many indigenous histories from colonial Latin America, the *Historia* serves as a guide wherein truths about the past and the lessons these truths teach inextricably intertwine. Susan Gillespie has described such histories as narrative charters for comprehending the world (1998: 233). And I believe this justly represents much of the *Historia*'s project. My inclination, however, is to push her claim further. In its quest to prompt remembrance, don Alonso's manuscript—and others of its ilk—shaped, and thus remade their own colonial worlds, not only the worlds of Pre-Hispanic actors and events. The work of these documents, in other words, lies in remaking the present no less than the past.[4]

In the case of the *Historia*, the truths most finely woven concern the proper relations between people who are at once potential allies and potential competitors. Great detail is also given over to the territories these people traverse and settle. In this chapter, I consider the *Historia*'s preoccupation with allies and rivals, and in the next, its obsession with their lands.

Divine Interventions

In the essay "The Aesthetics of Substance," Marilyn Strathern writes of images and events of such potency that, once witnessed, grow intractable; she considers what it might mean for certain things to become literally unforgettable. For her the issue is not precisely trauma or the scarring of memory, but rather the social process of disposal. The question she poses, and ultimately answers in the negative, is whether the elimination of an image or experience is possible. For the cultures that Strathern studies, there is no disposing of an image, only a refusal to consume it in the first place (1999). While we do not know don Alonso's age at mid-sixteenth century, the *Historia* tells us that he inherited the position of tlatoani in the year 1 Reed, when Cortés joined forces with the Tlaxcalans and "laid waste to the land in Cholula."[5] For him, any habits of ceremony or ritual—what we might today call religion— acquired before the Spanish conquest might well constitute the kind of indisposable element that Strathern describes. Certainly, by the time the *Historia*'s scribe began working, twenty years or so into colonial rule, don Alonso would have been Christian for a long time. More than this, he would have developed a rapport with friars in Cuauhtinchan and perhaps those of the nearby town of Tepeaca, and even Huejotzingo. Yet neither his dealings with mendicants nor his earlier conversion could have expunged all his memories of Pre-Hispanic deities and rites. He would have known such things too well. That pre-conquest gods rarely figure in the pages of the *Historia* underscores something so fundamental about the manuscript that it is almost impossible to see. Don Alonso's memories do not govern the narrative surface of his document, rather the stakes in his historical wager construe the remembrances to which his annals allude.

To be more precise, the *Historia* implies repleteness, but, in fact, organizes itself to stress certain kinds of memories. For instance, don Alonso's book hardly banishes pre-conquest divine actions, rather it reins them in. In this, the annals parallel other histories from Central Mexico of the same period. This may be a question of genre; that is, gods may have played only minor roles in certain kinds of histories that predate the Spanish conquest. Yet the treatment of deities in the *Historia* implies that, even in Christian New Spain, a persuasive account of pre-conquest times could not eclipse all references to ancient deities. And so, this book is quite particular about where the gods can appear. It allows no Pre-Hispanic gods to enter the altepetl of Cuauhtinchan, nor does it permit deities to take form via pictorial representation. When Pre-Hispanic gods do play a role, they do so strictly in the alphabetic text and are relegated to the deepest past. That is, after the twelfth century, no direct human interactions with the gods are recorded.[6] Divine interventions are confined to three named, and at times interchangeable, figures— Ipalnemouani, Quetzalcoatl, Tezcatlipoca—all of whom act as harbingers of good fortune. At crucial moments in antiquity, they enable the *Historia*'s heroes to acquire desired territories and achieve stunning battleground victories. In sum, the gods offer guidance that propels the deeds of ancestral leaders and, by extension, the narrative across difficult terrain.

Aggressive militancy combined with strong ethnic tensions define the contexts in which these deities surface. Indeed, all of the occasions upon which gods appear involve severe discord, the kind of dissension that threatens ruin. Although many occasions beg for divine intervention, only two groups, the Nonoualca and Tolteca—both of whom made a home in Tollan—converse with the gods. Of these two, only the Tolteca profit from multiple communions. According to the annals, deities did not often contact mortals but when they did, they chose their interlocutors carefully and offered them very explicit forms of advice. And we should not be surprised that in every instance their words tipped the balance of power in favor of the ancestral allies of the Cuauhtinchantlaca.

The first interaction between humans and deities occurs after the Nonoualca and Tolteca clash on a battlefield in Tollan. The Nonoualca decide to abandon their homeland and their leaders appeal to Ipalnemouani, the Giver of Life, who answers by directing them to settle new lands (fs. 2v–3r, ms. 54–58). While the exchange between deities and leaders is succinct, the *Historia* indicates that the mortals addressed the gods via song and penitential deeds. Such ritualized utterances signal holy moments in the *Historia*, implying that only heightened forms of speech penetrate the sacred realm. Within the larger narrative, the Nonoualca exchange with Ipalnemouani sets the stage for a similar interaction between two Tolteca leaders who, thirteen years hence, would appeal to Quetzalcoatl for settlement land of their own.[7] In doubling the ways and occasions upon which the Nonoualca and Tolteca leaders interact with the gods, the *Historia* solidifies the reader's perception of these two groups and their utopic existence in Tollan. In addition, the manuscript makes clear that on the human plane, the fates of the Tolteca and Nonoualca intertwine even as they diverge.

Within the annals, all of the other circumstances that warrant unmediated discourse with the gods trace their origin to a single Tolteca desire: rule over Cholula. This requires the ousting of a rival group, the Olmeca Xicalanca, and the military subjugation of their supporters. Here emerges one of the *Historia*'s structural subtleties. The Tolteca pit themselves against the Olmeca Xicalanca, but, in their longing to become the new lords of Cholula, they also aspire to a role that parallels that of their rivals. At key points in this adventure Ipalnemouani and Tezcatlipoca appear, animating the Tolteca leaders in their pursuit of hegemony. Ultimately, of course, the Tolteca succeed—triumphing through cunning and military valor. Yet the gods never offer to lead their efforts, nor do they rally with the Tolteca on the battlefield. The Pre-Hispanic deities only supply sage advice at critical moments. Florine Asselbergs reminds us that crises are intensifiers (2004: 197); thus, dangerous moments in antiquity would rightly call for sustained engagement with the sacred. In the *Historia*, as is to be expected of divine omniscience at such moments, the gods never err. Even so, the military victories of the Tolteca at Cholula unfold as events inspired and catalyzed by, but not directly dependent upon, divine intervention.

On its surface, then, the *Historia*'s treatment of Pre-Hispanic deities suggests that in ancient times deities intervened in the human world only at moments of extraordinary need. These moments inevitably turned on the dissolution of one social and political order and the formation of a novel one. The *Historia* is cagey in its silences, however. For nowhere does it reveal whether a life lived in the absence of direct guidance from Pre-Hispanic divinities represents a misfortune. Any sense of loss harbored by the annals' writer or patron—whether wrought by colonial events, the introduction of Christian practice, or just the daily passage of time—is held at bay. Reading between the lines of the written text, readers gradually grasp the fact that in special circumstances, exceptional mortals—not gods—command the political destiny of altepetl. On more than one sixteenth-century occasion this would have been a lesson, if not a verity, with profound resonance for don Alonso and his compatriots.

Birthing Ancestors

If Pre-Hispanic deities, those who came to be known as *tlacatecolotl* (literally man-owl) in the first generations after the conquest, rarely command the historical stage of the *Historia*, groups with markedly distinct ethnicities play leading roles. Opening the first page of the annals is a description and roll call for the twenty groups that together comprise Tollan. Each is invoked by name and, even prior to the annals' first date, ancestral identities are forged, in written text and pictorial form, through an alliance of difference. Through this emphatic inventorying the mixed constituency of the altepetl is foregrounded.[8] Yet the *Historia* hardly offers all the members of Tollan fair billing. Rather, the annals enlist narrative and pictorial strategies that at once chronicle alliances and skew the tale to feature don Alonso's ancestral moiety. The work is almost novelistic in the way it privileges, via text and image, the adventures of a few among many. For the *Historia* never explicates why a select ethnic group or lineage is more deserving than others. It just pushes ahead along its editorial vector. And in the end it leaves little doubt as to how much more some ancestral actors matter than others.

Although the Tolteca are on stage when the annals' curtain is raised, and continue to figure prominently over a sixty-year-span in the manuscript, it is the leaders of Cuauhtinchan who must capture the spotlight. In order for them to found the altepetl that is at once the source for and raison d'être of the annals, the locus of significant action must shift. This is accomplished in bits of descriptive prose and a pictorial scenography that portray the virtues and accomplishments of the ancestral Cuauhtinchantlaca. The labor of lending this collective protagonist its historical substance thus emerges as one of the *Historia*'s major narratological burdens. Given the importance of ancestors and origins in this tale, however, it is not the people of Cuauhtinchan themselves who must first enter history's theater but their progenitors, intrepid warriors known as the Chichimeca.

Our first glimpse of these warriors comes when two Tolteca heroes arrive at their subterranean lair, a cave in the mountains in a remote desert. Following divine counsel, Icxicoatl and Quetzaltehueyac journey to the sacred place known alternately as Colhuacatepec (Place of the Mountain of the Ancestors) and Chicomoztoc (Place of the Seven Caves). It is this site and revelatory crossroad in the narrative that the resplendent scene in plate 5 announces. Toward the bottom of the scene, near the mouth of the cave, the Tolteca heroes, blackened in soot in the manner of holy men, negotiate with two Chichimeca warriors. The wispy speech scrolls fluttering between the figures offer visual evidence of the prolixity of their discussion. The alphabetic text underscores what the image reiterates—extraordinary diplomatic perseverance was required to lure the Chichimeca into the fractious world of combat against the Tolteca enemies at Cholula.

As the birthplace of the Chichimeca and site of their initial encounter with the Tolteca, Colhuacatepec is the archaic pivot around which don Alonso's history book turns. While the founding of his altepetl ultimately becomes a seminal episode in the annals, the narrative of illustrious birth and privilege rotates around transactions conducted in and out of the mountain cave. Had the Chichimeca failed to be seduced from Colhuacatepec, two debacles would have ensued: the Tolteca would have had to cede control of their homeland at Cholula, and Cuauhtinchan would never have been founded, for the ancestral settlers of the altepetl—the first Cuauhtinchantlaca—numbered among those who dwelt within the cave.

To birth this brood from their womblike crypt, then, the annals resort to especially subtle and sophisticated means, enlisting both the painted and written registers to flesh out the sacral diplomacy at Chicomoztoc. The alphabetic text of the *Historia*, for instance, trades on oral cadences derived from recitation. To stage full conversations at the mountain cave and transcribe the lyrical content of songs and prayers consumes much ink, which in turn opens a digression in the annals' main narrative stream. As the Chichimeca are coaxed into this world, the speech of antiquity flowers like the flora atop their mountain home.

At Colhuacatepec time also slows. Until the Chichimeca become well settled in the realm of regular existence, day-by-day, rather than the typical year-by-year, narration is required to tell their story. Indeed, prior to, and after the events at Colhuacatepec, the annals faithfully register events in a year-by-year fashion. The Tolteca expedition to the mountain cave, however, interrupts the regular flow of time (fs. 15r–25v, ms. 46–50, 54–58). In the year 6 House, we read of twenty-six days (two cycles of 13), during which Icxicoatl and Quetzaltehueyac go to Chicomoztoc, coax the warriors within to emerge, prepare these figures for battle, and return to Cholula to trounce their (now mutual) enemies. Shortly after the victory celebration, as the Chichimeca warriors head into the wilderness to found their own altepetl, the *Historia* resumes timekeeping in yearly measures. Since this is the only break in the annals' practice of annual entries, the shift in registers highlights the significance of these events. As if to underscore the point, several full-page images are also associated with this emergence scene, many of which are the most elaborate in the entire *Historia*. In the visual register as well, then, all sense of hurry is suspended as pithy details come into view.[9] From this, we understand that the very language and temporality of the annals must shift to incorporate the Chichimeca warriors into the larger narrative of don Alonso's Pre-Hispanic tale.

While the episode at Colhuacatepec and those that immediately follow evoke meaning on multiple levels, I am particularly interested in a series of juxtapositions that allows the ancestral founders of Cuauhtinchan to emerge from the mountain cave with a unique claim to historical importance. According to the *Historia*, these people are at once allies of the Tolteca, allies of other Chichimeca, and allies of no one but themselves.

The links that chain the Chichimeca warriors to the Tolteca are forged largely of pictorial and appellative components. The episode at Colhuacatepec, for example, reiterates a primal scene. In the distant past, the Tolteca heroes had been Chichimecas. As barbarous hunter-warriors born from the mountain cave, they entered the world seeking their fortune. Now, the Tolteca heroes return to their birthplace to entice warriors like themselves from the same cavernous site. Early in the *Historia*'s alphabetic narrative there is parenthetical reference to Tolteca heroes coming from Colhuacatepec, thus hinting at the latter emergence. Through pictorial evocation this pattern—in which the Chichimeca exodus mirrors, and supercedes, that of the Tolteca—becomes especially clear.

The annals include two full-page images of Colhuacatepec-Chicomoztoc. The first shows the Tolteca emergence from the cave (pl. 1) the other depicts the Chichimeca warriors still sequestered in inside the cavern's recesses (pl. 5 and fig. 8). While not identical, the two paintings rely upon a single pictorial model. Such reiteration—which brings the large, painted cavern into view twice, and the second time returns us to a more elaborate version—produces a visual and mnemonic echo that links the two emergence tales. Because the doubling is not a literal repetition, however, our perception is colored, literally and figuratively, by the second scene. When the Tolteca return to Colhuacatepec-Chicomoztoc, this time to fetch the Chichimeca, the scene erupts into chromatic ebullience, implying that much time has passed since the traumatic events of the first exodus, and that both the cavern and the annals' reader have undergone a rite of passage.

The *Historia* further affirms kinship between the Tolteca and Chichimeca by fashioning Colhuacatepec in the lexical image of Cholula. The mountain cave is a supernatural setting, a sacred place invoked through a series of metaphorical sobriquets. Some of these designations evoke white rushes, white willows, or the blue-green color associated with Cholula. In this way, the repetition of names not only connotes preciousness, it also draws Cholula to Colhuacatepec, rendering them into parallel utopias. Moreover, although hundreds of places are mentioned in the *Historia*, the annals reserve the special distinction of having multiple, metaphorical appellations for just three sites: Cholula, Colhuacatepec, and Cuauhtinchan. Through a wealth of names, then, the *Historia* binds these places together even as it separates them from other sites. Yet the annals do not assign to Cuauhtinchan any of the same metaphorical names they offer to Cholula and Colhuacatepec; the altepetl of Cuauhtinchan participates in a constellation of sites worthy of multiple monikers, but does not emerge as the same kind of sacred, ancestral place as the other two.

Cuauhtinchan will never become as revered as Cholula, nor as miraculous as Colhuacatepec, nevertheless the *Historia* aligns these sites with care. The annals cannot merely explain the connections between the Tolteca of Cholula and the Chichimeca of Colhuacatepec, it must also assay the mettle of the ancestral Cuauhtinchantlaca so that they may come to rule their own altepetl. A fundamental index of this appraisal can be found in the ways that speech operates in the environs of Colhuacatepec. Throughout much of the annals, spoken language is an unproblematic, transparent medium. So, for example, honorific metaphorical exchanges are common among actors of high stature. Rarely are any spoken words obstacles to communication. Once the Tolteca assemble before the mountain cave, however, speech morphs into a sign that marks ethnic difference. According to the *Historia*, after four days of prayer, Icxicoatl and Quetzaltehueyac make contact with a lone Chichimeca warrior, Coatzin. From this moment of first encounter, Coatzin is identified as "the interpreter." He and only he speaks directly with both Tolteca heroes and Chichimeca warriors. Shuttling in and out of the cave, Coatzin translates the Tolteca tongue into the language of his fellow Chichimeca and then reverses the feat. Here linguistic difference calls attention to boundaries separating groups. Drawing this point out further, in this setting language also signifies Chichimeca solidarity. In designating one spokesperson for all of the warriors, the annals channel the cacophony of Chichimeca speech into the cunning voice of a unitary individual and thus resolve Chichimeca identity, an identity distinct from that of the Tolteca. Language therefore signs a way of life and position in the world, not merely a way of speaking.

As if to reaffirm this point, clothing also plays a role in separating the two groups, although only in pictorial imagery. The alphabetic text makes no mention of apparel, yet the painting of Chicomoztoc devotes considerable attention to the dress of the actors. In plate 5 the Tolteca appear richly attired in quetzal-feather headdresses and elaborate back ornaments, their skin blackened with soot. The Chichimeca warriors, on the other hand, are distinguished by pale skin, headdresses of short feathers, and animal-skin cloaks. Through clothing and skin color, the painting capitalizes on the representational possibilities for signing ethnic and status differences in visual terms. What makes one Chichimeca is thus the language one speaks as well as a physical way of being in the world.

Yet the ancestral founders of Cuauhtinchan were not, as the careful reader learns, merely Chichimeca. This is one point that the pictorial register makes far more apparent than the lexical one. In the painting of Chicomoztoc, each of seven Chichimeca groups holes up in a lobe of the cave. Named via a diminutive glyph at the back of each recess, the Malpantlaca are separated from the Texcalteca and Cuauhtinchantlaca in niches of the grotto.[10] Social divisions among the Chichimeca are therefore signed through the geomorphology of the cave. The painting in plate 5 also suggests that distinctions in status do not go unmarked. All the warriors inside Chicomoztoc wear identical headdresses of short feathers except for the Cuauhtinchantlaca, whose leader wears jaguar headgear (fig. 8). Within his recess alone we are shown an eagle and a jaguar. The eagle functions as a name glyph, identifying the Cuauhtinchantlaca as People of the Home of the Eagles. The coupling of raptor and feline, as avatars of the preeminent warrior societies in Pre-Hispanic central Mexico, also infuses this cavelet with a martial aura. To underscore this, the Cuauhtinchan eagle brandishes the *atl-tlachinolli*, a sign of sacred warfare, in his beak. Of all the Chichimeca warriors, then, the Cuauhtinchantlaca are the most militant.

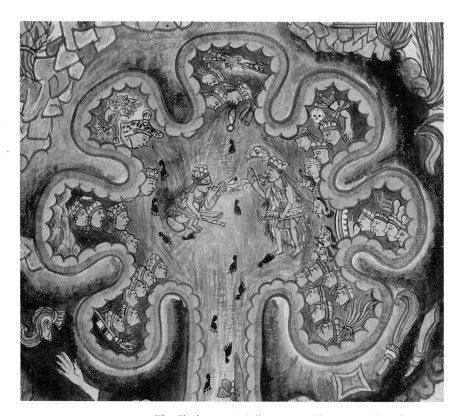

Fig. 8 The Chichimeca in Colhuacatepec-Chicomoztoc (detail), *Historia Tolteca-Chichimeca.* Pigment on European paper. Bibliothèque Nationale, Paris, f. 16r, ms. 51–53. *Photograph courtesy of the Bibliothèque Nationale, Paris.*

This is not insignificant, for according to the *Historia*, the Chichimeca warriors earned their badge of distinction, the right to found an autonomous altepetl, through military service. Consequently, the greater their soldierly contribution, the more deserving of autonomy and its privileges the ancestral Cuauhtinchantlaca became.

To further emphasize the exceptional position of the Cuauhtinchantlaca, the episode at Colhuacatepec provides a setting that establishes the priority of Moquihuix, one of the Cuauhtinchantlaca leaders. Identified in the painting by a black stripe across his cheek, Moquihuix assumes a unique role in the activities at the mountain cave. He appears at the center of Chicomoztoc and is the only Chichimeca warrior to have words with Coatzin, the interpreter (see pl. 5 and fig. 8). From this, the painting convinces us that Moquihuix was also a spokesman for the Chichimeca. Furthermore, the painting identifies Moquihuix as the first Chichimeca warrior to emerge from the cave. Aside from Coatzin the interpreter, he is the only warrior the visual image allows to venture outside the protective walls of Chicomoztoc.[11]

By distinguishing Moquihuix and the Cuauhtinchantlaca from other warriors at Colhuacatepec, the annals confirm their position as distinguished paragons of the Pre-Hispanic past. And for don Alonso, this distinction was no triviality. Moquihuix was not only an ancestral founder of Cuauhtinchan, he was the ancestral father of don Alonso's lineage. This, no doubt, helps to explain why the *Historia* so intently renders Moquihuix and the Cuauhtinchantlaca as extraordinary actors. Yet whatever the *Historia* agenda may have been, it does not unravel just one strand of ancestral achievement. Rather, the *Historia* consistently intertwines don Alonso's ambitions and desires with the fates of others. This book not only recounts the history of an illustrious lineage, it also binds that story into a metanarrative on the larger destiny of a whole altepetl.

To Found and Unfound Altepetl

The *Historia* goes to some trouble to demonstrate that Cuauhtinchan was not founded in a historical vacuum. Rather, don Alonso's hometown comes into its own alongside the altepetl of Totomihuacan, a site whose ancestors wielded authority through the same primal circumstances as his own founding fathers. That is, the first settlers of Totomihuacan were, likewise, warriors lured from Colhuacatepec to fight beside the Tolteca, and who, in the wake of victory, inherited their own territorial dominion. From the moment of its inception, then, Cuauhtinchan's existence and identity as an autonomous altepetl were mirrored in a sister community. Yet the manuscript does not relay this in an uncomplicated manner. The joint narratives of altepetl and autochthony follow patterns of alignment and divergence that we have already discerned, yet they also elaborate and refine these tropes. In so doing, they lend the *Historia* both complexity and an authoritative edge. Cuauhtinchan's foundation scene thus performs two tasks: it establishes the altepetl's initial boundaries, and it charts the moral high ground from which its distinctions shine, presumably diminishing the luster of its neighbors. The strength of Cuauhtinchan, the *Historia* asserts, derives from no ancient coincidence; rather, the altepetl's fate turns on the fact that it came into being as one—indeed, the most exceptional— among numerous ancient competitors.

In recounting this kind of tale, don Alonso's project is far from unique. Modern interpreters have teased similar tactics from many Nahua annals. What is significant here though, and what I draw upon below, is not simply the story of Cuauhtinchan's "exceptions to the rule" or "rule of exceptions," but key visual and lexical idioms that the *Historia* painters put into play to distinguish their homeland from its allies and rivals. Their idiosyncrasies suggest what we might call, for lack of a better phrase, "stratagems of convenient silence." By this I mean something closer to a narrative latticework than the censorious repression of controversial fact. An under-over-under-over pattern with blank spaces separating the lath produces absences that, while fundamental to the trellis structure, go largely unnoticed because of the busyness of the weave. What results is a history in which little appears intentionally struck from the record. There are, in other words, no dark lines obscuring unwelcome facts in the manner of spy documents in Hollywood Cold War dramas. Instead, the annals are so packed with minutiae that nonappearance in, or disappearance from, the historical record creates meaning in a subtle but significant manner.[12]

In its recollection of Cuauhtinchan's founding, the *Historia* rests, in two particularly acute ways, on such economies of silence. On one hand, the annals simply write many sites and groups of people out of the historical record. So, for instance, the manuscript identifies seven Chichimeca tribes who exit Colhuacatepec and fight the good fight in Cholula, yet only two of these valiant clans are rewarded for their valor: the Cuauhtinchantlaca and the Totomihuaque. The others—the Acolchichimeca, Tzauhcteca, Zacateca, Malpantlaca, and Texcalteca—quite literally disappear from the account (see Reyes García 1977: 28). In distinguishing just two groups, the Cuauhtinchantlaca and Totomihuaque, in pulling them away from the Chichimeca rank and file, the *Historia* compounds their significance at the expense of their fellow warriors. A second, more common, stratagem distinguishes Cuauhtinchan from its neighbor via analogy. Narrative or visual incidents alternately draw parallels between Cuauhtinchan and Totomihuacan and set them into hierarchical relations. This seesawing often signs a dangerous narrowing of similarity and difference; it indicates a sensitive (if not sore) spot where Cuauhtinchan's fate and identity coalesce in delicate social and political intercourse with a community that is nearly indistinguishable from itself.

Compiling clues from the annals' written narrative, we detect two versions of the founding of Cuauhtinchan and Totomihuacan.[13] These accounts concur that the leaders of the Cuauhtinchantlaca and the Totomihuaque are none other than the original Chichimeca warriors who, through military deeds, shored up the Tolteca; the *Historia* also admits that the two altepetl (Totomihuacan and Cuauhtinchan) settled their sites at the same crucial moment. Their mutual boundaries and political destinies therefore required painstaking differentiation. One narrative separates the history of the Totomihuaque from that of the Cuauhtinchantlaca, and fleshes out the internal composition of each. In this recollection of genesis what emerges are assertions of autonomy in the face of uncanny resemblance. The second nativity narrative is closer to a foundation myth, wherein the role played by the Tolteca heroes Icxicoatl and Quetzaltehueyac is heightened. Here the culture heroes not only lead the fathers of each altepetl to the places they will found, they also mark the boundaries at the juncture between them. Hence this account cultivates the nuanced relations of power and status among Tolteca, Totomihuaque, and Cuauhtinchantlaca.[14]

Read together, the two foundation accounts project Totomihuacan and Cuauhtinchan as altepetl cast into a single die. Yet the visual imagery of the *Historia* proceeds otherwise. The pictorial register treats in considerable detail the asymmetrical relationship between the polities such that Cuauhtinchan's importance emerges at the expense of Totomihuacan's. Three double-folio paintings in the *Historia* depict the altepetl foundation myths, one represents the settling of Totomihuacan (pl. 13) with the other two focusing upon Cuauhtinchan (pls. 15 and 16). In addition to their common thematic preoccupations, all use similar compositional mechanisms. Extending across two pages of the annals, each image locates signs for the newly established altepetl and its founder(s) toward the center of the painted rectangle. Smaller toponyms, which signify boundary markers, limn the perimeter, conceptualizing outlying places as a circuit framing an epicenter. By repeating this configuration three times, the *Historia* aligns the scenes as it offers its readers thematic variations on the founding of altepetl. The format here is important, for these are the only three paintings in the annals to employ this compositional layout.[15]

When the first two images are placed side by side, however, we grasp how much less indulgent the *Historia* is in its treatment of the founding of Totomihuacan. Comparing plates 13 and 15, we see a parallel relationship between a center and its periphery—between a core of an altepetl and its boundaries—diagrammed in each painting. Yet the relative degree of detail sharply separates the images. In the painting of Totomihuacan, for instance, only one named leader, Aquiyahuatl, makes an appearance toward the center of the page. Across from him and at his back, stands the sign for his altepetl: a small hill glyph that, except for its placement and green color, resembles the other place signs in the painting (pl. 13). Apart from the central elements and their frame of boundary markers, the ground of this painting lies fallow. The land between Totomihuacan (represented here as Basket Hill, Chiquiuhtepec) and its boundaries appears devoid of human settlement and utterly lacking in landscape ambition. In contrast, the crowded and busy depiction of Cuauhtinchan not only defines the migration route of its founders with trails of footprints, it shows footprints passing before each boundary marker at the perimeter of the page. This evokes the ritual "walking of boundaries" that was performed at the altepetl's installation (pl. 15). In addition, the painting salts the ground with scenes of military victories that sealed the auspicious fate of the ancient Cuauhtinchantlaca, allowing them to rule over this land.

As in the Totomihuacan painting, the central toponym in plate 15 has been set apart from the boundary markers at the periphery of this scene, yet Cuauhtinchan hardly appears here as just another altepetl among many. Rather its toponymic sign dwarfs all of the conquered sites in its environs as well as those that limn its territory. Moreover, the glyph for Cuauhtinchan evokes the features of an actual place in the landscape. Jagged cliffs and a stream of water divide the toponym in half; its hilly edges have been shaded with tones of green and gold and dotted with plants. In contrast, the other hill glyphs in the painting have not been depicted as landscape vignettes. With the exception of Matlalcueye (upper left corner), which has been modeled in green and gold, the toponyms surrounding Cuauhtinchan take a traditional Pre-Hispanic form: affixes and standardized hill glyphs, or streams of water, are used to evoke the names of places. As a result, Cuauhtinchan visually dominates its mapped extremities—and by extension, its territorial region—in a way that Totomihuacan does not. When the two images are read together, we see that the birth of Cuauhtinchan has been rendered in more detail and with greater nuance than that of her twin. Although Totomihuacan's origins appear, at least at first, to receive significant attention, the pictorial implication is that the history of one altepetl's founding ultimately supercedes the other.

The third painting in this sequence underscores the point, but through different visual language (pl. 16). This image focuses on the establishment of boundaries that took place when Totomihuacan and Cuauhtinchan were settled, and it shows Icxicoatl and Quetzaltehueyac engaged in this boundary rite, conversing with delegates from both altepetl. A written commentary on the right side of the painting notes that both Totomihuaque and Cuauhtinchantlaca took part in these boundary rites. And at each edge of the painting, just below Icxicoatl and Quetzaltehueyac, a pair of delegates appears. To create balance and indicate that neither party has the upper hand, the painter shows Cuauhtinchan's leaders to the left, Totomihuacan's representatives to the right. Although harmony and impartiality are suggested by this composition, the painting nevertheless privileges Cuauhtinchan, for the position of honor at the center of the image is held by toponyms for only that altepetl. This, combined with the fact that even among the boundary sites the toponym for Totomihuacan is absent, establishes Cuauhtinchan's eminence over its sister community. The painting has eclipsed from view the altepetl of Totomihuacan even as it pictures the delegates of both altepetl marking their boundaries.

While the three paintings of altepetl foundings reveal that Cuauhtinchan defined itself as both kindred to and more important than Totomihuacan, there is more to their story. A comparison of these images also suggests that from the very beginning Cuauhtinchan's identity as a political body was fractured and diverse. The first painting of Cuauhtinchan's settlement, for example, portrays the altepetl as a hetero-geneous entity with military ambitions (pl. 15). Five leaders of the altepetl are shown near the center of the scene, each commanding his own region of Cuauhtinchan.[16] In addition, multiple conquests are pictured. Two men are sacrificially dispatched by arrows, and severed heads metonymically sign Cuauhtinchantlaca victories over neighboring communities. An alternative perspective on both the foundation and identity of Cuauhtinchan is shown in the second of Cuauhtinchan's birth images (pl. 16).[17] Suppressed in this composition are the internal divisions of the previous foundation scene. Instead, the altepetl appears with only two founders stationed near the toponymic signs at the center of the composition. The other leaders and disparate parts of the altepetl have been subsumed by these actors and place glyphs. Moreover, compared to the other representation, this scene of Cuauhtinchan's establishment has been purged of the altepetl's subsequent military endeavors. Speech scrolls displace bleeding heads as negotiations replace conquest.

The divergence between the two pictorial accounts largely stems from the fact that the paintings represent different aspects of the foundation narrative. The first image sets forth the priority of military conquest in the establishment of Cuauhtinchan's autonomy; the second brings to the fore negotiations over terri-torial domain. Because the paintings were meant to be seen in sequence within the context of the annals, Cuauhtinchan emerges as an altepetl with multiple identities. It coalesces even in its heterogeneity, as a military power and as a product of inter-corporate boundary negotiation.

These two foundation paintings therefore betray an important aspect of Nahua historical imagination. It is here that we sense most keenly their morality tale. Once, long ago, two ways existed to assert claims to territory and political autonomy—negotiation was the means of interaction with superior (such as the Tolteca) and collateral (such as the Totomihuaque) groups, while combat leading to conquest epitomized rapport with people of inferior status and/or alien ethnicity.

The paintings also indicate that the people of Cuauhtinchan presented a full array of virtues when they founded their altepetl: they exhibited fierceness in battle, they excelled as cunning negotiators, and they had the prescience not to overvalue any of these skills to the exclusion of others.

Dynastic Coupling

So far my reading of don Alonso's book has inspired the following assessment: the *Historia* memorializes not one man's take on the deep past, but rather, through the confluence of anecdotal threads—some visual, others alphabetic—sustains don Alonso's aspirations to pin his heritage to the birth of illustrious ancestors, to the founding of his altepetl, and to the distant horizon of collective living memory. Moreover, the literary stage of his book features the play of silence against prolixity, of paucity against abundance. As historians working at the turn of the twenty-first century (rather than the mid-sixteenth), we have learned that the implications of certain silences, not just their location and form, require comment. In Cuauhtinchan in the 1540s or 1550s, it was seemingly proper for a history book to remain mute about those who did not matter. Today such reticence would provoke a more complicated response, especially if it hushed, even without malice, women and men whose economic and political autonomy remained stunted by the reigning hierarchies within altepetl like Cuauhtinchan. Indeed, much current scholarship in ethnohistory, archaeology, and art history seeks to write back into Pre-Hispanic antiquity those who lived their lives outside the limelight, whose experiences of splendor and prestige were far more limited than even those of don Alonso and his kin. This kind of history seems to have been of little value to indigenous leaders in the sixteenth century, and so the *Historia* provides precious few insights into the bit actors that must have filled its hometown and the communities of the ancients.

There is of course, no compulsion to take the manuscript at face value, yet my primary concern lies with the construction and meaning of the *Historia*'s Pre-Hispanic history, and so, in this instance, I choose to follow its lead. Only in the realm of gender relations do the annals provide thin cracks from which a story of marginal figures can be drawn out. Among the most absent and underarticulated of all the people in don Alonso's past are women, and yet they are not wholly invisible. Appearing at critical junctures in the account, certain women—such as those rejected by Huemac at Tollan—set events into motion that lead to the realignment of power relations between male-dominated factions. Within the *Historia*, females can assume the role of narrative catalyst, and thus sometimes fulfill roles similar to those described by Susan Gillespie in her structural analysis of Mexica imperial histories (1989: 61–78). It is this "nearly but not quite" arrangement that calls for reconsideration. To close this chapter on allies and rivals, then, I turn to one last trope of social relations, that of intermarriage, for I believe that the boundaries of don Alonso's history were drawn not only upon the land, when his altepetl was born alongside that of Totomihuacan, but also through the literary and matrimonial exchange of women, women who were hardly commoners, but rather the Pre-Hispanic equivalents of Guinevere of Arthurian fame.

[handwritten marginal note: BUT IS THIS REALLY DIFFERENT? PERSONAL INTERPRETATION MUST INTERSECT W/ COLLECTIVE MEMORY SO AS NOT TO BE DISMISSED]

[handwritten marginal note: SA!]

On the bridal theme, the annals hardly falter. Marriages *Historia*-style are of a piece, they are local events cast before a narrative backdrop of male prerogative and agency. Highly valued for their exchange value, well-born brides were precious— not quite as commodities, but certainly as desired beings. In this, the annals' tale is indistinguishable from many sixteenth-century histories from central Mexico. In this particular telling, the paradigm for the leaders of Cuauhtinchan hinges on an ideal of manhood given substance by great leaders of the Tolteca. That is, the rulers of the Cuauhtinchantlaca earn the right to govern only as they labor in the shadow of these legendary male heroes. Moreover, altepetl foundation scenes, scenes that ostensibly mobilize entire communities, coalesce in the *Historia* as the designs of men alone. Even genealogy, one of the most basic historical topoi to draw male and female actors together, occupies the *Historia* scribe only rarely. Far more consequential than the notation of family trees are dynastic histories that trace the passage of rulership from father to son across generations. The *Historia*, for example, registers the dynastic lines of several sixteenth-century leaders of Cuauhtinchan, some of which take form as lists of male names that (miraculously) engender only male progeny. It is true that in a few genealogies the names of both mothers and fathers are recorded, but these are rare occurrences. And the offspring of these unions invariably turn out to be male. Female progenitors, when identified, most frequently are revealed to be non-Cuauhtinchantlaca by birth. One of the support roles women perform in this book is to signal admixture with foreign, usually ancestral, blood, and thus parse those who are wholly autochthonous from those who are not.

The pictorial component of the *Historia* also favors the primacy of men, largely through representational visibility. Whereas principal male figures appear frequently in the annals' paintings, their female counterparts are almost wholly absent. Even when their visages and bodily forms do surface, these women are ciphers. They are, for the most part, nameless figures who appear as if to remind readers that the world of the ancestors was not comprised only of males (fig. 9). In this, the *Historia* differs from Bernardino de Sahagún's works, *Primeros Memoriales* and *Florentine Codex*, both of which assign women more prominent roles in their painted images than in their written texts (Brown 1983; Hellbom 1967). It also stands apart from several of the imperial histories from Central Mexico that feature named women (Diel 2005; Gillespie 1989). Indeed, in the annals from Cuauhtinchan, the representational channels of script and image run parallel in their near silence.

If text and image conspire in a similar androcentricity, we recognize nonetheless that the *Historia*'s imagery cannot be taken as representative of Nahua social reality. Scholars of gender have taught us much in the last two decades. Not the least of their lessons is that "looking for women" to balance the narratives of highly visible men is but one project of many. To grapple persuasively with questions of gender requires considerable imagination, since the ways in which people wield their bodies and forge meaningful male and female (and other) experiences is no simple, or even predictable matter (see, for instance, Conkey 2001).

In the case of the *Historia*, gender was, I believe, a source of some anxiety; otherwise its insistence on male actors would not have been so marked. In modern

Fig. 9 Chichimeca women. *Historia Tolteca-Chichimeca.* Pigment on European paper. Bibliothèque Nationale, Paris, f. 22v, ms. 54–58 (detail). *Photograph courtesy of the Bibliothèque Nationale, Paris.*

parlance, we might say the annals do not merely privilege the lives of men, they seek to construct a vision of paradigmatic male identity. Who men could, and should, become is one of the annals' most crucial lessons. As such, the scarcity of females may be read as a narrative scrim that heightens the complex hierarchy of altepetl-building and warrior society. The entry of a female actor is a kind of epiphany given her more common absence, and from this we understand that these annals fashion an ideal masculine agent whose traits depend, at least in part, upon the near occlusion of female counterparts. Men, to put it bluntly, are their best selves when dealing with other men and, upon occasion, when marrying significant women. Surely the representation of both women and men in the *Historia* bore some relationship to lived reality; indeed, we know that texts interpolate their readers and vice versa. Yet the points of intersection, between representation and actual lives, are not easy to know. As with so many Central Mexican histories, the task set for these annals did not lie in describing what ethnohistoric research suggests were the lived experiences of gender.[18]

Ultimately, intermarriage fulfills a substantial need in securing the legacy of Cuauhtinchan's male leaders, and perhaps most obviously, if not also most importantly, marital bonds tie Cuauhtinchan to the sacred site of Cholula. The founders of Cuauhtinchan were not only warriors who emerged from their mountain cave to fight on behalf of their Tolteca allies, they were also grooms who married the daughters of Icxicoatl and Quetzaltehueyac. In the history of Cuauhtinchan these intermarriages sutured an enduring graft between two heterogeneous groups of people—the civilized Tolteca and the warlike Chichimeca—and, by extension, the two altepetl. Beyond this, nuptial unions are significant within Cuauhtinchan itself. Two intermarriages stand out as exemplary in this context. The first, which has just been mentioned, joined the Tolteca and Chichimeca, not only binding Cholula to Cuauhtinchan but also elevating two Chichimeca leaders, Moquihuix and Teuhctlecozauhqui. According to the *Historia*, of all Cuauhtinchan's leaders only these were offered the daughters of the Tolteca.[19] The lineages of Teuhctlecozauhqui and Moquihuix, then, embody the primal connection with the Tolteca heroes. The second intermarriage of Cuauhtinchantlaca with outsiders follows a pattern initiated by this very union. The men of Cuauhtinchan, who live in a well-established community, offer their daughters to recent Mixteca arrivals. Within the annals, this alliance becomes meaningful because it reiterates the match made years earlier by the Tolteca and Chichimeca. One marriage takes on meaning as the founding paradigm, the other as replicating instance. At the same time, these marriages align the habits of the ancestral Cuauhtinchantlaca with the well-honed practices of high-status individuals in Central Mexico who sought to bind social groups along both horizontal and vertical axes of economics and prestige (Berdan 2006).

Other marriage alliances occur in Cuauhtinchan's history, but these two auspicious unions crystallize into the two principal parcialidades that cleave Cuauhtinchan. The Nahua groups descend from the marriage of Tolteca and Chichimeca, whereas the Pinome spring from the coupling of Cuauhtinchantlaca with Mixteca. Throughout the sixteenth century, distributions of power in Cuauhtinchan were structured by this division. This is one reason why the *Historia* features the origins of these ethnic groups. There is, however, another reason. These annals do not merely register community history, they are also a history of an illustrious lineage, and don Alonso de Castañeda claimed Nahua descent. That the *Historia* establishes the priority of his ancestors—as the first settlers in Cuauhtinchan who emerged from Chicomoztoc and married Cholulans—is hardly trivial. For it is through such genealogical skeins that his lineage commands a status so prestigious that Mixteca immigrants and their Pinome descendants could never hope to unravel them. And, if we can trust the *Historia*, this status was bound into don Alonso's heritage for time immemorial.

In relating the history of the Nahua and Pinome parcialidades, and in promoting the Nahuas as the more distinguished faction, the *Historia* employs, once again, a divisive partiality. Patterns of similarity and difference create both collateral and hierarchical relations. I am thus claiming that, in addition to beckoning toward ideal maleness, the *Historia* intermarriages performed another semiotic function. In this regard, the Cuauhtinchan annals resemble to no small degree the Mexica royal histories that Susan Gillespie (1989) and Lori Diel (2005) have examined. Conjoining their insights with the analysis here, a broader question might be posed. Although the *Historia* was neither royal in inspiration or function, nor produced in

Fig. 10 Teuhctlecozauhqui and Tepexoch ilama at Cuauhtinchan (detail of Cuauhtinchan foundation scene), *Historia Tolteca-Chichimeca*. Pigment on European paper. Bibliothèque Nationale, Paris, f. 33r, ms. 46–50. *Photograph courtesy of the Bibliothèque Nationale, Paris.*

Mexico-Tenochtitlan, its alignment with those that were is too similar to be simply coincidental. The query that hovers at the margins is whether Pre-Hispanic women entered Nahua annals and chronicles across Central Mexico less as historical actors than as signs, and, if so, what was the range of their semiotic powers?

If we pursue the narratives of intermarriage in the *Historia*, we see that when taken up by the literary and pictorial apparatus of the manuscript women do not merely color male identities or distinguish key Nahua lineages, they also align Nahuas and Pinome even as they separate these two groups from lesser factions in Cuauhtinchan's history. In calling attention to the first leaders of the Nahua parcialidad, however, the annals focus attention on one primordial Nahua couple, the altepetl-founder Teuhctlecozauhqui and his Cholulan consort, Tepexoch ilama. No other couple in the annals figures so prominently or so often. Nor does any other couple play such a conspicuous role in the historical narrative.[20] Moreover, the *Historia* painters represent Teuhctlecozauhqui and Tepexoch ilama in a manner that accentuates their exceptional status. They are the sole male-female pair to appear in the painted imagery of the annals. It is in fact their story that establishes the boundaries of don Alonso's historical gambit, and, ultimately, defines the semiotic scope of his literary and pictorial endeavor.

The *Historia* recounts that, in the twelfth century, a man named Teuhctlecozauhqui played an instrumental part in Cuauhtinchan's founding. This hero emerged from the cave of Colhuacatepec-Chicomoztoc and fought for Quetzaltehueyac and Icxicoatl at Cholula; the Tolteca invested this man with sovereign authority, and Teuhctlecozauhqui went on to rule over those who settled Cuauhtinchan. Moreover, this man wed a Cholulan woman called Tepexoch ilama. Two centuries later, the annals tell of warriors from Tlatelolco who invaded Cuauhtinchan and subjugated it. The ruler these warriors defeated was named Teuhctlecozauhqui and his consort was also a woman called Tepexoch ilama. While the *Historia* does make extraordinary claims, suggesting that one man and his bride ruled Cuauhtinchan for over two hundred years is an unlikely one (Leibsohn, n.d.: 390). Rather, in this titular replication the annals convey something more complex.

To grasp this point, it is necessary to consider more fully the pictorial aspect of the *Historia*. While neither precisely a redundancy nor a replication, the paintings bear upon and reiterate content covered in the alphabetic text: a dynastic couple named Teuhctlecozauhqui and Tepexoch ilama is present at both the founding of Cuauhtinchan and its defeat at the hands of the Tlatelolcans. We see this in two painted scenes. In one, the first of the altepetl's foundation scenes, Teuhctlecozauhqui perches atop a stone seat next to a house that signifies his palace and, by extension, his settlement within Cuauhtinchan (fig. 10 and pl. 15). The trail of footprints approaching his palatial home marks his migration to Tepeticpac (Mountain Summit), the region over which he reigned. Across from him kneels a woman in Pre-Hispanic–style accoutrements; a hill-glyph and flower identify her as Tepexoch ilama (Hill Flower). The couple therefore appears here in the guise of altepetl-founders. Because Teuhctlecozauhqui is the sole founder-ruler to appear with a consort in the painting, the couple's relationship accrues further significance.

Fig. 11 Tepexoch ilama with Teuhctlecozauhqui (detail of Cuauhtinchan battle scene), *Historia Tolteca-Chichimeca*. Pigment on European paper. Bibliothèque Nationale, Paris, f. 42v, ms. 46–50. *Photograph courtesy of the Bibliothèque Nationale, Paris.*

The pair visually testifies to the ruler's connections with the Tolteca lords of Cholula, who invested him with the authority to govern and bestowed upon him one of their daughters. At one level, then, these figures symbolize a link in the chain of dynastic power forged between Cholula and Cuauhtinchan.

Yet there is more to this story, for two arrows pierce the couple's palace. The barbs receive no mention in the alphabetic text, but herein lies one of the *Historia* painter's more skillful ruses. A kind of visual prolepsis is put into play, the arrows foreshadowing events that will occur two centuries hence, when Tlatelolcans conquer the latter-day Teuhctlecozauhqui and Tepexoch ilama. Further support for this reading of the image comes from another depiction of the couple. Staged within the last major painting of the *Historia* is a pitched battle between the forces of the Cuauhtinchantlaca and Tlatelolcans (pls. 17/18). Reappearing, but this time centered at the apex of an oversized hill, Teuhctlecozauhqui and Tepexoch ilama sit across from each other, flanking their palace (fig. 11). The composition of this vignette closely resembles that in figure 10, although here Teuhctlecozauhqui sits upon a bench and his consort is seen in a more elaborate dress. Because the battle still rages below them and, presumably because the forces in the battle are so evenly matched, the outcome of this fray is a hard to foresee. Arrows do not yet pierce the edifice of the leader and his consort.[21]

Fig. 12 Tepexoch ilama with Quauhtlatoa (detail of Cuauhtinchan's defeat), *Historia Tolteca-Chichimeca*. Pigment on European paper. Bibliothèque Nationale, Paris, f. 43r, ms. 54–58. *Photograph courtesy of the Bibliothèque Nationale, Paris.*

Ultimately, this battle between the Cuauhtinchantlaca and Tlatelolcans will leave the Nahua faction crippled. For in the wake of the Tlatelolcan victory, those of Pinome descent oust the Nahua governors of Cuauhtinchan, and two hundred years of Nahua hegemony comes to an ignominious end. Hence, we gather that Teuhctlecozauhqui and Tepexoch ilama represent the alpha and omega of Nahua power in Cuauhtinchan. In picturing the same couple twice, in nearly identical vignettes, the annals imply that one lineage's rule arcs back over Cuauhtinchan from the time of its founding to the time of its conquest by the Tlatelolcans.

In his 1947 essay on the *Historia*, Paul Kirchhoff suggested that this lineage was anchored by two leaders with a shared name. He also proposed that this doubling was meant to symbolically align the two leaders across centuries of Cuauhtinchan's history.[22] Because Kirchhoff was more concerned with questions of dynastic chronology than with the codex's visual convergences, he makes little of the fact that Teuhctlecozauhqui does not rule Cuauhtinchan alone. Yet the visual point is crucial. The ruler appears with his consort, Tepexoch ilama, and together, the pair reinscribes the inauguration and closure of Nahua dominance at Cuauhtinchan.

Whether or not Tepexoch ilama actually had any power to govern in Cuauhtinchan remains an open question. The *Historia* is silent on this point, yet in representing Teuhctlecozauhqui and Tepexoch ilama in both the foundation and battle scenes, the manuscript accomplishes several ends. First, the reiteration avers that Teuhctlecozauhqui's alliance with Cholula remained symbolically viable for at least two hundred years. Tepexoch ilama's presence renders the leader's tie to this sacred city, quite literally, a visual plausibility. Second, in showing Teuhctlecozauhqui with his Cholulan consort at the time of his defeat, the annals suggest that although Nahuas were thrown over by their Pinome rivals (and their Tlatelolcan allies), they hoarded a vast store of symbolic capital to be leveraged via claims to illustrious heritage. Finally, the *Historia* reaffirms the role played by Nahua leaders in antiquity, for it bypasses the founding couples of the Pinome dynasties, which dominated Cuauhtinchan politically at the time of the manuscript's production but against which we might reasonably suspect don Alonso harbored some enmity.

For readers of the *Historia*, then, a visual bracket built upon the enduring legacy of Teuhctlecozauhqui and Tepexoch ilama is proffered on don Alonso's behalf. Yet don Alonso was a cagey man, and his historical wager concerned the future as well as the past. Thus his tale of intermarriage does not end with the fall of Teuhctlecozauhqui, but rather with Tepexoch ilama who, according to the *Historia*, was whisked away after the defeat of her husband to become the bridal spolia of the Tlatelolcan victor (f. 43v, ms. 54–58). The point is made visually in plate 18 and figure 12, in which Tepexoch ilama sits as consort across from Quauhtlatoa, the Tlatelolcan ruler, just as she did on the previous page, as the consort of Teuhctlecozauhqui. According to the annals, then, it is the marital eligibility of this woman, rather than any particular skill or personal deed, which makes her significant. And in sending her off to marry into another line, don Alonso's book at once draws a boundary around his own lineage ambitions but leaves an opening for the return of a gift—if not in the form an ancestral bride, then perhaps in the restitution of those boundaries that her absence created.

Notes

1. Images of Chicomoztoc—sometimes as Colhuacatepec, sometimes as a separate site—appear in a number of sixteenth-century historical manuscripts, including the *Mapa Sigüenza*, the *Codex Azcatitlan*, the *Codex Mexicanus*, lienzos from Coixtlahuaca, and *Mapa 2* from Cuauhtinchan. Discussion of this originary cave also surfaces in Diego Durán and Geronimo de Mendieta, among other sources. See, for instance, Heyden (1981, 2000, 2005), Manzanilla (2000), and, for perspectives beyond central Mexico, the essays in Brady and Prufer (2005).

2. We sense this from the fact that, in the last twenty-five years, this image of ancestral Nahua origins has been more frequently published than any other representation of Chicomoztoc, and it has certainly become the most commonly reproduced scene from the *Historia*. The painting

appears, for instance, in Boone (1994), Carrasco and Sessions (2007b), Fields and Zamudio-Taylor (2001), Gruzinski (1992), Pasztory (1983), Roman Castellon Huerta (2001), Solís (2004), Townsend (1992a, 1992b). It is posted on Wikipedia and the websites of the Foundation for the Advancement of Mesoamerican Studies, the Mesoamerican Research Foundation, and universities in California, Massachusetts, and Wisconsin. The painting has also been redrawn and pictured in Aguilar Moreno (2006), Bernal-García (2006), Brady and Prufer (2005), Brotherston (1992), and Heyden (1981). While not as commonly published as some images from sixteenth-century New Spain—such as the frontispiece of the *Codex Mendoza* or scenes from the *Florentine Codex*—this *Historia* painting has become the most visible and accessible image of the Nahua primordial cave.

3. For a range of perspectives on this, see Bruner (1994), Connerton (1989), Cohen (1994), Fentress and Wickam (1992), Kuhn (2000), and Passerini (1987, 2007).

4. The recasting of indigenous history in colonial Latin America—and the implications of this process—are topics that have received considerable attention in the scholarly literature. Yet discussion most often focuses on the ways in which colonized peoples have reworked their ancient history, not on my concern here, which is how the production of Pre-Hispanic history remakes a colonial present. Joanne Rappaport's study represents an important exception (1990); other arguments I have found particularly helpful for analysis of the *Historia* are those of Gillespie (1989, 1998), Salomon (1982), and Urton (1990). See Chapter 4 for further discussion.

5. *Historia*, f. 50v, ms. 54–58, pp. 423–424. The Nahuatl for the entire year's entry reads, "1. Acatl. xiuitl. Inic acico yn castillantlaca auh yn ualla yntoca marques. auh yn acico ompa yn tlaxcallan yeuantin quinamique yn tlaxcalteca yn tlatoque quitlapolloque quitlatlauhtique yuan yc tlalpolloque yn chollalla ca no ypan yn ce acatl xiuitl."

6. From the twelfth-century founding of Cuauhtinchan to the sixteenth-century events registered at the manuscript's end, only one reference to a deity appears. This is when two ethnic groups, the Huexotzinca and Acolhuaque, attack Cholula in the year 3 Reed (e.g., in the 13th century, *Historia*, f. 38v, ms. 46–50). The deity Quetzalcoatl is mentioned in this scene, although he is not described as explicitly interacting with humans. Many centuries later, the *Historia* records the introduction of Christianity, but only by noting the arrival of a friar, Juan de Rivas, in the area (*Historia*, f. 51r. ms. 54–58). Thus the annals create the impression that, from the time of its origin, Cuauhtinchan had no sustained relationships with deities; furthermore, if the annals are to be believed, the altepetl apparently experienced no momentous catastrophes that required an appeal to the gods. Just one textual cue contradicts this construction, hinting that the interaction of humans and gods on a daily level continued well into the colonial period. A series of inscriptions appears on the outer, first page of the *Historia*. All were added well after the manuscript was produced, by hands other than those who wrote the *Historia*. One Nahuatl and Popoloca inscription seems to be an invocation that, among other appeals, asks the reader to come sit with the gods to hear this tale. On the implications of this, see Swanton (2001).

7. In this case, the Tolteca seek to settle in or near Cholula, and the deity is called both Ipalnemouani and "the *tlacatecolotl*, Quetzalcoatl" (f. 5v, ms. 54–58). The word *tlacatecolotl* literally means "man-owl," and was used by friars to refer to all Pre-Hispanic deities. It is often translated as "devil" or "demon" (Molina 1977; Karttunen 1983). While it is possible to read the word in the *Historia* as evidence that Nahuas were well Christianized by this point in time, and had even come to see their own Pre-Hispanic deities as demonic, this was not necessarily the case. The appearance of the term in and of itself sheds little light on how Nahuas understood either tlacatecolotl or their Pre-Hispanic deities more generally.

8. The written text identifies the residents of Tollan as the Pantecatl, Ytzcuitzoncatli, Tlematepehua, Tlequaztepehua, Tezcatepehua, Nonoualca, Cuitlapiltzinca, Aztateca, Tzanatepehua, Tetezincatli, Tecolotepehua, Tochpaneca, Cenpohualteca, Cuetlaxteca, Cozcateca, Teuhxilcatli, Zacana, Cuixcoca, Quauchichionlca, and Chiuhnauhteca. The first image of the annals shows four culture heroes at Tollan, two of whom are Tolteca-Chichimeca, two Nonoualca. Through hieratic scale, wherein full-figure images of Icxicoatl and Quetzaltehueyac dwarf the representations of Xelhua and Huehuetzin, the painting signals who will become the primary players in this tale (fig. 7).

9. Interestingly, while the songs and invocations of this portion of the text are presumed to have deep roots in Pre-Hispanic times, the images in this portion of the *Historia* are among those most closely related to European models, in terms of composition and style (see Appendix 1). This reminds us that the *Historia*'s commentary on the Chichimeca, as the ancestors of the Cuauhtinchantlaca, was translated from many media and significantly renovated to create the form it exhibits here.

10. Moving clockwise from the top, the seven groups within the cave are: Totomihuaque, Acolchichimeca, Tzauhcteca, Zacateca, Malpantlaca, Texcalteca, and Cuauhtinchantlaca.

11. The written text of the *Historia* also distinguishes Moquihuix and his lineage, the Moquihuixca, from the other Chichimeca. On these alphabetic and prose strategies, see Reyes García (1977: 27–31) and Kirchhoff et al. (1976: 11).

12. Silences, or "places of forgetting," are familiar in the literature on memory. These necessarily function as part of any binding memory of the past. We can reasonably presume that patterns of memory and forgetting were well honed in Cuauhtinchan in the 1550s, and that they may well have shaped the patterns on display in the *Historia*. Yet the representational strategies of the annals cannot be conflated in any simple way with the gestures and rituals of daily life and its psychologies (see, for instance, Kuhn 2000). This is one reason the *Historia*'s images and texts are worth parsing: they both organize and impose upon lived realities, but do not literally mirror or record the material and bodily experiences of the past. Rather the *Historia* opens (and occupies) a space between actual memories and their imagined intensity.

13. The first account appears in the *Historia*, fs. 28v–33r, ms. 46–50, the second rendition follows immediately in fs. 35r–36v, ms. 46–50.

14. Interactions between local people and the Totomihuaque and Cuauhtinchantlaca are not addressed in either foundation narrative. The implication is that the Chichimeca warriors established themselves on empty land. This was not the case, however; see *Historia*, f. 37v, ms. 46–50, Reyes García (1977: 66–73), Dávila (n.d.), and Dávila Zaragoza (n.d)

15. At one level, the similarities among these images are not coincidental. All three paintings depend upon the same source for much of their imagery: the *Mapa Pintado*. Yet the *Historia* painters have significantly refashioned their model, thus the redundant composition represents more than slavish copying (see discussion, Chapter 3). See also Hanns Prem for discussion of the "reality" of the boundary arrangements suggested by the three paintings (1997).

16. These men are Moquihuix, Xiuhtzon, Tonatiuh, Teuhctlecozauhqui, and Cuixin quauhman ycac, heads of five of Cuauhtinchan's seven subgroups. Reyes García claims that these were probably the five most important groups comprising the altepetl (1977: 31–37). Moreover, each appears here occupying a different region of the altepetl. For example, Moquihuix settled at Tepetitlan (The Foot of the Mountain), Xiuhtzon at Tollan (Place of the Rushes), and Teuhctlecozauhqui at Tepeticpac (Mountain Summit). Finally, the painting indicates diversity within Cuauhtinchan by dividing the five leaders into two groups. Moquihuix and Teuhctlecozauhqui, the leaders most closely linked with don Alonso's ancestral line, perch on stylized stone seats while the others sit upon rectangular benches. Reyes García believes that this may be a way of signing cultural, political, and/or religious distinctions (1977: 35). On the representation of Cuauhtinchan as a heterogeneous entity, see also Leibsohn (1994).

17. In this scene, the strategy of eclipsing historical actors and sites is brought to bear on Cuauhtinchan itself. For the regions settled by Xiuhtzon, Tonatiuh, and Cuixin quauhman ycac are rendered invisible. According to this image, Moquihuix and Teuhctlecozauhqui are no longer two of several altepetl-founders, they are the sole founders. Two other Cuauhtinchantlaca do appear in this painting; at the left edge, below Icxicoatl and Quetzaltehueyac, are the figures of Tonatiuh and Teocon. The painting does not show them as founders of Cuauhtinchan, however, but rather as delegates sent to confirm the boundaries with the Totomihuaque.

18. Among the most provocative assessments of gender in sixteenth-century histories and manuscripts are still those of Clendinnen (1995)

and Gillespie (1989). For recent ethnohistory and broader theories of gender relations in Pre-Hispanic and early colonial Mexico, see the essay collections edited by Klein (2001), Lavrin (1989), Restall et al. (2005), Sigal (2003), and Schroeder et al. (1997), as well as Sousa (2007, n.d.).

19. *Historia*, f. 28v, ms. 46–50 and f. 35r, ms. 46–50. Even though the Cuauhtinchantlaca were one of several Chichimeca groups who left Colhuacatepec and warred alongside the Tolteca, the *Historia* claims that only the leaders of Cuauhtinchan were "rewarded" with women. Since no other altepetl can claim such intimate connections with the illustrious city of Cholula, these marriage alliances function as signifiers of Cuauhtinchan's extraordinary status. Other instances in which men of high status marry their daughters to those of lower economic and/or social standing are well known in central Mexican accounts. See, for example, Carrasco (1984), Gillespie (1989), Pohl (2003) and Sousa (2007, n.d.).

20. According to the genealogy outlined by Kirchhoff et al. don Alonso could trace his ancestry to the union between Moquihuix and Teuhczohuatl Xiuhtlatzin as well as to the marriage of Teuhctlecozauhqui and Tepexoch ilama (1976: 250–251). Although don Alonso's ties to Moquihuix are stronger, and although the *Historia* goes a long way to place Moquihuix on par with Teuhctlecozauhqui, the latter seems to have been the more important Nahua leader. This would seem to be why don Alonso's bond to Teuhctlecozauhqui and Tepexoch ilama was so significant. On the relationship between Teuhctlecozauhqui and Moquihuix as rulers of Cuauhtinchan, see Kirchhoff (1947: lii–lv).

21. On the next page of the annals (f. 43r, ms. 54–58), Teuhctlecozauhqui's defeat is clearly signed: Tepexoch ilama appears seated across from the Tlatelolcan victor, Quauhtlatoa, not the Cuauhtinchantlaca leader. See discussions in Appendix 1 (pls 17/18) and in Chapter 3.

22. In this capacity, the two Teuhctlecozauhquis are not unlike Moteucçoma I and Moteucçoma II in Mexica history. According to Susan Gillespie, these two men stand as boundary figures and occupy structurally similar positions within dynastic histories (1989: 123–133). This is not to suggest that Cuauhtinchan's history followed the same structural patterns as Mexica imperial accounts in every respect, yet to present a narrative compelling to sixteenth-century Nahuas in Central Mexico, it would have had to share some basic principles. Given Elizabeth Brumfiel's argument that certain aspects of Aztec imperial ideology were not embraced by provincial leaders (2006), this aspect of history-making garners significance as a practice that did align local elites with Mexica expectations and conventions of representation.

CHAPTER 3

WRITING THE LAND

AS IT WOULD TURN OUT, when Tepexoch ilama left Cuauhtinchan for Tlatelolco in the fifteenth century, neither she nor a namesake ever returned. Hers was a one-way journey from a defeated altepetl to a victorious one, from the palace of one ruler-husband to that of his conqueror. When don Alonso trekked to Mexico City, close to one hundred years later, he too traveled as a vanquished noble. While his lot and condition were in certain regards quite different from those of his ancestral kin, the fate of the deposed consort nevertheless tainted his. To wit, the boundaries don Alonso sought to defend in 1546 were the very boundaries established by Mexica lords just a few years after the conquest of Cuauhtinchan, which forced the departure of Tepexoch ilama. Exactly how territorial limits born of defeat came to be those most sought by noblemen from Cuauhtinchan is something we shall never know. The documents make clear, however, that the restitution of these particular boundaries was indeed their goal. The proper recovery of territorial abutments must have been of profound concern in the latter half of don Alonso's life, for the *Historia* is almost compulsively fixated on the description and depiction of borders. Yet in every instance, the estates at issue are less "real" than mnemonic—divisions of territory derived through travel across the deep historic past.

In her introduction to the book *Text and Territory* Sylvia Tomasch raises the provocative question of geographical desire. For her, it stems from the double and reciprocating action of two "associated processes—the textualization of territories and the territorialization of texts" (1998: 5). While focused on European examples, Tomasch's notion offers a seductive entry into the dual-edged processes that bind the *Historia*'s preoccupation with land. Fundamental to the annals are the tensions between territorial evocation and texts. The *Historia*—through both alphabetic writing and visual imagery, as well as through its material objecthood, the booklike form of the manuscript itself—implies that don Alonso's territorial enthusiasm was not an uncomplicated affair. It also suggests that the acquisition of new tracts of property was, at best, a remote consideration. For the annals dwell exclusively upon

Fig. 13 Merced map of Otumba, 1590. Pigment on European paper, ca. 30 cm (height) × 21 cm (width). Archivo General de la Nacíon, Mexico City, Tierras, vol. 2782, exp. 15, f. 17 [Mapoteca 2160]. *Photograph courtesy of the Archivo General de la Nación, Mexico City.*

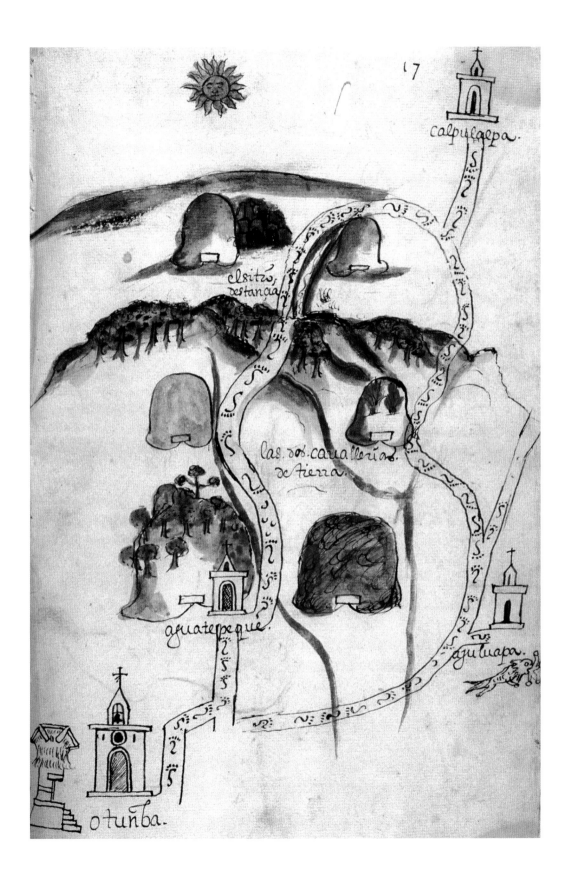

calpulaepa.

elsitio, destancia

las .sos. cavallerías. de tierra.

aguatepeque.

ajuluapa.

otunba.

the lands of antiquity, the boundaries of ancestors. Fidelity to genre may explain part of this; records about the past were not, for sixteenth-century Nahuas, also records of contemporary lands. Yet the disjunction remains striking.

Across the sixteenth century, indigenous people painted hundreds of *pinturas*, scenes of land and territory that today we often assimilate into our category of map. Most of these works, such as that in figure 13, were created for the *merced*, or land grant, process, in which parcels of land were dispersed by the Audiencia to individuals or communities who petitioned for them (Mundy 1996: 181–188, 233–234). Born of acquisitive desires for property—among Spaniards and indigenous people and communities—these images feature the sixteenth-century composition of land, community, and boundary. In the painting from Otumba of 1590 (fig. 13), for instance, we see a church and temple in the lower left corner signing a community nestled at the base of a hilly landscape. A string of hill forms marches up the page, and roads with footprints meander among them. At the very center of the painting is a short alphabetic text, identifying the land under petition. Among other things, its placement implies how, in order to fulfill particular kinds of geographic aspiration, writing and territory intertwined in the visual exposition of New Spain (Leibsohn 2000; Russo 2005).

In contrast to those registered on the merced map of Otumba, the *Historia*'s geographic obsessions concerned not the physical territories of sixteenth-century daily existence—at least not in any overt way—but rather narratives of lands and boundaries traversed and claimed by ancestors. In this the *Historia* exhibits a strong penchant for the archaistic. Yet we also know that don Alonso found older methods of recording boundaries and ancestral migrations to be weakening in their appeal. Had this not been the case, no commission for an extensive suite of new writings and paintings, a project that departs so significantly from Pre-Hispanic models, would ever have been necessary. Herein lies one of the most difficult aspects of the *Historia*. Ancestral sites had to be born anew, yet at the same time, tap the authority of antiquity. Put bluntly, to satisfy don Alonso, ancient lands had to wield contemporary symbolic means, but not lose themselves in contemporary innovation. This represents the extraordinary paradox of his geographical desire. And it places stringent demands on alphabetic texts and frames. For how can written words take the place of painted images and oral recitations, which were, before the Spanish conquest, wholly adequate modes of territorial evocation?

This question is not merely rhetorical. For the processes at hand involve not only the ways in which the *Historia* textualizes territory, but also the degree to which the annals succeed in this endeavor. The specter of failure, in other words, looms large. Tomasch warns us that a successful writing of the world is simply not possible (1998: 11). Yet don Alonso's was a more optimistic endeavor. Had he suspected the *Historia*

Fig. 14 Nonoualca boundaries (with highlights added), *Historia Tolteca-Chichimeca*. Pigment on European paper, ca. 28.5 cm (height) × 20 cm (width). Bibliothèque Nationale, Paris, f. 4v, ms. 54–58. *Photograph courtesy of the Bibliothèque Nationale, Paris.*

Eucyztli ytancas.
Eyaçpalan xiacall.
tochtli yanochahapotla
motolyn yyapan
tlallan calleo.

Tohcocl capotlan.
Quauhtetelpan.
tofotlan.
Eovaialeo.
hatzitepec.

· x x ·

ychtectlan
Ecall ycamac
Ayrauhtlan.
Tetlaco
Micaoztoc.

chicavaztepetl.
tochpatepetl.
xallapom.
Omiquilla
matlal cueyecan.

Nepovalli.
Quevetzillatl.
Eeliztlom.
Eovatepetl.
tlamacazcatzinco.

yzvatlan
Euezcomatlan.
cacalloll.

teodn yocan.
villovac.
petzpolla
yllacatzquauhtla
meyocan.

tzovactlatlacpac
yztepetl.
tlachnioltepetl.
Auatlatlacpac
viztquhtelinhcan.

Vayaexocotella
Queçexce grtoc.
yxmatlatzinco.
auixtepetl.
Teteltlicpac.

Aychquialleo.
Aztahatl.
vetzmalloyocan.
Temallacayo.
nopaltelixhcan.

tepetlatepu napan
xotitlan tlalli.
teponaztlan.
Eemelleaca.
xiithquilla.

Eovatepetl.
Anauhtzinco.
Eacaticpac.
tepona vaztla yac.
teqnavitlan.

Cacalloll. Scan.
tlami ytepath.

· x vj ·

Aztahatl.
tecollo guyo.
xonacatepetl.
Ollayo.
avecaltzotecomatla

· x x ·

Lontlapanalonya.
yztaquavia.
yttexyo.
dichicayo.
Necovaya.

tlillantepetl
Eovaxolloc.
tepocepochtli icac.
qohtlatcaapom.
Tetobincan.

incapable of sustaining the memories he sought to invigorate and preserve, he would have commissioned another kind of document. But hope is not the same thing as achievement, and aspiration is hardly interchangeable with success. Hence don Alonso's gamble, thus his gambit.

"Chronicles of the Impossible" is the phrase Frank Salomon invented to describe early colonial works from the Andes which, in their struggle to symbolize post-conquest truths, intertwine indigenous and European modes of recordkeeping (1982). The results are works that speak clearly to almost no one—too few had, or developed, the fluency required to disentangle the cacophonous mix of representational systems. The *Historia* skirts similar ground. We know from the previous chapter how the annals negotiated anxieties of similarity and difference in the social realm, but what of territory? The questions that now beckon concern a different tension, that between innovation and preservation. This chapter poses two queries on this theme: how does this manuscript turn text into territory and territory into text, and are there signs that *Historia*'s renovating ambitions proved too risky?

Writing Boundaries

Concerns about text and territory are, perhaps, neither the most obvious queries to pose about the *Historia*'s representation of land, nor the easiest to answer. To my mind, however, they are crucial for at least three reasons. First, in casting his history into alphabetic signs, and then binding that writing into a European-style codex, don Alonso made it clear that relationships between territory and textuality—although he would never have used such words—did, indeed, preoccupy him. The structure and expense of the annals indicate that this Nahua man doubted whether memories of ancient territories could abide, unless they were in some way, literally, written out. Second, in its presentation of ancestral lands, the *Historia* relies upon the material and visual substance of writing, not merely the denotative sense of alphabetically inscribed words. The annals thus transform many folios into miniature territories, mapped through the disposition of writing or glyphic signs on paper (fig. 14). Third and finally, the lands in the *Historia* are unmistakably the lands of literary and visual representation; to define their location in some "real" or chartable place in the world was not this manuscript's mission. Even if this had been don Alonso's aim, he could not have achieved it—any more than we can—apart from the mediation of images, words, and material objects.

There are many in the fields of history and cultural studies who have written about the play between inscription and landscape, the tensions that bind writing and geography. David Smail's descriptions of the intersection of notarial writing, imaginary civic space, and the realities of lived experience in Marseille offer an evocative model (1999). I also take suggestive cues from Tom Conley's work on writing and mapping (1996) and Louis Marin's semiotic reading of writing about, and on, utopic space (1990). Yet the path I pursue here also passes between these theoretical projects. For my primary goal lies less in connecting the *Historia* to any overarching graphic phenomenology, than in assessing a more local concern: how

Pre-Hispanic territory took shape in, yet ultimately drove don Alonso's ambitions for, a book about the past.

When don Alonso commissioned the *Historia*, indigenous people in New Spain had already developed numerous techniques and graphic conventions for representing and documenting their lands. Some had Pre-Hispanic roots, some were born after the conquest and drew, as well, upon European imagery. In addition to the pinturas of mercedes and other official projects such as the Relaciones Geográficas, Nahuas made and maintained cadastral registers, bills of sale, and cartographic histories (works that wound events from the ancestral past into territorial vignettes). With the exception of one European-style landscape painting, however, the *Historia* opts for a restricted purview and a conservative representational scaffold. That is, the book focuses upon patrimonial boundaries and migratory routes, and it represents them largely through toponymic glyphs and alphabetic writing. Don Alonso's manuscript may have been innovative, but it did not range widely across the field of representational possibilities when it came to territory.

If passage across the land is one of the prime territorial tropes of his annals, the extremities of Pre-Hispanic domains is the other. In both instances alphabetic writing plays a fundamental role. Even the most elaborate pictorials representing ancient lands—such as the boundary images of Totomihuacan and Cuauhtinchan at the time of their foundings—do not function apart from writing.[1] To call forth memories of territory in don Alonso's history, then, was to call upon word signs inked onto paper, if not also uttered aloud.

It is not hard to imagine that the rituals of writing—the preparation of materials, the sketching of guidelines, and the fashioning of page after page of calligraphic uncials and minuscules—had their own implications and meanings in Cuauhtinchan at mid-century. Books of similar intricacy would have been few in this altepetl, and largely, if not wholly, inaccessible outside Christian settings. The other primary milieu for the production and circulation of writing was that of local notaries. Although by 1560 many an altepetl had one or two notaries capable of providing local documents in Nahuatl, their works were not fancy, nor were refined, deluxe documents their forte. While the *Historia* scribe would have been familiar with both of these metiers and their associated rites, don Alonso's annals were ultimately foreign to both. And there would have been sense in this as well.

Much has been written on the changes wrought by alphabetic writing in indigenous communities in the first generations after the Spanish conquest. For some scholars, alphabetism is a quintessential sign, almost a scar, that marks the cultural violence of colonial rule (see, for instance, Gruzinski 1993; Mignolo 1989, 1992; Rabasa 2000). For others, the infusion of writing was not inconsequential, but it was nonetheless a far more benign, almost mundane event in the history of Nahua culture (Karttunen and Lockhart 1987; Lockhart 1992). My reading of the evidence suggests there is something to both positions. What is fundamental for under-standing the *Historia* is that the manuscript offers no signs of alphabetic resistance, no reluctance to rely upon written forms. Yet it would be a mistake to presume that writing, in and of itself, was seen as sufficient—at mid-century, pictorial representation and oral recitation were still very much necessities. Further, as we see below, don Alonso's manuscript betrays some profound anxieties about both writing and picturing. My point, nevertheless, still holds—alphabetic writing was in no way shunned by the *Historia*.

For those with an eye for trajectories, this may seem unsurprising. Throughout the sixteenth century, dependence upon alphabetic writing in Nahuatl did increase, although few in any given altepetl could ever read or write. Trajectories, however, chart the broad trends and rarely reveal a whole story. We know from local records, for instance, that a written account of ancestral boundaries was not don Alonso's only alternative. Between 1530 and 1580, painters in Cuauhtinchan made at least four cartographic histories. Known today as the *Mapas de Cuauhtinchan* 1, 2, and 3, and the *Mapa Pintado*, these works all eschew writing. In formal and material terms, all are far more conservative than the *Historia*. And although none of these mapas replicates precisely the story cued by don Alonso's annals, all find some parallels. The decision to map ancestral lands with written words thus did not represent the default option.[2]

While we do not know the name of the *Historia* writer or of its painters, it seems likely that the creators of this history project would have been male. The sons of nobles, more often than daughters, were taught to read and write in both the Mexica empire and in New Spain. Moreover, when don Alonso commissioned this set of annals, he did not seek, nor have to rely upon, untutored hands. The annals' writer was well practiced in scribal conventions, well versed in the mechanics and structure of contemporary European bookmaking. In spite of this, he used alphabetic script in ways that diverge from Nahua notaries who worked in the region (Leibsohn n.d.). We sense this most viscerally in the scribe's attentiveness to the visual texture of the written manuscript page. Here I do not mean simply the density of ink, the chroma of paint, or the rhythm of the script, but rather the patterned dispersal of words across the page. Rather like footprints on a sandy beach that, through their depth and direction, permit one's eye to discern the gait and stride of an absent passerby, so too the writing in the *Historia* defines the signature of its draftsman. My point is simple but central: how writing occupies the field of the manuscript page is no less significant than "what the words say." The notation of territorial landmarks extends well beyond denotative means.

A striking example of this occurs in figure 14. Here the names of the Nonoualca boundaries appear as bundled pentads. The arrangement of boundaries as groups of five appears throughout the annals, and, I would claim, derives in part from mnemonic formulae employed in the memorization and reproduction of long lists of boundary stations.[3] Other boundary lists in the *Historia*, such as those pertaining to the foundation borders at Totomihuacan and Cuauhtinchan, also cluster into groups of five, aligned as lists of vertical columns (for instance, fig. 15). The degree

Fig. 15 The boundaries of Cuauhtinchan and Totomihuacan (in alphabetic script with highlights added), *Historia Tolteca-Chichimeca*. Pigment on European paper, ca. 29 cm (height) × 20 cm (width). Bibliothèque Nationale, Paris, f. 36v, ms. 46–50. *Photograph courtesy of the Bibliothèque Nationale, Paris.*

Centepetl.	Tapetl xoxouhcan.	
Atoyatl.	Tecolquauhtla.	Covatepetl.
Atvayo.	cavetzinco	Quauhtepetl.
Yztenenetl.	Tecpoyotl.	Ocellotepetl.
Covatepetl.	chingin molli.	
		Centlipalacá
Tecciztitla	pachocan	Mitli ymacan.
yepancovac.	Litlaltepetl.	vavauhtla.
Tecollotl.	Hacotepetl.	
Ytzocan.	yecatepetl	Maltlalcueye.
Tepipilolco.	Acapavazq	Acapavazq
Covacuitlachdichiquilco.	Atvayo.	Atvayo
chapol metzco.	Cotepetl.	Centepetl.
Macacholco.		
Acatla.		
petlatzinco.		
Teyoca		
chitla		
Acayavalolco		
Oztoyavallco.		
Atlavi molleo.		
Tempatzacapa		
Quauhyavalolco.		
Yztac tetla.		
Cuecueyoca		
chollotecamilla		
ychcopinalloya		
Techinapa milhca tlacollyteca çacallyteca		
Teachtlan		
Macuixochtlan		
Ytztleyocan.		

to which the visual patterns of written words follow precedents set in Pre-Hispanic pictorial imagery is not known—although the number five was of considerable symbolic importance throughout Mesoamerica, with connections to the cardinal directions, numeric notational systems, and calendrics. Moreover, the number figures prominently in a variety of painted codices. In the *Codex Borgia*, for example, certain pages are composed in pentads (pp. 27–28) and calendrical dates are also organized with five to a column (pp. 1–8).

Even if the full suite of specific meanings eludes us today, for Nahuas who used the *Historia* pentads would have evoked connotative fields that were at some level symbolic, not simply descriptive. At the same time, it seems likely that toponymic signs were also laid out in clusters and/or patterns to parallel oral recits. The organization of lists into bundles of five punctuates the *Historia*: boundaries, individuals, and social groups all respond to this format. This repetitive dispersal of pentads signals how lengthy lists and items for recall would have been summoned from memory and spoken aloud. Alphabetic script in this case visualizes not only the subject matter of the recit (territorial boundaries), but also its Pre-Hispanic, and subsequent colonial, rhythmic and formal structure.

In certain respects, the list of Nonoualca boundaries resembles a leaf from a European codex or manuscript (figs. 14, 16). Yet the writing also points to a conflation of Nahua geographical knowledge, oral recitation, and mnemonic pattern. The sole pictorial element—a large toponymic glyph—occupies the position traditionally reserved for a decorated initial, and the words that descend in parallel columns resemble a concordance in a European biblical commentary. In fact, the toponymic glyph here emulates the function of a European initial in signaling a beginning, in this case, the beginning of a list of boundaries. Unlike its European counterpart, however, the Nahua place glyph does not direct the reader to the first name in the list (just below it). Rather, the glyph combines linguistic referents for two separate sites—the three shells refer to Tecciztli ytencan, which is the first place listed to the right of the glyph, and the four-sided emblem refers to Nepohualli, the first place written just below the glyph. In this, the toponymic glyph mimics European scriptural practice, but does not fulfill precisely the roles assigned to decorated initials in European books.

Unfortunately, the source of this list is not preserved, although evidence internal to the *Historia* and drawn from other mid-sixteenth-century manuscripts suggests that this page recasts a diagram of toponyms that sets forth a circuit of boundaries. Originally each place name would have been represented as a place glyph, and these signs would have been arranged in a schematic way spanning the field—perhaps in a manner analogous to the boundaries of Cuauhtinchan and Totomihuacan that appear on the *Mapa Pintado* (fig. 17). The written words on this page therefore coalesce as a kind of cartographic itinerary that traces the armature of the Nonoualca homeland.

When Paul Kirchhoff plotted the names of these Nonoualca sites on a twentieth-century map, he discovered that the list described a circuit enclosing an irregular polygonal area (1958; Kirchhoff et al. 1976). In the physical geography

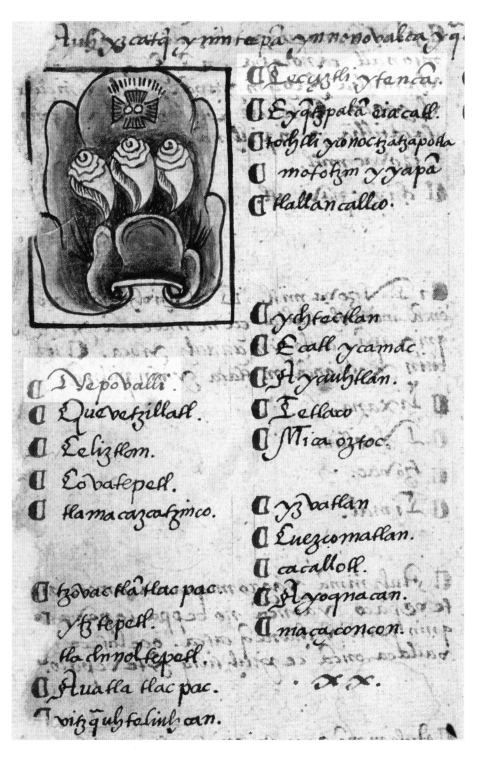

Auh yçatq yn rn repa y nnonoualca y q

Ⓘ Lecyztli ytanca.
Ⓘ Eyaspatā diacatl.
Ⓘ tochtli yronoczaçapotla
Ⓘ mofohzm yyapā
Ⓘ tlallan callco.

Ⓘ Nepoualli.
Ⓘ Quevehzillatl.
Ⓘ Leliztlom.
Ⓘ Coʋatepetl.
Ⓘ tlamacazcatzinco.

Ⓘ ychtactlan
Ⓘ Ecatl ycamac
Ⓘ Ayauhtlan.
Ⓘ Tetlaco
Ⓘ Micaoztoc

Ⓘ yzoatlan
Ⓘ Euezcomatlan.
Ⓘ cacalloll.
Ⓘ Ayoqnacan.
Ⓘ maçaconcon.

Ⓘ Izoac tla tlac pac
yztepetl.
tla chnyoltepetl.
Ⓘ Auatla tlac pac.
vitzquhtolintycan.

· x x ·

Fig. 16 Nonoualca boundaries (detail of initial glyph with highlights added), *Historia Tolteca-Chichimeca*. Pigment on European paper. Bibliothèque Nationale, Paris, f. 4v, ms. 54–58. *Photograph courtesy of the Bibliothèque Nationale, Paris.*

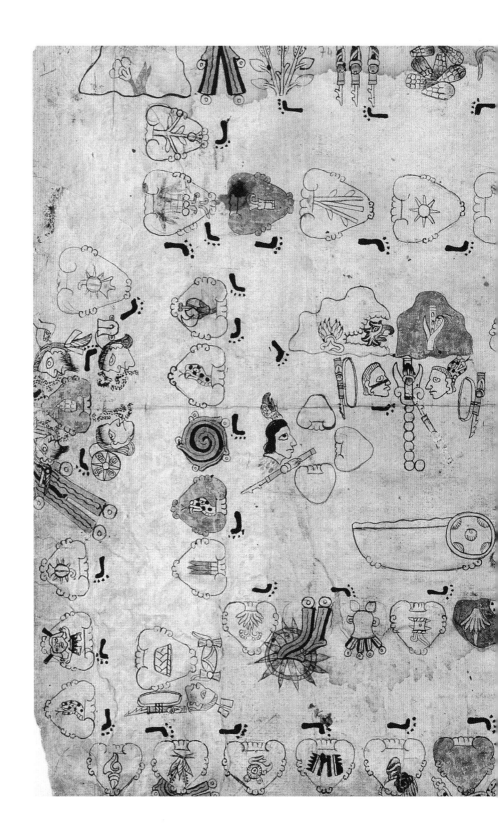

Fig. 17 *Mapa Pintado*, ca. 1532. Pigment on European paper, later attached to native-made paper, ca. 30 cm (height) × 44 (width) cm. Bibliothèque Nationale, Paris, ms. 54–58, p. 1/2. *Photograph courtesy of the Bibliothèque Nationale, Paris.*

of modern Mexico, the sites of Coatepetl and Temalacayo, which appear near the beginning and end of the list, lie proximate to one other, toward the northeast. Sites in the middle of the list, such as Ey quetzpalan ei acatl and Ayauhtlan, stand near one another at the southeastern region of the Nonoualca homeland. As readers scan the roster of place names (or listeners hear the sites recited aloud), they follow a path that travels out and then back toward its point of origin. In listing rather than picturing the Nonoualca boundaries, the writer privileges narrative sequence over visual diagram, yet he also uses alphabetic script to circumscribe a specific territorial zone. Consequently, the writing not only cues the names of ancient Nonoualca boundaries, it also charts the territory these emigrants from Tollan staked as their homeland. The folio thus becomes an alphabetic map, half-textualized and half-territorialized. Writing and land engage each other in a play of referential signage that complicates, but does not force either one or the other to forfeit all its meaning.[4] This venture is made even more explicit in another list of boundaries, that which defines the initial lands of Totomihuacan and Cuauhtinchan. In figure 15, for example, we see the name Centepetl written thrice. The word appears once at the opening of the list in the upper left corner, and then twice at the end, where the scribe has set the words side by side. The route recorded here thus starts and ends at the same site. Comparison with a pictorial representation of these boundaries (pl. 16) reveals that the arrangement of words into double columns mimics the array of glyphs along the upper left edge of the painting, which also stand in dual rows. Here, then, we find the most explicit instance in which writing behaves according to the rules of mapping and scriptural itineraries trace a circuit across the land.[5]

The story of written boundaries is, however, more complicated still. For the written lists of border sites resonate in a social, as well as a territorial register. To grasp what this means we must return to the Nonoualca borders (fig. 14). As was the case just above, a unique name in the list makes multiple appearances. Cacallotl occurs at the halfway point, in the thirty-eighth position, and again at the very end, in the seventy-sixth slot. Kirchhoff has argued that two separate towns with identical names were located on this boundary circuit—one in the northeast and one in the southwest. If he is correct, then the two Cacallotls constitute hinge points on the itinerary and the doubling of their names provides a key to the shape of the Nonoualca homeland. That is, starting at the first position in the writer's list, Nepohualli, the itinerary leads in an outbound direction until the first Cacallotl is reached. There, the path turns and heads homeward. The loop is complete when the second Cacallotl is reached. Unfortunately, we cannot be sure how the Nonoualca borders in the *Historia* would map onto a modern representation of territory— too many sites cannot be affixed to places now extant in Central Mexico. Boundary itineraries that record circuits and succumb to doubling do appear elsewhere in this manuscript, and, indeed, in telling locales.

Fig. 18 The boundaries of Totomihuacan (in alphabetic script with highlights added), *Historia Tolteca-Chichimeca.* Pigment on European paper, ca. 29.5 cm (height) × 20 cm (width). Bibliothèque Nationale, Paris, f. 31v, ms. 46–50. *Photograph courtesy of the Bibliothèque Nationale, Paris.*

¶ Tepoxocho
¶ Covatepetl.
¶ Temomoztli
¶ Atzontli
¶ Tecollotl.

¶ Tecacavilli.
¶ Yztac auixtla
¶ Atl patlavaca
¶ Totoll quetzalle.
¶ Techimalli

¶ Tecaxitl.
¶ Tochtopetl.
¶ Temallacayo
¶ Tecpatepetl.
¶ Quauhyavalolteo:

¶ Tenpatzacapa
¶ Atlavi molleo.
¶ Oztoyavalleo.
¶ chiltec pintla.
¶ petlatzinco.

¶ Acatlan
¶ Macacholteo
¶ chapolmetzco.
¶ Covaatlachichiqilco.
¶ Tepipillolteo.

¶ yztoca
¶ Epacovac
¶ Tecaciztlla
¶ Covatepetl.
¶ yztapanec.

¶ Quauh yavalolteo
¶ Centepetl.

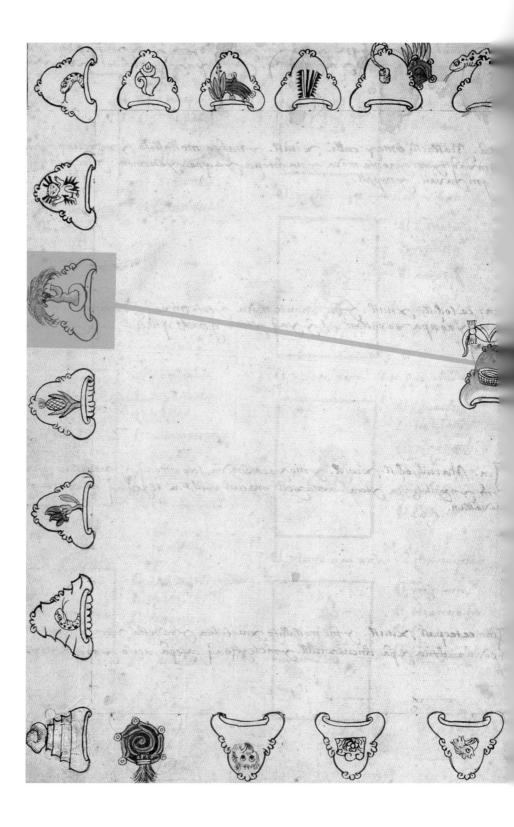

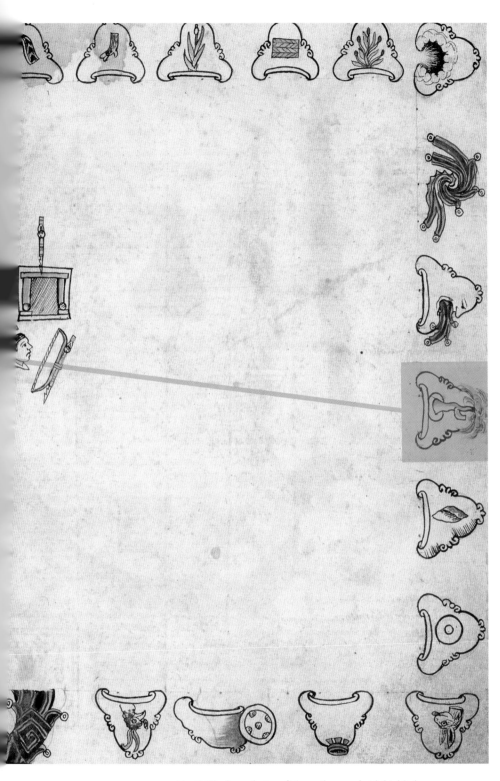

Fig. 19 The boundaries of Totomihuacan (with highlights on
the sites named Quauhyahualolco), *Historia Tolteca-Chichimeca*.
Pigment on European paper, ca. 29.5 cm (height) × 40 cm
(width). Bibliothèque Nationale, Paris, f. 30v–31r, ms. 46–50.
Photograph courtesy of the Bibliothèque Nationale, Paris.

We see a similar instance of both glyph and written boundary list, for instance, in the description of Totomihuacan's founding. Again, one place name, Quauhyahualolco, appears twice within a list of boundary sites—at the halfway point and at the end (fig. 18). And on the accompanying boundary painting, toponymic glyphs for Quauhyahualolco stand almost directly opposite each other, at the center left and center right edges of the painting. A line drawn between them creates an axis of reflection. Sites below this imaginary line stand on one side of Totomihuacan, those above stand near the other (Kirchhoff et al. 1976: 259). And like Cacallotl on the Nonoualca boundary list, the site of Quauhyahualolco seems to operate as an axial or isometric hinge (fig. 19).

This enigmatic doubling of two significant entities itself has a double in the social order of the *Historia*. Just as Teuhctlecozauhqui and Tepexoch ilama, the twin dynastic couples, signed the alpha and omega of Nahua rulership in Cuauhtinchan, the doubling of place names here—especially at such auspicious locales, at the half-way mark and the culmination of an ancestral domain—implies more than a simple compulsion or need to use the same name twice in describing an ancestral homeland. Indeed, a careful reading of the annals reveals that this arrangement is reserved for the boundaries of particular groups of people. Specifically, this form of territorial representation describes only the borders of the Nonoualca and not those of the Tolteca, only of the Totomihuaque and not of the Cuauhtinchantlaca. This kind of territorial list is, I suggest, not merely a description of a path through the lands of antiquity. Rather, the doubling of boundaries and their placement at specific sites on the page also functions to sever don Alonso's ancestors from those who are most like them but cannot, ultimately, share the same fate. The circuit mapped through writing (and, in the case of Totomihuacan, also in painting) is thus born of an anxiety we have seen before—an anxiety about desires for distinction from those who are most nearly the same.

It would, indeed, be fascinating to know how the boundaries of the Nonoualca and Totomihauque actually spread themselves out into a lived landscape. Yet the point here, which I would argue is an even more significant one, is that Pre-Hispanic territory took form in the *Historia* in ways that were patterned—both in terms of itinerary and social hierarchy. The use of alphabetic script to summon borders reveals how writing could describe a territorial expanse, that is, both through the sequencing of named sites and the disposition of those appellations on the paper folio. Alphabetic script was thus used to both establish and enclose a specific region of ancestral territory. This territory, however, was not strictly physical. For the written itineraries we have just traced also mapped the place of social groups in the larger narrative of historical destiny. From this we glean one primary way that graphic expression enabled the *Historia* to chart geographical desires, desires stoked by the potential rewards of social and political distinction, desires that thus extended well beyond any particular physical landscape.

Recit and the Migration of Words

In the *Historia* it is not merely Pre-Hispanic territories, but the rituals of ancestral transit across these lands, that command the lion's share of graphic and lexical space. The writing of territory here, however, does not perpetuate the fiction of land tread upon for the first time—don Alonso's book was, instead, persuasively reinscriptive. This underscores a significant feature of Pre-Hispanic geographic sense: sites were subject to reformation as they were remembered. The shape that lands exhibited, in any given showing or telling, was not entirely open to negotiation, but neither was it tacked down to immutable points on a grid. Land made memory, and memory, land.

Tim Ingold asserts that the very perception of landscape is predicated on acts of remembrance (1993: 152–153). For the *Historia* this is certainly true. In this case, it is not simply ancestral migration, but rather migrations that could anneal pre-conquest political identity that became the privileged trope. In this, the annals parallel other Central Mexican histories wherein the founding of illustrious altepetl (including that of Tenochtitlan) requires peripatetic ancients to cross difficult lands, weather the menace of enemy assault, and overcome all manner of hardship before finally alighting upon a district where they can settle. The *Historia* adumbrates not one but multiple migration tales, including those of the Nonoualca, the Tolteca, the Totomihuaque, and, of course, the Cuauhtinchantlaca. In so doing, it insinuates that all of these peregrinations are the stuff of don Alonso's lineage history. This is a strategic point. The migrations that mattered were not those undertaken only by don Alonso's ancestors. Instead, the wanderings of selected, intertwined social groups comprised the geography of his history.

As was the case with ancestral boundaries, the *Historia*'s commentary on migration routes requires vigilant readership. For the moral lessons of these pilgrimages are rarely rendered in explicit terms. Further, because transit is quintessential to migration narratives, the annals must march the reader through time and territory, at once textualizing and territorializing the traveler's vantage. The migration tale that receives the most protracted attention in the *Historia* figures as part of the larger story of Tolteca struggle for dominance at Cholula. To secure their position as rulers, Icxicoatl and Quetzaltehueyac wind their way to Colhuacatepec-Chicomoztoc to summon the Chichimeca warriors. Initially, theirs is an egressive mission. The narrative later parades these culture heroes back from the mountain cave, and so the lands they cross on their way to the sacred cavern must in some fashion be recrossed on the homebound leg of their journey. It is this recrossing, or reinscribing, of the land that proves most revelatory, bidding readers (and perhaps listeners) to imagine environments "pregnant with the past" (Ingold 1993: 153).

According to the annals, Colhuacatepec-Chicomoztoc was elsewhere. Not only was it physically far from Cholula, the events that occurred at the cavern transpired, quite literally, in another time. Writing in this portion of the annals thus works to suggest an otherness of both time and place. The paths that lead to and from the cavern are painstakingly identified in the annals; in this way, written words script don Alonso's ancestors into an exceptional territorial realm. At the same time, alphabetic writing summons a (remembered) physical world, and it inscribes the manuscript page with the trace of Tolteca and Chichimeca passage. According to the *Historia*, the journey to Colhuacatepec is something more than just a casual jaunt. It requires five days of travel, and an equal number of overnight rest stops. What matters most in the *Historia*'s telling are the dates, the points of origin, the names of intermediary sites, and the destination. All other activity is digression. The return, although recounted in a similar vein, is less brisk. This excursion requires ten days and passage through more than a hundred sites. Certainly the annalist could have summarized the return route. Instead, as the *Historia* treats this journey, it is a major exegesis of particulars, replete with names of sites never before mentioned. This verifies for the annals' reader that between Colhuacatepec and Cholula, lacunae simply did not exist; the ancestors crossed through the landscape everywhere in-between.

In recounting the trek to Colhuacatepec and back, the *Historia* could equally have emphasized any number of aspects of the migration experience, describing, for example, what the Tolteca said during their journey, what songs they sang or prayers they uttered. It might have also described the magical, shamanic labor and danger required to move from the mundane plane of existence to the sacred cave, as recounted by Diego Durán (1993). Instead, the geographical contours of the expedition are defined in the *Historia* strictly by site—their names and their order. Ancestral land takes form through the contingent vantage of the trekker, and the tentative position of rest in *media res*. The physical morphology or qualities of any given place matter very little in this written land. Who passed where: this is the territorial knowledge required, a geographic longing fulfilled.

There is, as well, a social dimension to this ancestorscape. In following another path home, the *Historia* narrative underscores the power of ritual travel. The Tolteca heroes who set out for Colhuacatepec returned to Cholula, but their encounters with the sacred mountain cave remade them. The asymmetrical path creates not merely a more replete physical territory, but also a territorial foil that is meant to mark ancestral difference, to register heroic transformation. We know that among the Mexica, Pre-Hispanic migrations coded social metamorphosis. This is one point that Nigel Davies made in investigating the "rags to riches" trope (1980, 1987), and Elizabeth Boone elaborated in her argument about migration. According to Boone, migratory movement was, at its root, a performance that remade the Mexica into a people specially destined to dominate and control Mesoamerica (1991: 118). Something similar seems to be lurking within don Alonso's ancestral narratives. The *Historia*, however, provides yet another vantage onto Boone's "transfiguring migration" idea.

Using divergences in the itinerary to cue ancestral metamorphosis, the annals suggest that territorial descriptions open more than physical arrangements of place in space. That is, the *Historia* marshals descriptions of Pre-Hispanic land as social charters. This is not to say that land is, or was, a literal social charter, although in some instances it may have been. Rather, I am arguing that the *Historia* demonstrates that Pre-Hispanic land, when properly textualized (i.e., properly registered and recorded), adhered more to the rhetorical device of metonymy than to metaphor. This distinction is key. I do not believe that the *Historia* convinces us that territory was like an ancestral social order; instead, in a part-for-whole fashion, the description of territory is also a description of a moral and social constellation. This fact, I suggest, helps explain why don Alonso so wanted a book like the *Historia*, a book wherein the disposition of ancestral lands was a prime topos. This manuscript became, in other words, a documentary record that could render the mutual fashioning of community and place visible and thus, in some ways, ever more real.

There is one final aspect to chart in this vein. Although the *Historia*'s text describes both the route to Colhuacatepec and its return, the relevant pictorial materials do not. No painted map indicates the direction of travel or the arrangement of sites in the landscape; neither are there representational images of this journey or the places visited along the way. The lexical register of the annals lists the name of each site in sequence and relays a bare skeleton of toponymic glyphs. In accounting for these circuits, however, the writer adopts a rote pattern: each day unfolds in a nearly identical manner. This is especially vivid during the return trip, when, as they head towards Cholula, the Tolteca and Chichimeca wake, travel, and rest in an almost numbing (and perhaps ritually transformative) routine. Only the territory traversed each day alters. As with the boundaries of ancestral lands, this repetitious litany of days, in which each list mirrors the one from prior days, must derive from formulae that permitted memorization and performance as oral recit.

A visual component comes into play as well. For every day of the migration, the writer notes in red, "And when it dawned, they went to. . . ." Immediately below this comment there appear the date glyph and, in black, the written itinerary. Consequently, a mimetic call and response emerges between the patterned narrative and the visual repetition of script and glyphs across the page (fig. 20). Through their formal cadence and syntax, then, written words not only register the route of ancestral movement, they also exhibit its recitational surface. Since much of the writing in the *Historia* fulfills a role similar to that played by oral performance in Pre-Hispanic histories, the interlacing of alphabetic script, territory, and recitation is not wholly unexpected. At one level, we may imagine the *Historia*'s writer working by transcribing the patterns of oral performance directly into the visual language of writing across the page. This kind of writing, which cues ritualized speech action, may rest upon Pre-Hispanic precedents. John Monaghan, in a discussion of the relationship between pictorial images in the *Codex Vienna* and contemporary Mixtec oral performance, points to visual properties in the codex that mimic the structural action of oral performance; he notes that "the structure and composition of the codex would be designed to facilitate an oral, public reading, signaling to the reader not only the way certain figures are to be identified, but also the poetics of reading" (1990: 139). Something similar may undergird the *Historia*. Nevertheless, the annals never worked along paths that established one-to-one correspondence; the picturing of ancestral migration routes is not merely a transcription of speech. We know this because there are many characteristics of oral performance that surface in the *Historia* apart from territorial description; also, throughout the annals, writing sometimes exhibits only attenuated links to oral mechanisms of recitation. I therefore suggest significance adhered in the fact that descriptions of land so consistently cue, through visual

ꟳ Auh ymygnac ovallat vic m man yaye
movica ꟳ gñauhnavac. yca.

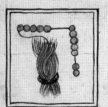

ꟳ.xij. mallinalli. to
nalli. ymic val peuh ꟳ
yn yi gm pileo ꟳ chicheme
ca yn m̄ moq m̄ vix̄e moco
chitito gñauhnavac.

ꟳ Tevevec. ꟳ si m̄a yavitze.
ꟳ Teocalhne yaca. ꟳ si m̄a yavitze.
ꟳ Atroyatzinco. ꟳ si m̄a yavitze.
ꟳ Hallicamatlaponcan. m m̄a yavitze.
ꟳ Tlacopan. ꟳ si m̄a yavitze.

ꟳ Quavaca. ꟳ si m̄a yavitze.
ꟳ Quauhtitlan. ꟳ si m̄a yavitze.
ꟳ macavacan. ꟳ si man yavitze.
ꟳ Tetlilpian. ꟳ si m̄a yavitze.
ꟳ Veveychocayom. m m̄a yavitze.

ꟳ Ticolleo. ꟳ si m̄a yavitze.
ꟳ mallinalleo. ꟳ si m̄a yavitze.
ꟳ Quauhnavac. ꟳ si m̄a yavitze.
ꟳ Tepoztepec. ꟳ si m̄a yavitze.
ꟳ Ayacatlan. ꟳ si m̄a yavitze.
ꟳ Coyovacan. ꟳ si m̄a yavitze.
ꟳ Acaxochic cencalleo m m̄a yavitze
ꟳ Chapoltepec.

ꟳ Auh ymygnac ovallat vic m m̄a yaye
movica ꟳ chapoltepec yca.

ꟳ.xiij. Acatl. to
nalli. ymic val peuh ꟳre
yn gñauh navad yn chi
chi meca ꟳm̄ valh mi ca
ymic yil edvatl. ꟳgnexal
teve yac mocochitito cha
poltepec.

ꟳ Tepoztepec. ꟳ si m̄a yavitze.
ꟳ ayacatlan. ꟳ si m̄a yavitze.
ꟳ coyovacan. ꟳ si m̄a yavitze.
ꟳ Acaxochic cencalleo. m m̄a yavitze.
ꟳ Chapoltepec.   Lochico.

ꟳ auh ymygnac ovallat vic. M̄ m̄a ya
ye movica yna maq m̄ac̄ yca.

ꟳ.i. Ocelotl. tonalli
ymic vallevaꟳ ꟳ chapol
tepec yn chichimeca
yn gñauhtli tencolloll
ꟳm̄ valh mi ca ymic ꟳrio
vall ꟳgne ꟳ alteve yac
mococchitito ꟳ amaq ne
mecan yntlatoꟳ ꟳ chichi mca.

ꟳ Tenochtitlan. ꟳ si m̄a yavitze.
ꟳ Vechachtecatitlan ꟳ si m̄a yavitze.
ꟳ Azcaxochitepec. ꟳ si m̄a yavitze.
ꟳ Tzitzintepec. ꟳ si m̄a yavitze.
ꟳ tzitzimatlanio. ꟳ si m̄a yavitze.

means and structure, the oral epoch of history keeping. Seen in this light, the *Historia* becomes a document with literary ambitions, wielding the written word as signal of antiquity and its performative authority.

From this we begin to grasp how and why the *Historia*'s geographical desire took the form it did. To wit, the annals most likely update ancestral land narratives by translating them into written, alphabetic scores. Yet by relying upon the visual presentation of written words (and glyphs) to evoke both patterns of recitation and the Pre-Hispanic tendency to paint in ways that prompt such recits, the Pre-Hispanic migration routes become at once older and newer than what had come before. These lands become textual records that, in turn, describe on paper, via reference to an oral legacy, a shifting travelscape. Moreover, we know that throughout the sixteenth century, in many indigenous communities, texts continued to be compulsively read aloud. And so, if don Alonso had the story of the Tolteca and Chichimeca migration read aloud, the territories it set out would have conformed to a patterned cadence that accustomed colonial gazes, as well as mouths, ears, and imaginations. In a certain way, this mode of writing opened a door onto ancient territory, which allowed Cuauhtinchantlaca to re-experience the migration of their kin. By means of visual and performative mimicry, readers and their audiences scanned and revoiced the word and picture play—as they traveled through antiquity and its lands.

On the Slippage of Texts and Their Territories

Over the last fifteen years, several historians of medieval, early modern, and modern history have proposed ways of construing alphabetic writing as literal and figurative maps that chart life worlds, historical scenes, and imaginary landscapes. After reckoning with the written territories of the *Historia*, I am particularly open to the suggestive studies by Tom Cummins and Joanne Rappaport (1998), Donna Merwick (1997, 1999), and Brinkley Messick (1993) on the scribal practices of notaries. These scholars examine distinct historical settings, yet demonstrate how a world in flux is mapped in the daily rituals of writing. Merwick, for instance, has argued that when the English conquered New Netherland in the seventeenth century, among other new practices, a dual register of written record was engendered. Notaries who had once written in Dutch, now found themselves compelled to write in English as well. Their task was complex, for only in rare instances was the same text required in each tongue; it was not enough to translate from one language to the other. Rather, English colonizers introduced novel forms of documentation, and with them, new ways of registering experience. It was the job of Dutch notaries to reconcile older and more familiar modes of legal scripture with those that now, increasingly, superceded them. To document daily life in the context of colonial Albany thus required a kind of stilted linguistic dance.[6]

Fig. 20 Migration route, patterned glyphs, and alphabetic script, *Historia Tolteca-Chichimeca*. Pigment on European paper, ca. 29 cm (height) × 20 cm (width). Bibliothèque Nationale, Paris, f. 24v, ms. 46–50. *Photograph courtesy of the Bibliothèque Nationale, Paris.*

Certainly don Alonso's annals contended with a different set of circumstances. Before the arrival of Spaniards, pictorial and oral, not written, records had dominated, and the *Historia* is quite distinct from the writings of Nahua notaries. Nevertheless, there are striking similarities in the cultural dimension and performative challenges that this nobleman's book and the colonial documents of Albany needed to negotiate. For both found themselves caught in a dense web of changing expectations for written records and their evocative powers. We see in the *Historia*'s cracks and fissures how the annals' writer struggled with this, as he sought to alphabetize Pre-Hispanic records, if not also pre-conquest memories. The final example of the *Historia*'s brush with territory and text that I want to consider concerns precisely one of these fissures.

Until this point, my analysis has focused on the alphabetic writing in the *Historia*, acknowledging, but passing hastily over, the differences between written script and painted glyph. This has been necessitated by my larger argument, but it is not representative of how Nahuas generally regarded graphic symbols. Indeed, a number of Mesoamericanists have focused on just this gap, the one that sets glyphic expression apart from written expression, to show how the oscillation between Pre-Hispanic and colonial expression played out (Galarza 1980; Lockhart 1992; Scharlau 1986). What don Alonso's manuscript reveals, however, is that alphabetic script, like toponymic glyphs and oral recits, could map space. Nonetheless, distinctions between written and painted signs (which were not linguistically marked as separate categories in Nahuatl) were of some consequence. Moreover, the manuscript demonstrates that neither technique necessarily commanded a chronicler's full respect. This is made clear in the doubling that occurs when the boundaries of Totomihuacan and Cuauhtinchan get depicted in two registers, one glyphic (pl. 16) and one textual (fig. 15). The redundancy, which may strike us as inefficient, marks both the recognition of, and attention to, difference. The connotative fields signed by written words versus those opened by glyphic elements are difficult to discern. Yet the *Historia* offers at least one persuasive clue that no medium of territorial presentation—word, glyph, or image—surfaced in the annals haphazardly.

Throughout the annals, painted images of place, be they sacred "elsewheres" such as Colhuacatepec-Chicomoztoc, or more "urban" sites, such as Cholula, tend to cast toponymic forms against a blank expanse of ground. The first entry of Icxicoatl and Quetzaltehueyac into Cholula, shown in plate 2, displays one of the more extreme examples of this glyphic dispersion; the foundation scene of Totomihuacan, with its more carefully plotted hill forms at the perimeter of the page, is yet another (pl. 13). Even when painters work in styles more heavily inspired by European example, as did the one who created the twin trees in the ball-court scene (pl. 6), the pictures are bereft of "landscaped" backgrounds. Objects associated with setting, place, or territory hover in a kind of pictorial indeterminacy. This inclination derives from Pre-Hispanic graphic conventions, which set distinct pictorial and glyphic elements—often, but not always, one and the same—against the blank grounds of hide, cloth, and bark-paper supports. That the *Historia* painters continued this tradition is not, given the date and substance of the annals, remarkable. What is more striking is the prevalence and consistency of these pictorial conventions. While certain glyphic elements have the appearance of landscape vignettes, with touches of color modeling their forms, there is only one scene in the entire annals that breaks rank, as it were, and reinterprets, in its figure-to-ground relationships, European landscape imagery.

This scene is one examined earlier, representing Tepexoch ilama and Teuhctlecozauhqui at the battle of Cuauhtinchan's warriors against combatants from Tlateloco (pls. 17/18), in which the site of Cuauhtinchan takes form as an enormous hill studded with thorny maguey plants. A few toponymic and name glyphs are present, yet in contrast to all of the other images in the *Historia*, this one situates human figures in a landscape whose conception is more mimetic than glyphic. The visual rhetoric of territorial space not only takes form through the name glyphs that chart territory according to familiar appellations (i.e., a representation of an eagle to cue the moniker Cuauhtinchan, "Home of the Eagle"), it also evokes the appearance of an actual landscape through illusion—albeit in a highly conventionalized manner. This breach in the pictorial regime of the annals is neither incidental nor immaterial. For this scene depicts the very juncture, after a two-hundred-year span, when the Nahua factions of Cuauhtinchan lost power. This rupture in the annals' pictorial style thus signals a break in ancestral political life. Moreover, the writing associated with this image, in contrast to all other territorial evocations, simply names the key actors in the scene: Tepexoch ilama, Teuhctlecozauhqui, and Quauhtlatoa. There is no territorial inscription, no evocative summoning of land through written word play. In many senses, this picture, and the battle it evokes, stands alone.

The *Historia* offers no explicit comment upon this lapse in its pictorial scheme. Yet the break does reveal an awareness—conscious or half so—of the dramatic differences in graphic expression and style that separated alphabetic word from glyph, and both of these from pictorial landscaping. The manner through which territory was inscribed elsewhere in the annals should not be taken for granted. It was no default arrangement. We sense this in the fact that the most important sites in the annals make their appearance through both alphabet and glyph, through writing and painting that parallel one another. Redundancy thus also seems to signal territorial significance.

But what happens when text and image refuse to "line up" as it were, or when the two produce a dissonant clash? As far as I know, with one exception, the sources for the *Historia* have been lost. The only physical trace of the writer's models is a pictorial document, also from sixteenth-century Cuauhtinchan, the *Mapa Pintado* (fig. 17).[7] According to Reyes García, this work predates the *Historia* by several years, with the initial imagery having been set down in 1532. While the original context of the *Mapa Pintado* is not known, Kirchhoff et al. argue that it was created for a legal inquiry into boundaries (1976: 8–9). Yet examination of the original reveals the document was not completed all at once. Additions were made throughout the sixteenth century, and at some later date, the painting's support of European paper was glued to a piece of amatl or bark paper. This suggests that the *Mapa Pintado* was asked to address more than one intended function, more than one set of readers' interests. The document did remain in Cuauhtinchan through the mid-eighteenth century, until collected, along with the *Historia* and *Mapa de Cuauhtinchan 1*, by Lorenzo Boturini. At the very least, this local collection and preservation of documents implies a perception that these paintings were related—through their antiquity if not also their narratives and original purposes. It is true that no single portion of the *Historia* replicates the *Mapa Pintado* in its entirety: in some places material is excluded, in others the earlier painting is elaborated upon. Yet each of the three *Historia* images and three written folio pages relies heavily upon this source, and all of them portray the borders of Totomihuacan and Cuauhtinchan.

To sketch in broad strokes the relationships between these two sixteenth-century documents is no easy task. Yet it seems that those who helped compile and create don Alonso's book reinterpreted the *Mapa Pintado*, adapting it so that it was appropriate for his codilogical framework. Images were excerpted and these details made into three new paintings, each with an accompanying page of writing. Placing all of these transpositions within the leaves of the *Historia* successfully "preserved" the original, even as it also produced gaping chasms between the model and its "copies."

Today no written text accompanies the *Mapa Pintado*, nor do glosses label the image. Although the painting itself is clearly not Pre-Hispanic, the absence of a textual component suggests that an oral recitation, probably following Pre-Hispanic conventions, was the performative frame for the document. While we cannot know precisely how the *Mapa Pintado* functioned as a visual score for oral performance, in moving back and forth between the *Historia* text and the *Mapa Pintado* the outlines of these narratives begin to emerge. They concern themes that are by now quite familiar: the foundation of Cuauhtinchan and Totomihuacan, the boundaries established for each altepetl, the role played by Icxicoatl and Quetzaltehueyac in marking these boundaries, and Cuauhtinchan's domination of nearby communities. Laid side-by-side and interlaced, the footprints of each of these stories are spread across the painting (see fig. 17), and just as elements from several narratives appear to crowd in upon one another, their assemblage seems to invite many ways of reading. Boone describes the reading order and historical sequence of the narrative as ambiguous (2000: 181), and, indeed, some images require decoding from left to right, other sequences unfold top to bottom, and yet others call for the painting to be rotated 90, 180, and then 270 degrees. Whether this produced ambiguity for sixteenth-century eyes—or only modern readers, whose expectations have been cultivated by the predilections of alphabetic texts—remains an open question. Surely, though, woven into the very fabric of the *Mapa Pintado* is a constellation of narrative possibilities, a situation that runs against the grain of alphabetic texts and their fixation on an orthodox reading pattern from top to bottom, left to right, and line to line.

The three *Historia* scenes that draw upon the *Mapa Pintado* replicate its syntactic features, features that were fundamental markers of the boundary-painting genre.[8] For example, the *Mapa Pintado* sets toponymic signs for Cuauhtinchan near the center of the image and then encloses the site in a frame of boundary stations. Likewise, all three of the *Historia* images depend upon a central toponym and a border of boundary markers (see pls. 13, 15, and 16). In giving the toponymic glyphs at the perimeter of the page multiple orientations, the *Historia* paintings further cleave to their model. On both source and derivatives, some glyphs face upright while others are inverted or turned sideways. In this way, the *Historia* creators adhered to the genre despite alterations: boundary painting thus begat book-bound boundary painting.

The *Historia* painters' interest in updating an older source, however, caused them to adopt several strategies as they reworked the *Mapa Pintado*. A comparison of the first boundary painting in the *Historia* that features the settling of Totomihuacan (pl. 13) with that in the *Mapa Pintado*, reveals a painting significantly less replete. In a sense, the *Historia* presents an exegetical unpacking of one section of the *Mapa Pintado*, investing it with the qualities of a self-sufficient scene. The painter moved the toponym for Basket Hill (the toponymic sign for Totomihuacan), for example, from the lower left corner of the *Mapa Pintado* to the center of the new painting, and rearranged a suite of toponymic glyphs from the original to make up the perimeter of the new image. In transferring elements from the *Mapa Pintado* to the *Historia*, the painter arranged many of the boundary-markers in the same sequence; in so doing— that is, by faithfully preserving the signs used on his model and their sequence—the annals-maker emphasized the status of his own painting as a copy. Indeed, these resemblances underscore the decision to rework the *Mapa Pintado* model only in very specific ways. In addition, the annals' writer inscribed on the back of the painting a full list of the boundaries that limn the picture on the obverse (fig. 18). In changing the frame of the *Mapa Pintado*, the painter and writer (who may have been one and the same) at once adhered to the content and the form of the original painting, and created an "other" species of image. So configured, the *Historia* painting displays a curtailed set of core meanings. The former spectrum of historical pathways narrows as the image is recast into an account of a single leader and one set of boundaries.

A second boundary painting in the *Historia* develops in a similar vein (pl. 15). While it focuses on the foundation of Cuauhtinchan, the image is also organized around a selection of glyphs and events from the *Mapa Pintado*. Here, however, nearly all of the sites on the Totomihuacan image are excised such that only four toponymic signs appear on both paintings (i.e., Atzontli, Coatepetl, Tepexocho, and Temalacayo). Instead, the painter develops another, equally coherent, set of images that, when coupled with the written list of boundary sites that accompanies it in the *Historia*, cues a different narrative. Visually, the differences between the two "redactions" are not subtle. In contrast to the first boundary painting, which was emptied of narrative cues, the second redactive painting is considerably more elaborate. Not only did the painter copy more of his source, but, using these elements as a framework, he added new images to evoke other aspects of the foundation narrative. The two scenes of arrow sacrifice, one in each corner of the painting, represent additions, as do the images of Moquihuix drilling fire, the five leaders of Cuauhtinchan, and the arrows piercing Teuhctlecozauhqui's house. With regard to place signs, the painter has maintained the same sequence as that of his source; however, several of the affixes have been reworked. From this we gather that something more complex than the strict replication of an original was at stake for those painting the *Historia*.

Indeed, when the *Historia* painters created their boundary paintings they reworked the *Mapa Pintado* into pictures and texts they regarded as suitable for a European-style codex. And instead of reproducing one image with multiple narrative paths, they fashioned a multitude of paintings—each one presenting a single strand of the larger story. We sense from this that the narrative elicited by the *Mapa Pintado*, the boundary-painting genre, and the European book prototype were all important. It was not possible to juggle these conflicting elements, however. The writer and painters cut their losses to safeguard the meaning of their source and in so doing sacrificed much of its original complexity. They also altered the status and syntactical connective tissue by which boundary paintings made their visual claims.

The last of the three paintings in the *Historia* to display elements from the *Mapa Pintado* references stories excluded from the other images (pl. 16). For the sake of comprehensiveness, this last installment in the boundary series collects the missing pieces and, so to speak, explicates these remnants from the *Mapa Pintado*. This pictorial "compilation" shows the Totomihuaque and Cuauhtinchantlaca raising their boundaries under the direction of the Tolteca. As was the case with its companions, the painting corresponds closely to the written narrative in the annals, and its back bears a territorial inscription that aligns, through visual composition and appellation, the sites depicted in glyphic form. Here, however, some of the challenges of reworking the *Mapa Pintado* leave a visible mark.

A comparison of model and source indicates that the *Historia* "neatened up" the details of the *Mapa Pintado*. The spaces between toponyms are regularized and, over all, the painting is fitted into a more symmetrical arrangement. From one perspective these changes are trivial formal adjustments; however, the realignments and stylistic revisions result in crucial shifts in meaning in the new image. On the *Mapa Pintado*, the culture heroes Icxicoatl and Quetzaltehueyac appear opposite each other on either side of the painting: they converse at Centepetl (Green Corn Hill) on the left, and again at Tetl inepaniuhcan (Place Where the Rocks Join) on the right. In the *Historia* painting, the figures also assemble at the left and right edges of the page. Yet a shift in the story has occurred. Again the men greet each other at Centepetl, but now, after walking along the boundaries, they appear at stage right, at Atlahuimolco (Place Where the Water Bends) not Tetl inepaniuhcan. The site of their original meeting has instead been shifted to the top of the scene. Hence, the visual imagery cues a different conclusion to the narrative than that of the *Mapa Pintado* (fig. 21).

Because of the addition of an inscription that runs across the right side of the *Historia* painting, we know that the annals-maker recognized in this image the possibility of an aberrant reading. To preempt this, at the site of the original meeting, and in line with the toponymic sign for Tetl inepaniuhcan, he wrote, "There at Tetl ynepaniuhcan, the Chichimeca, the Totomihuaque and the Cuauhtinchantlaca, the

Fig. 21 Places where the ancestors meet (detail of Cuauhtinchan foundation scene: second view), *Historia Tolteca-Chichimeca*. Bibliothèque Nationale, Paris, f. 36r, ms. 46–50. *Photograph courtesy of the Bibliothèque Nationale, Paris.*

Dieq ynapamvsca mo namiq. ynfnibimea tofo ynvrq ymalytadsdiftaca ymniqaia
ynelbaca dihhi meca ymic ytilovad ymmcbgalleveg del ymic qm nbnahdyscavq
by yca finilloyiaca fi xifiili qm nbnahdyscaro q

complement of the Tolteca Chichimeca Icxicoatl and Quetzaltehueyac, all met in order to raise the boundaries. In the year 8 Reed they agreed to even it out."[9] This written passage functions quite differently from any other territorial gloss we have seen thus far. Indeed, nowhere else in the *Historia* does Nahuatl script penetrate the pictorial plane, nowhere else does alphabetic writing interrupt and impose upon pictorial representation. On one level, then, this text does not territorialize the manuscript page, but rather interrupts the illusion of the map and poses a contrameaning in the complementary register. We might say, à la Tomasch, that the script intervenes here to deterritorialize the visual and mnemonic field called up by the glyphic scene.

But this is not all. The alphabetic script also fills the gap that emerged between the old graphic configuration and the new codex painting. The "corrected" pictorial image indicates that the annals-writer knew that, in an important way, his painting no longer worked as the original did. Moreover, the adulterated image reveals his need to remedy the problematic contortion in the narrative cued by the new image. The culture heroes could not meet at Atlahuimolco instead of Tetl inepaniuhcan— although they could, apparently, meet at one place pictorially and another via an alphabetic label.

I believe that when the writer of the *Historia* emended his image with alphabetic script he enlisted the specificity of the written word against the considerably more open possibilities that accompanied the interpretation of pictorial record and oral performance. The turn to alphabetic writing as a hook or gaff, reveals that the writer redressed anxiety about the misreading of the image via word signs. More important, it makes clear that purely open readings were not permissible. The juxtaposition of text and image on this boundary painting further reveals that the writer recognized that earlier historical accounts could sometimes become broken during the translation process. Although the "correct" narrative emerged by linking two channels (painting and writing), the aberrant reading was itself an unanticipated byproduct of this union. This reading occurred when the symbolic fields of the codex and the boundary map merged. Since the boundary painting points back in time to an earlier form of recordkeeping, the written text undermines the consistency of the image, noting (as corrections do) that the painting does not convey in good faith an acceptable "truth." From this we gather that the *Historia* represents less an experiment in new forms of recordkeeping than an attempt to span a void—to fix historically friable meanings in very particular ways.

Taking this all one step further, I would suggest that this painting in the *Historia* confirms that the status of pictorial imagery was shifting in Nahua communities. This was, to borrow Donna Merwick's words, one of the "costs of conquest"; the conquered had to change, they had to read their environment, their social and moral space, in fundamentally different ways (1999: 186). The boundary painting teaches us that images were still regarded as highly persuasive signs. As yet only certain things were in flux. Had images ceased fulfilling their semiotic duties, the annals' writer might have created a book that was strictly alphabetic, that fully territorialized text, as it were, in the manner of the Nonoualca boundary roster (fig. 14).

And so, in a very basic way, I sense that don Alonso might have agreed with Tomasch: a writing of the world could not be successful unless it also made room for painted images. If we shift the light, however, and read the *Historia* less literally, we see that geographical desire, especially for Pre-Hispanic territory and its history, was inextricably bound into the letters and signs of this manuscript. And yet, as I conclude this reading of territory, this expedition into lexical spaces, it only seems fair to ask whether don Alonso's companions or kin would have shared his obsessions, would have found his textualized territories compelling? Indeed, to whom would his bookmaking matter? Unfortunately, no dust-jacket testimony survives to suggest how, on any given occasion, the *Historia* was relished, how many lives its canny reading of sixteenth-century arcana changed. A reasonable conjecture would be that its circulation was limited, its audience select. Moreover, scholars of literacy and orality tell us that communities of readers would have been more likely to notice only when a work such as the *Historia* failed, when it stretched familiar narratives too far or elaborated them in an unsuitable manner (see, for instance, Clanchy 1979; Kuhn 2000; and Stock 1984). That is, the narrative twists did not have to make consistent sense at every turn, only at those that would keep one from losing the proverbial way.

In certain crucial ways the textual territory of the *Historia* was built to facilitate traverse, to create complexity, and then to find a clear and satisfactory resolution. Given that these annals survived as a family heirloom, we may surmise that much of their textual landscape was acceptable. This is not to say that we read the same things into tales that don Alonso or his kin would wish. Nor is it to say that don Alonso harbored no anxieties about which parts of his story, which ancestral landscapes, would truly pass on to his heirs.

WHAT IF IT WAS
— LIKE PRE-HISPANIC CODICES —
MORE LIKE AN AIDE MÉMOIRE?
IT WAS MADE TO MEMORIALIZE
AND EVOKE A PAST THAT
WAS LEGACY & KEY TO
ALTEPETL IDENTITY — OR
TEZALLI IDENTITY... THE
FORMER SEEMS MORE LIKELY
IN VIEW OF THE INVESTMENT

Notes

1. The exception to this rule is the sole European-style landscape painting in the *Historia* (pls. 17/18). On this image, see discussion in Chapter 3 and in Appendix 1.

2. For discussion of the relationships among the *Mapas de Cuauhtinchan* and the *Historia*, see Simons (1968) and Yoneda (1981). Elizabeth Boone discusses very well the relationship of *Mapa de Cuauhtinchan* 2, in particular, and the *Historia* (2000: 173–182), and several essays in Carrasco and Sessions (2007b) engage this topic. Descriptions of the *Mapas de Cuauhtinchan* are given in Appendix 2, this volume.

3. Paul Kirchhoff has suggested that some of these pentads represent a regrouping of units originally bound together as quartets. In particular, he explains that the twenty altepetl that comprised Tollan—listed in the *Historia* in four groups of five altepetl each—were originally conceived as five groups of four altepetl. Each of these five groups was associated with the cardinal directions (north, east, center, west, and south) and fundamental Mesoamerican concepts of the universe (1961: 248–265). Although his argument has merits, I find it unconvincing because multiple units of five (rather than four) predominate in the *Historia*. See also Prem (1997: 481–488) on the ideological implications of these pentads vis-à-vis Mesoamerican history-keeping practices more broadly.

4. For the shape and dimension of this territory to be summoned, one must already possess considerable knowledge of the past and its cultural geographies. The written list of appellations, itself, serves as a poor map if one lacks all familiarity with the lay of this ancestral land. Even in spite of its demands for background knowledge, the scriptural roster as a prompt for memory and map of territory seems to have been popular with the *Historia* writer and painters.

5. This is not to say that the written list of boundaries and the glyphic scene cue precisely the same narratives. Rather my point is that the alphabetic itinerary and distribution of toponyms at the perimeter of the manuscript page create parallel descriptions of the same geographic "space." Were annals readers to begin at Centepetl, and move down the list of alphabetic names on folio 36v, they would "pass by" the same sites, in the same order, as would readers of the glyphic scene were they to start at Centepetl, where the footprints enter, and trace a counterclockwise circuit around the page. For discussion of the narrative cued by this glyphic scene, see discussion in Chapter 3.

6. As Donna Merwick points out, some were more successful at mastering the new cadences than others. Indeed, it is her claim that success or failure vis-à-vis shifting demands for things as "simple" as documents represents an arch site in the entanglement between historical subjects and the cultural violence of colonization (1997).

7. The manuscript is currently housed in the Bibliothèque Nationale de France, with the *Historia* (fols. 1–2, ms. 54–58). In the facsimile of the *Historia* published by Mengin (1942), the *Mapa Pintado* was presented as part of the *Historia* itself. Heinrich Berlin and Silvia Rendón also included the *Mapa Pintado* as one of the plates of the *Historia* (1947). Luis Reyes García, however, has conclusively demonstrated that the *Mapa Pintado* predates the *Historia* and is not, properly speaking, part of the annals (1977: 12–13). This argument is elaborated in Kirchhoff et al. (1976: 8–9). See also Simons (1968) and Prem (1997) for a discussion of the relationships between the *Historia* boundary paintings and the *Mapa Pintado*.

8. Such paintings have a wide geographical distribution, with examples known from Veracruz to the Isthmus of Tehuantepec. The genre is discussed by Boone (2000), Glass (1975), and Smith (1973). Arthur Miller has proposed a post-conquest, as opposed to pre-conquest origin for similar kinds of indigenous cartographs (1991); although, see also Boone (1992). The literature on specific indigenous maps (or groups of them) is extensive; but good discussions of indigenous mapping, more broadly, appear in Mundy (1996), Russo (2005) and, in comparison with Spanish practices, Kagan (2000).

9. *Historia* (f. 36r, ms. 46–50). The Nahuatl reads, "Oncan tetl ynepaniuhcan monamique yn chichimeca totomiuaque quauhtechantlaca yn imacica yn tolteca chichimeca yn Icxicouatl yn quetzalteueyac ynic quiquetzque yn tepantli yca chicuey. acatl xiuitl quineneuhcauique."

CHAPTER 4

IN THE GUISE OF A
PRE-HISPANIC PAST

IN MORE WAYS THAN ONE, the *Historia* remains a work in progress. Because the final pages of the document are missing, it is difficult to assess whether the annalists concluded the work, or whether they anticipated a continuation that a shortage of energy, resources, or perhaps unforeseen circumstances prevented. Clearly the clock ran out. Colonial life could be treacherous to ambitious men of don Alonso's circle—which is not to imply that such individuals accustomed themselves to tasks perennially undone. Nonetheless, even significant projects were thwarted by the vicissitudes of fortune. And yet, in the end, the *Historia* offers few hints that don Alonso and his scribal allies harbored qualms about which ancient narratives deserved record and relay. A reader might have been left to elaborate from memory or other sources, to fill in details now and again, but the story of Huemac and the Nonoualca, of Totomihuacan and Cholula, of Tepexoch ilama and her consorts, was there in essence. These were the characters and events who required safekeeping and reperformance; to get their stories right was no minor task. For don Alonso the dilemma of history turned out to be less one of memory, than of documents, and particularly the insufficiencies of certain kinds of documentary record. Neither writing nor painting wholly fit the task at hand. But in the 1550s, what were his choices? How best was he to stack the deck favorably for ancestral players, how best to vouchsafe their achievements?

It is hazardous to stretch a single instance too far, yet before concluding my commentary it seems useful to take stock, to assess what the *Historia* reveals about the making of Pre-Hispanic history, if not the Pre-Hispanic fabric, of New Spain. To do this ultimately requires that we turn away from Cuauhtinchan and from don Alonso's dossier—at least briefly—and consider our comportment toward both colonial manuscripts and the pre-conquest histories they register. While the *Historia*'s pages have been carefully inscribed and its folios covered in complex painting, the annals remain obdurate in the face of our quest to chronicle the visceral realities of Pre-Hispanic antiquity; further, they cannot, in and of themselves, sketch for us how sixteenth-century Nahua memory figured into early colonial history-making. This is not to say that the document is somehow flawed in its movement through memory into history. Rather, the point is this: our curiosities and those of don Alonso do not neatly align. If his manuscript offers any historical lesson about the sixteenth century, it is that even those with personal experiences and memories of Pre-Hispanic life hardly had either the occasion or means to recompile their totality. Moreover, our wish to have Nahuas perform, in documentary installments, such totalizing work, is precisely a confusion of our desires for theirs. Put simply, don Alonso's manuscript demonstrates that Nahua productions of history, the fashioning of an authentically Pre-Hispanic past, were artful. They were not, as such, a salvage operation. That kind of history would only arrive much later, under quite other colonial conditions (Florescano 1994; Haskett 2005; Rabasa 2000).

It is an article of faith among scholars of indigenous histories that the past is, and will always remain, a construction. In one regard, the *Historia* bears this out. The Pre-Hispanic tales this manuscript sets forth are, indeed, honed to a point by sixteenth-century circumstance. For had don Alonso's life turned out differently, so too would have his bookmaking. But this kind of relationship, in which present contingencies shape the past, is oversimple on numerous accounts. Most obvious is the presumption that the present wields the upper hand, giving the past its ultimate shape—even if this past refuses to speak willingly at the master's command. Yet as we know from many an example, histories and memories are unruly, their relationships fickle.

In their investigation of the social production of memory, James Fentress and Chris Wickham suggest that "[i]t is the process of passing down possibilities from the past to the present which produces the subject" (1992:51). This notion of begetting is useful here. For history and memory make us just as we make them. Following Fentress and Wickham, what remains to be resolved is less the substance of Pre-Hispanic history that don Alonso's book passes down than the manifold possibilities of that passage.

Pre-Hispanic Traces

To pursue this facet of Pre-Hispanic history shifts the traditional terms of inquiry in a subtle, but decisive, direction. For the issue at hand is one of lingering potential and possibility, rather than cold, hard fact. This approach, I believe, offers the advantage of bringing to the foreground a fundamental matter. For don Alonso and others like him the past was never *merely* an assemblage of facts or recorded events. Of course there were veristic hooks upon which the stuff of personal and lineage history was hung. Yet the past itself was—and to this day remains—perennially in flux, shifting in its contours. Hence a patron or author's ability to craft new accounts, to build distinctive records. The *Historia* demonstrates how one Nahua noble sought to stabilize his history through the instruments of script and paint. In undertaking this task, however, don Alonso foreclosed on other possibilities, other kinds of records and remembrances.

In these closing remarks, I acknowledge that which we cannot know about either the *Historia* or don Alonso's motives. Principle among the undecidables are the following: a) whether the annals confound or stint their sources; b) whether, or how, the *Historia* misconstrues the past to promote don Alonso's—or any other— particular agenda; and c) whether the *Historia* reflects, accurately or not, the unique subjectivity of its owners. Readers of a certain mind might identify these themes as misguided obsessions. Indeed, one could argue that all three implicate history and subjectivity in a rather static, unchanging state of affairs. These undecidables also rest on presumptions about historical truth vis-à-vis the process of mediation that are at best disputable, at worst unsustainable. Nonetheless, many of us who work on post-conquest manuscripts are not yet ready to relinquish our hands. We are still in the game, optimistic that don Alonso's manuscript is not strictly a colonial document to its core. It is a work on, and about, the possibility of Pre-Hispanic pasts.

With this I would concur. Beyond this, the *Historia* reveals how fundamentally different a sixteenth-century Nahua vision of the Pre-Hispanic is from our own. Perhaps this represents an awkward observation: our histories draw heavily upon the horizon created by sixteenth-century works such as don Alonso's book. Even so, modern accounts of the Pre-Hispanic past resemble the *Historia* in neither form nor structure. The differences are not insignificant, and to deny or even minimize them is to refuse don Alonso and his compatriots a purchase upon the past that cannot be subsumed by our own. This is something about which Gary Tomlinson has written eloquently (1996). His point—about the capacity of colonial documents to resist our categories of knowledge, and our responsibility to respect such distinctiveness even as we seek to interpret and understand colonial histories—is one I take seriously. The challenge in this (some might say the game) lies in understanding how to weigh the inscrutable against the knowable. To my eye, the *Historia* does proffer compelling insights into the possibilities of Pre-Hispanic history in the first generations after the Spanish conquest, even as it resists our compulsions to grasp Pre-Hispanic actualities. The issue is what to make of this.

Scanning the *Historia* for historical perspectives, I would isolate four primary vantages it opens onto the Pre-Hispanic past. Admittedly, there is no single site within the manuscript, no specific image or paragraph, that articulates what, truly, was at stake for don Alonso, what truly carried weight. It is only by reading and assessing the work as a complex whole, by acknowledging both its commentaries and its silences, its pictorial imagery and alphabetic script, that such knowledge begins to coalesce. First, and perhaps foremost, the *Historia* betrays a profound sense of optimism that the past was knowable and, no less significantly, translatable. The past, this manuscript seeks to persuade its readers, could be brought forward to the colonial present. The manuscript also contends that such an enterprise was worthwhile, if not precisely inevitable. These may seem obvious points, yet their implications are hardly so. For given all that don Alonso and his colleagues found themselves negotiating in 1550, even procuring the paper and paint to craft a new history book was an enterprise of consequence. To undertake the renovation of old records, to follow with fidelity, yet simultaneously recraft, the glyphs and narratives of yore were not insignificant endeavors. And they suggest how desirable a good Pre-Hispanic history could be for those living in the sixteenth century in New Spain.

The *Historia* is quite clear, however, that preservation of the past was not don Alonso's sole concern, nor was the remembering of all the ancestral knowledge that he or his community could command. In the sixteenth century, this kind of information gathering was not unknown; it infused the history projects sponsored by friars,

[handwritten margin note: ISN'T THIS A BASIC PREMISE OF ALL HISTORIOGRAPHY?]

men such as Bernardino de Sahagún (Klor de Alva et al. 1988; Schwaller 2003). Indeed, the differences between the *Florentine Codex* and the *Historia* are striking. For Sahagún's history, through questionnaire and interview, baited the production of memory (1950–1982, 1982, 1993), whereas don Alonso's project betrays many a sign of culling and opportune forgetting. We sense this most clearly from the *Historia* writer's occasional "etc." Written into the annals, this abbreviation suggests that the identification of omission was an acceptable part of the history-making process. The manuscript thus made no secret of the fact that it presented highly selective memories about the past. In signaling that the Pre-Hispanic history resulted, at least in part, from the deletion of certain details, songs, or memories, the *Historia* also demonstrates how much labor and expense could be devoted to selectively remembering aspects of the Pre-Hispanic past—and, no less significantly, willingly so.

In seeking to make the old new, the *Historia* depends upon a counterintuitive move. It asserts that the past does its most productive work when only part of it is translated into the present. This is something quite apart from the collecting and appraising of workaday historical enterprise. In choosing to update and recast history—and in allowing the manuscript to signal this labor and process—don Alonso's bookmaking project reveals an extraordinary confidence in the flexibility of pre-conquest knowledge. Had this patron and his manuscript makers lacked such faith, had they believed the familiar boundaries of the past to be incapable of stretching to accommodate the novelties and demands of life in sixteenth-century New Spain, they never could have afforded the wager that became the *Historia*.

The second vantage onto Pre-Hispanic matters that the annals provide centers on the shape of Nahua history itself. For don Alonso's past did not have just one plot or point. From the very outset, the history that takes form here is disjunctive and ruptured. Not only are there the gaps we would expect from any annalistic record-keeping (White 1978, 1981), but the different sections of don Alonso's annals refuse to cohere. Their narrative fragments impinge upon one another only indirectly, in a mediated and mitigating fashion. We need only think of the Nonoualca exodus from Tollan and the roll call of the boundaries inscribing their new homeland that open and conclude the *Historia*'s first chapter. The relevance of this history to the founding of Cuauhtinchan or the achievements of Moquihuix, don Alonso's illustrious ancestor, is no easy thing to resolve, at least not today. Yet the presence of this tale, especially given that the annalist was clear about his decision not to copy all that was available to him, suggests that an acceptable Pre-Hispanic history could be a sum of disparate parts.

There is, of course, some temptation to perceive in this the colonial dissolution of the Pre-Hispanic world, to presume that before the conquest there existed more coherent perspectives on the past. And perhaps such perspectives did exist. James Lockhart has found, however, that in both concept and practice, an aggregation of distinct units characterizes much of Nahua social life (1992). Moreover, we know that although colonial rule produced remarkable hardships for indigenous people and forced momentous change upon them, in pre-conquest times Mexica kings destroyed the histories of their predecessors and had them written anew. Even in antiquity, the past invited revisionism; it hardly fused into a single, crystalline narrative. So we must exercise caution when it comes to documents, no less than to paintings. For both have their own rhetorical strategies, their own internal lives. The ruptures in the *Historia* reveal not colonial conditions per se; rather, they remind us how accounts of Pre-Hispanic history, perhaps even long before the Spanish arrived, were subject to the fragmentation of genre and not merely of memory.

Beyond this, and this is my third point, this set of annals compels us to accept that Pre-Hispanic narratives rarely featured singular, exceptional lives. Across four hundred years of deeds and dates, no single actor bears the protagonistic burden of the *Historia*'s tale. There are figures who exhibit a luster of accomplishment that overshadows those who take the historical stage beside them. Indeed, we have seen how only certain kinds of historical actors—men of eminent status, their brides, and their allies—repeatedly catch the narrative's limelight. Yet those who matter most in the annals are ultimately collectives—pairs, or at times constellations, of players. By way of example, we might recall the Nonoualca and Tolteca at Tollan, Icxicoatl and Quetzaltehueyac at Cholula, Teuhctlecozauqhui and Tepexoch ilama at Cuauhtinchan, and, finally, the altepetl of Cuauhtinchan and Totomihuacan. The *Historia* compulsively concentrates on the time when ancestral figures acted within a community of peers. Great figures of antiquity were never renowned on their own terms. This is not to say the annals present a perspective onto Pre-Hispanic times that is essentially corporate or collective. Instead, the *Historia* is best read as a history in which a major preoccupation lies in describing those ancestors who, although dangerously close to one another, merit distinction. Competition and alliance take form in don Alonso's book as primordial conditions of the Pre-Hispanic epoch. I stress this point because, if Fentress and Wickham are correct and subjectivity emanates from a field of possible transactions through history, then the *Historia*'s fixation on the fine lines between nearly identical communities and individuals could be constitutive of don Alonso's future, not only his past. As he looked ahead, his sharpest anxieties would have hinged on his contradistinction to those closest to him, rather than those he could know little about—Spaniards, friars, and colonial officials making their homes in Madrid, Puebla, and Mexico City. This was not inevitable: many a community harbors greater anxiety about what lies distant rather than near; if don Alonso's preoccupations with the local seem unsurprising, this is one more testimony to the pervasive (and persuasive) legacy of things Pre-Hispanic.

Finally, and this represents the fourth perspective onto Pre-Hispanic history, in the *Historia* land never signifies as a purely territorial phenomenon. It is impossible to find any places, any sites of memory, in the annals that abide apart from the unfurling deeds of human actors. Tollan is the home of the Nonoulaca, the Tolteca, and their allies. Cholula is the altepetl first of the Olmeca Xicalanca and later the Tolteca. Indeed, territorial description takes one of two forms in this manuscript; either it is constituted as an inventory of community boundaries or it looms piecemeal as the plane of ancestral migration. This nexus, where land and people actualize one another in memory, infuses not only the annalist's scriptural oeuvre, but also the painted scenery. For nowhere does the *Historia* posit territory, or even define a spatial setting through glyphic appellation, apart from references to ancestral contours of action. The ties between particular lands and specific ancestors are not necessarily permanent; people in the *Historia* do not once and forever lay claim to a piece of territory or mark it with their presence. In fact, the opposite may be closer to the truth. Much of don Alonso's book details how people come to settle upon or rule a named place in the world. Yet the annals are consistent on one point: there was no land in the ancestral past without occupants. Territory simply did not exist without a concomitant chain of historical events. What I see in the *Historia* is at odds with the terrain proposed by Philip Arnold in his study of Tlalocan. In that study he distinguishes between land, which is necessarily independent of human creativity, and landscape, which articulates land-human interactions (1998: 17). In don Alonso's book, the former does not exist. Territory comes into being only as a crucible for the deeds and founding gestures of ancestors.[1] Even something as "basic" as the names of places in the *Historia* plays into this. For there are no lands without names and, clearly, no names without people to bestow, wield, and remember them. The *Historia* is one of many manuscripts wherein territories unmarked by humans cannot exist. Consequently, the territorial cupidity of don Alonso's history is, fundamentally, also a social and historical form of desire. So too is his present. For the boundaries he sought to restore in 1546, the boundaries described at the end of his annals, are like those that surface elsewhere in the manuscript, no less cultural than physical.

In describing matters as I have, I cannot be sure that don Alonso would have assented. Yet in arguing that the *Historia* illuminates the Pre-Hispanic ground of colonial memory, I share with him the faith that a book may translate, and thus betray, significant narratives about antiquity. In effect, in reading the *Historia* now, in the twenty-first century, we are complicit with its objectives. We entertain the possibility that don Alonso might have been correct: his past was reformable without loss of crucial meaning. What seems less likely, however, is that in investing in writing and pictorial imagery, in making a book about the past, don Alonso's renovation of history has proven to be exactly the history that he bargained for.

The Gamesmanship of History

Throughout this study, I have underscored the *Historia*'s relationships with time and Pre-Hispanic experience, claiming that this is not a cynical, but a hopeful and self-discerning enterprise. Don Alonso and his bookmakers, as is the case with players deeply invested in a high-stakes game, could grasp only partially the likely outcome. Nevertheless, he, they, intuited all too well a fundamental stricture: who they could be—and beyond this, who they could become—in the sixteenth-century landscape of possibility, depended upon what and how they had wagered in games past. Put simply, Pre-Hispanic history was colonial destiny, not merely the other way around. In round-robin fashion, however, specific colonial destinies begat very particular and very peculiar Pre-Hispanic histories. Consequently the present did not so much remake the past as it foretold its future in a cunning way. The two constructed and constrained one another. While prima facie this may seem rudimentary, it is a point that has largely eluded our scholarship, for the contingency of past and colonial present are not easily reckoned with as a dynamically unfolding game of chance and tactic. Nonetheless, a primary objective of my analysis has been to seize something of this unstable arrangement. Beyond this, I have sought metaphors that allow for the pleasurable play in which don Alonso's manuscript so perceptibly revels. The combination of a predictable calculus mixing with the slippages of memory epitomizes the *Historia*. Indeed, the pictorial language that presents the remembering process is itself inventive and mercurial within its formulaic tropes.

But innovation can be risky. It seems more than likely that the *Historia* could not have ranked among the riskiest prospects that don Alonso undertook in his life. After all, the annals are merely a book of stories, and not one that seeks to undermine Spanish authority. Yet because it was so alien to other histories circulating in Cuauhtinchan it embodies a calculated risk. The *Historia* thus reveals possibilities for passing Pre-Hispanic narratives onto progeny and it indicates how that enterprise is riddled with chance. Memories and material traces must be spun together. The facts of ancient history—the deeds at sites settled—are not the only things to be resolved, so too are the visual and material convergences of history. In no small way the *Historia* suggests that for don Alonso the most promising aspect of the Pre-Hispanic past was its pregnant elasticity. To look different, yet mean the same, that was his hope, if not also his folly. Ultimately, then, the *Historia* operates as any good wager might: it stakes a claim upon present realities, past experiences, and the future they portend. And in many ways, don Alonso's bookmaking operation turned out to be one of his better investments.

The nuanced roles and responsibilities thrust upon the *Historia* in Cuauhtinchan in 1550 may largely elude us but the manuscript seems to have scored well in later rounds. By the seventeenth century, the book had matured into a family heirloom of considerable symbolic value. This represents the first of many returns on don Alonso's wager. We also know that the annals were kept in don Alonso's altepetl, alongside other historical documents, including the *Mapas de Cuauhtinchan*, well into the eighteenth century. In the 1740s, the *Historia* began its migration from Cuauhtinchan to Mexico City and then, within a few decades, on to Paris. With other painted histories, the manuscript left the community archives of Cuauhtinchan and entered the acquisitive grasp of Lorenzo Boturini Benaducci, an Italian collector who gravitated to New Spain, smitten by the legacy of the Virgin of Guadalupe. Boturini's appetites for pictorial documents were wide-ranging and pantagruelian. Within a few short years he amassed an enormous cache of indigenous paintings. Legal wranglings with Spanish officials landed him in jail and ultimately led to his deportation. His painted spoils were confiscated by Mexican authorities and ultimately lost or dispersed. Not surprisingly, none of Boturini's manuscripts made their way back to the communities from whence they came. Most eventually reached Europe via a network of collectors. In effect, his collecting endeavors set into motion a European siphon that drew sixteenth-century pictorials away from their contexts of creation. No longer the history of a single community or lineage, each work now joined a larger corpus of "indigenous manuscripts."

How, exactly, Boturini carried off his collecting remains obscure: whether people or communities were coerced into the forfeiture of documents, whether payments were arranged, or whether indigenous mediators smoothed the acquisition process, is undocumented but imaginable. What is certain is that when Boturini took possession of three of Cuauhtinchan's histories—the *Historia*, the *Mapa Pintado*, and the *Mapa de Cuauhtinchan 1*—he seized community documents. For the *Historia* and other maps were, by that time, holdings of the local archives. This is a second return on don Alonso's wager. Since being sent to Paris, where it now resides, the *Historia* was copied in the nineteenth century by several bibliophiles and has, in portions, been published and republished numerous times. This suggests that the bets that don Alonso hedged when he invested in ink and paper futures were well chosen. Although he could not have known it at the time, the *Historia* has become a monument in our modern reckoning of Pre-Hispanic history.

Reception Histories

Ultimately, for modern readers of the *Historia*, an interpretive conundrum remains: how to understand the fullness of the Pre-Hispanic past if, within less than a quarter century of the Spanish conquest, indigenous people sought to record only select events and representational traditions culled from the deep past? This dilemma is, I believe, more intractable than meets the eye. Put simply, for whom, and in what ways, could (or should) a manuscript, constructed as is the *Historia*, matter? Early on in this study I insisted that the material forms and words used in writing the past are without innocence. Our metaphors of description are not trifles. I also asked whether the annals of don Alonso might have implications for debates that extend beyond the parameters of Pre-Hispanic and early colonial visual culture and history. Admittedly, these queries broach themes external to a monographic manuscript study, but I wish to argue that they are nonetheless relevant to the broader designs of don Alonso's project, perhaps even having an impact on the notion of an "incorporated" self with Pre-Hispanic roots. And in closing, it is to these topics that I turn.

Even in Cuauhtinchan, the *Historia* represented but one Pre-Hispanic construction of the past, competing among many for authority. In the mid-sixteenth century, these annals jostled amidst an amalgamation of local histories and images—the *Mapa Pintado*, and *Mapas de Cuauhtinchan* 1, 2, 3, and 4, the *Libro de los Guardianes*. They also accompanied oral histories that were as surely performed as they were unlikely to leave material traces. Outside this altepetl, in neighboring towns as well as communities across Spanish America (and even Spain), a myriad of indigenous history-keepers set their accounts to paper and cloth. To line them up side-by-side—*Codex Xolotl, Codex Selden, Mapa de Sigüenza, Mapa de Cuauhtinchan 2, Nueva corónica y buen gobierno, Anales de Tepeaca, Manuscript of Huarochiri, Comentarios Reales de los Incas*—is to confront an uncanny array of testimony. Although the *Historia* rests more comfortably alongside some of these documents than others, two questions persist: given all the modes and methods for conserving Pre-Hispanic images of past events, to what genre of history-keeping does the *Historia* properly belong, and is it a parochial or a worldly vision that characterizes it?

To specialists of the field, the *Historia* stands as a specimen of "Stage 2 annals" in the progression Lockhart has outlined for the corpus of indigenous writing (1992). Yet such an assignation sheds little light on the tactical and strategic ambitions that crisscross the *Historia*. The manuscript resembles certain imperial histories of Central Mexico structured, as it were, by deep narrative patterns and well-honed tropes. Don Alonso's annals could also be positioned within the genre of horizontal propaganda described for Mexica and Mixtec communities, in which local leaders tendentiously vied for privilege and distinction based on an interchange of symbolic and material tokens. Whether the *Historia* is also a "chronicle of the impossible" (Salomon 1982) and a form of colonial critique could also be compellingly argued. Ironically, given all that is just beyond reach with respect to the Pre-Hispanic past, the most crucial challenge we now face, as modern redactors of colonial manuscripts, is more methodological than factual. In the last twenty years a florescence of writing on indigenous histories has opened a surfeit of methodologies and models for analyzing documents like the *Historia*. How to choose among them? This is no rhetorical question. For more often than not, the reasons we settle upon one explanatory framework as opposed to another seems to evoke a disciplinary site of "social forgetting," a quiet space in interpretive scholarship. While Luisa Passerini rightly argues that a charged silence in the public sphere can have a positive meaning (2007: 26–27), is there nothing to be gained by more frankness about our interpretive ambitions?

In her book on myth, history, and writing in Pre-Hispanic Mexico, Joyce Marcus argues, more persuasively than most, for the propagandistic objectives of Mesoamerican histories (1992). A dominant line of this argument maintains that Mexica imperial histories were tendentious manipulations of historical events that serviced the controlling interests of state and ruler. She further contends that through creation and recreation of these "historical" narratives the past assumed a persuasive power, however distorting of social reality it might be. In this account Central Mexican histories become inextricably bound up with struggles over material wealth and symbolic capital. It is probably unwise to build too direct a conduit between the imperial histories of Pre-Hispanic tlatoque and don Alonso's annalistic project, but certain superficial parallels do pertain. The *Historia* was tailored to conform to the interests of a local leader and it could have supported claims colored by political desire. Indeed, because the *Historia* promoted don Alonso's social and economic position within Cuauhtinchan, a position inherited, rather than earned, one might be inclined to read his manuscript as an instrument of horizontal propaganda. That is, the annals could represent an elaborate and highly mediated form of historical competition, in which high-status Cuauhtinchantlaca checked each other via partial, if not also elaborate, accounts of the past. For many a Mesoamericanist, this interpretive strategy will strike a familiar chord (see, for example, Boone 1996; Marcus 2003). Yet its purchase on the broader predicament of history-keeping—in native communities, in early modernity, in colonial settings—is incomplete given the fragile evidentiary structure of the Pre-Hispanic past.

Rolena Adorno (2000) and, more recently, Cynthia Stone (2004) have argued that certain colonial manuscripts might best be construed as the product of cultural mediators, drafted by polyglot authors who exploited the intersections among multiple knowledge systems. These would be colonial writers effectively straddling boundaries (which were themselves in flux) between Spanish and native communities and creating hybridized genres of expression, as in *Nueva corónica* and *Relación de Michoacan*. One may identify in these projects, as Adorno asserts in her analysis of the *Nueva corónica*, a risky cultural gambit that ultimately grows into a line of cultural resistance. Given the complex and contradictory nature of cultural mediation as we now understand it, colonial resistance as opposed to accommodation appear to be just two options of the many that shaped and colored daily life in the cities and towns of Spanish America in the sixteenth and seventeenth centuries. History-keeping could also engage strategies and elements of subversion along with (and even alongside) those of collaboration or craven collusion. Could mediation be the deeper motive that drives don Alonso's manuscript project?

Here is a man who, at least on occasion, kept the company of friars and Spaniards, who appreciated the persuasiveness of alphabetic writing and European-style bookmaking, and yet remained firmly committed to Pre-Hispanic narratives and their nuances of value—at least in the context of his commissioned work. While he appears not to have enlisted Spanish readership, which adds a serious wrinkle to any autoethnographic ascription (Pratt 1994), don Alonso's "atelier" invested mightily in graphic innovation and lexical experimentation. Indeed, even as the *Historia* undermines the tropes of European recordkeeping, it challenges Pre-Hispanic forms of documentation and representation. Expertly stitched into the filaments of Nahua memory, the *Historia* sets itself apart from its Pre-Hispanic models and from other, contemporary Cuauhtinchan histories. Unlike fellow altepetl members who found cause to replicate Pre-Hispanic genres of recordkeeping and thus fashion documents such as the *Mapas de Cuauhtinchan*, don Alonso's bookmakers judged this manner of registry wanting. The *Historia* has instead rearranged the lineaments of traditional recordkeeping, even as it cleaves to precepts and teachings of Pre-Hispanic history and morality. If read in this light, the *Historia* seems to destabilize not only European forms of recordkeeping but also those of Pre-Hispanic origins. Because neither has the upper hand, we might say don Alonso's colonial project calls into question the figure-to-ground relationship of European and Pre-Hispanic history-keeping.

In this scenario, don Alonso and allies come dangerously close to achieving the status of hero-interpreters, committed to an agenda of cultural critique not commonly identified in indigenous historians, much less those who shouldered the mantle of provincial leadership. This reading of course, is not without its troubles. My point, however, is not to settle don Alonso's role as an agent of change, but to engage seriously a modern interpretive dilemma. Were we to align, rather than counterpose, this reading of the *Historia* with that outlined above—in which the annals served as a tool of local persuasion—we would see more clearly the complexity of the role imposed upon the Pre-Hispanic past in an altepetl like Cuauhtinchan.

Interpretive elasticity, of course, cannot be infinite: we cannot laminate our readings of indigenous histories one to the other ceaselessly, as if the underlying presumptions of each and every interpretation could mesh, as tightly as tongue-

and-groove, with all others. Yet when we elevate one proposition over another—say, cultural critique over propaganda (or vice versa)—what happens to don Alonso's history? Do we see it more clearly for what "it really was"? In the sixteenth century, of course, the annals could not just say "just anything," nor could they reliably do their work in any random setting. Community standards and expectations governed the documentary record's reception. Today, our interpretive options seem to promise a greater open-endedness. To read through the lens of subaltern politics, however, is to bring forward a very different sixteenth-century history than that focused on the daily pragmatics of indigenous life.[2] In both cases, the Pre-Hispanic past is construed as a mode of memory work; in the former, however, the politics and economics of submission loom large. The subtle subversions of colonial mimicry (Bhabha 1984), in other words, are hardly at issue for those who see Nahuas basically going about their daily business as best they could. And so the question cannot simply be that of obtaining an accurate read on the past; it must instead, and also, turn upon how wide a range of meanings indigenous documents can summon, today, in the present.

In Chapter 1, I underscored how different the *Historia* is from contemporary metropolitan narratives of sixteenth-century Europe. Much scholarly ink has been spilled since George Kubler analogized the survival of Pre-Hispanic cultural forms to the flotsam lingering in the wake of a proverbial shipwreck (1964). For Latin Americanists who focus on indigenous histories and visual cultures, comparison to European paradigms, against which colonial and Pre-Hispanic projects are subjected to validity checklists, remains dubious for so many reasons. Indeed, by reading documents written in Nahuatl, Maya, Mixtec, and other indigenous tongues, and by steeping ourselves in the semiotics of indigenous agency, much of the tenaciousness, resilience, and mutability of Pre-Hispanic history and colonial representations of it has surfaced—in ways and with a depth not often imagined possible. Nevertheless, if we step back from our objects of study, far enough to take in the wider horizon of history writing, Europe still casts a shadow over these claimants to historical relevance. The novel record-keeping gestures and rites of New Spain and Peru have barely made a dent in most historiographies outside of Latin America. Is this parochialism prompted by the documents themselves—their material and narrative forms, their "foreign" iconography and obsession with local sites and genealogies— or is there perhaps another issue at play?

We are fortunate today in being able to grasp so much more of Pre-Hispanic history—particularly, as it circulated in the sixteenth and seventeenth centuries— than was possible even thirty years ago. And indeed, this includes an acute sense of how lacking in consensus and homogeneity that past once was (Klein 2002). Yet the intersections between colonial memory and Pre-Hispanic antiquity produce strange bedfellows, and they don't really get out as much as they might. There is, of course, much that specialists in the field still seek to know, and ought to debate among themselves. In certain ways, it is still early days in the study of Pre-Hispanic history as manifested in colonial manuscripts. Yet the comparative scholars would make this point: the most compelling lessons the *Historia* offers about history-keeping are not likely to get resolved in Latin America alone. Rather, to know whether indigenous histories from New Spain and Peru are in any way unique—whether their impulses match those of any other histories elsewhere, or their modes of mediation are exceptional—it becomes necessary to set these works alongside documents quite alien to them. In the absence of such comparisons, there are no means to measure the broadest power of their Pre-Hispanic metaphors and colonial descriptions of the past, no way to appraise the potency of their ancestral narratives. Thus, the last crucial question prompted by the *Historia* (and manuscripts of its ilk) does in fact concern the longue durée. Seen from the present, are these documents unusual or representative modes of history-keeping produced on the cusp of colonialism? To put a finer point on it, do they signify practices uniquely Latin American, distinctly Novohispanic, or, for that matter, utterly local?

Ultimately, were I to pursue this project further, I would place my bets on this kind of question, on the comparative approach to history. For works like the *Historia* do, indeed, bear witness to the broader sense and scope of both early modern and colonial history keeping. In developing my interpretation of the annals here, however, I have observed don Alonso's tack and privileged more local events. I have also learned a trick or two in the course of the game. Tradition does indeed have consequence, and the worth of close reading, of collecting and parsing Pre-Hispanic from colonial images and texts, is not (yet) discountable. Yet tradition, as we know, requires constant cultivation, and this means keeping a hand in the forms and linguistic tropes of one's own time. Don Alonso's investment cum wager rested upon the convergence of paper and paint and ancestral narrative; mine likewise trusts marks on paper, and although the quest is different, I am ultimately concerned, as was he, with the flux of interpretation—of how Pre-Hispanic histories translate to the present, how best to assure for them a long life. Of course, Tepexoch ilama is hardly my kin and Tollan and Cuauhtichan are not my ancestral homes, and so my stake in their future differs from that of don Alonso, his granddaughter doña María, and their descendents whose names are no longer known. Yet if don Alonso's wager teaches us one thing, it is this: the past can hardly contain the ancestors, its history is never written for them alone.

Notes

1. In this, the conceptual and rhetorical work of territory in the *Historia* resembles that described by Keith Basso among the Navajos (1996) as well as certain Australian approaches to ancestral lands. It also aligns with modern philosophical approaches to landscape anchored deeply in phenomenology (as opposed to visuality). See, for instance, Ingold (1993) on the former, and Casey (2002) on the latter.

2. This point is made particularly eloquently, if not also somewhat contentiously, in the essays collected by Thurner and Guerrero (2003). The assessments in that volume, coupled with those of Klor de Alva (1989), Mignolo (2000), and the essays in Bolaños and Verdesio (2002), illuminate the range of the anthropological and historical writing on postcolonial studies vis-à-vis colonial Latin America. A primary counterpoint emerges in the work of Lockhart (1992), and many who work closely with indigenous-language documents (see Cline [1986], Haskett [1991, 2005], Horn [1997], and Terraciano [2001]); see also Restall (2003), who puts much of this latter work into a useful perspective.

MAJOR PAINTINGS FROM THE *HISTORIA TOLTECA-CHICHIMECA*

THE IMAGES DESCRIBED in this appendix comprise the suite of full- and double-folio paintings in the *Historia*. Descriptions focused on the composition, iconography, and narrative implications of each image appear here, along with brief commentaries about the style of each painting. These interpretations highlight what could have been seen in, and read from, the *Historia*'s pictorial vocabularies and compositions. What emerges is a sense of how significant and substantial were the roles played by images in the *Historia*, both denotatively and connotatively: these pictures were never mere illustrations. Even so, if unambiguous meanings were produced and consumed in the sixteenth century by readers of the annals, such details elude us today. As in any representational system, the imagery in the *Historia* calls upon a wide range of affects and logic, yet this evocative range had to be able to shift, like a view through a kaleidoscope, to accommodate distinct reading occasions and interpretive ambitions. Fluidity, however, should not be mistaken for indecision or elusiveness. The *Historia* was an account of the Pre-Hispanic past that sought to persuade local readers of its veracity. Consequently, the capacity of its imagery to summon meaning traced, and abided in, distinct patterns and limits. These patterns and possibilities represent the gist of the following descriptions.

The images appear here according to their order in the *Historia*. In order to help modern readers distinguish one painting from another, I have given each work a short title relating to the primary iconographic themes of the painting. The discussion of style highlights the range of visual conventions *Historia* painters drew upon as they worked. Alessandra Russo has recently argued, and rightly so, that sixteenth-century painters did not necessarily parse their images in terms of ethnic and stylistic origins; moreover, the desire to distinguish "the European" from the "Pre-Hispanic" represents a modern concern (2005: 17–28). Yet it is precisely because the *Historia* juxtaposes explicit redactions of earlier forms of image-making with newly invented forms of representation that I find it useful, as an interpretive strategy, to note the kinds of models painters would have known. The manuscript folio numbers parallel those of the Bibliothèque Nationale in Paris, which currently holds the *Historia*. Right and left, throughout, refer to the reader's right, the reader's left.

PLATE 1

FIRST EXODUS FROM COLHUACATEPEC

f. 5r, ms. 54–58

This folio opens the annals' second section, which recounts the Tolteca-Chichimeca migration to Cholula and their first victory over the Olmęca Xicalanca lords resident there. As is typical of opening scenes throughout the *Historia*, a short explanatory text, set down in red ink, appears above the full-folio painting. This text does not identify the Tolteca-Chichimeca figures that stand below the cave, nor does it address the cave scene proper. Instead, the writing summarizes events previously recounted in the annals, focusing upon the separation of ancestral groups: "Here is the story of how the Tolteca Chichimeca came from Colhuacatepec and arrived at Tollan with their complement the Nonoualca. At Tollan they left each other and divided so that the Nonoualca went to Atlahuimolco, Tepatzacapan, Quetzaltepec, and left the Tolteca Chichimeca behind."[1]

Meanwhile, the painting restricts itself to a single incident from the grander narrative and, through its compositional use of branching footprints, stresses the themes of departure and disunion registered in the alphabetic text.

Iconography and Composition

Originally framed on all sides by a solid black line, the painted scene offers a cut-away view of Colhuacatepec, the ancestral mountain, set against an unelaborated background. At the center of the image rests a darkened cavern, which, the painting suggests, lies directly below the mountain's curling peak. A single row of footsteps running along the painting's central, vertical axis leads from the interior of the cave to the bottom of the scene. Tracing a path of exodus from the dark recess at the folio's center, the footsteps diverge when they reach the figures standing below. Reading from left to right, Tololhuitzil and Tezcahuitzil stand facing Quetzaltehueyac and Icxicoatl. Each figure is named glyphically—with small painted signs placed near the crown of the head, or, in the case of Quetzaltehueyac, with a colored plume emerging from his mouth. Constituting a kind of figural frieze at the bottom of the scene, the four wear similar hairstyles, headdresses, and outfits. Apart from the name glyphs that identify each of these men, the painting contains just one other significant glyph: the mottled, curving form at the top of the cave homophonically evokes the name "Colhuacatepec." In keeping with Pre-Hispanic practices wherein visual forms cued specific words, this curving appendage ("col," or "something twisted") inaugurates the utterance of the cavern's name. The cave also exhibits its seven characteristic lobes, reminding readers

Pl. 1 First exodus from Colhuacatepec, *Historia Tolteca-Chichimeca*. Pigment on European paper, ca. 28.5 cm (height) × 18.5 cm (width). Bibliothèque Nationale, Paris, f. 5r, ms. 54–58. *Photograph courtesy of the Bibliothèque Nationale, Paris.*

¶ Yzcatgni ynm tlafollo ŷtolteca chichimeca ymcvallexa q ŷcolhnacatapec ymi
caeuo ŷtollom. ymi macica ŷnonovallca. onca ŷmocauhŝq ymopelo q ŷto
llan ymi macica ŷtolteca ymcyayaoi ŷnonovallca. yna tlavi molteo ŷ tepaŝa
capa ŷ qneʒaltepec. qni mocuhŝtevaq ŷtolteca chi chi meca.

that this site of Pre-Hispanic ancestral emigration is also Chicomoztoc, or Place of Seven Caves. The edges of the cavern, however, owe more of their graphic details to European-style landscape images than Pre-Hispanic–style paintings. Rocks and cacti, for example, fulfill a descriptive role here, underscoring that the seven-lobed cave lies within a mountain, in a far-off desert.

Style

The painter of this scene has mixed images and graphic conventions from numerous sources. Firm dark outlining—a technique often seen in Pre-Hispanic images— appears around the lobes of the cave and its curving, glyphic appendage. Yet shading and modeling, which rely upon European precedents, abound. The human bodies reveal an awareness of proportion and methods of depicting human anatomy with tangible roots in European representations, although the depictions of legs and faces are more convincing than the rendering of shoulders, arms, hands, or feet. It is also notable that the painter has chosen not to define the space between Colhuacatepec and the Tolteca-Chichimeca. Consequently, the mountain cavern and four figures seem to float in space. This, too, may derive from Pre-Hispanic conventions.

Narrative Implications

Scrutiny of the painting's overlapping forms and stratified paint layers reveals clues about the picture's genesis: the seven lobes of the cave and the name glyphs of the Tolteca-Chichimeca bear evidence of being set down before the addition of human figures or cacti.[2] For the painter, Pre-Hispanic–style glyphs seem to have anchored the composition, acting as guideposts for the picture's execution. While this scene does not literally illustrate the text above it, the painting accentuates a symbolic point. The four warriors are truly Tolteca-Chichimeca: they sport the headdresses of Tolteca, yet wear loincloths and grasp weaponry associated with Chichimeca— ancestral hunter-warriors from the north. Later in the annals, as they grow more civilized, the alphabetic text will call these figures simply Tolteca and the painters will render them with more refined garb and accoutrements, but not in this scene. This painting portrays the men as half-formed culture heroes and foreshadows a transformation yet to come.

PLATE 2

ARRIVING AT CHOLULA

f. 7v, ms. 51–53

This painting focuses on the arrival at Cholula of two Tolteca-Chichimeca culture heroes, Quetzaltehueyac (Quetzal Plume at the Lips), at the reader's right, and Icxicoatl (Serpent Foot), at the left. The top of the folio bears a short alphabetic inscription that identifies the two men and announces their arrival at the sacred site. This text was covered by a long strip of paper added to the top of the manuscript at some later date, but the writing remains visible in the original folio. It reads "[h]ere are those who arrive at Tlachiuhaltepetl, Icxicoatl, and Quetzaltehueyac" and thus refers to Cholula by the appellation Tlachiuhaltepetl.[3] The passage was penned in red ink, as is typical of texts set above full-folio images throughout the *Historia*.

Iconography and Composition

This is the first pictorial representation of Cholula in the annals, and two themes are underscored: the multitude of appellations—and thus identifying aspects—of the site, and the locale's link to the Tolteca heroes. Within a space defined by a solid black border, these two protagonists appear near the top of the painting, accompanied by glyphic nomenclature and dressed as Chichimeca wanderers not yet fully legitimized as Tolteca rulers. The arrangement of the figures' hair, for example, identifies Quetzaltehueyac and Icxicoatl as Tolteca; the two wear animal skin cloaks, however, and therefore appear here as neither fully Tolteca nor fully Chichimeca. Each figure raises a hand in a gesture of greeting or speech. Between them looms an imposing hill, itself surmounted by an oversized frog. In addition to the amphibian, the hillock supports six blossoming flowers and from its base flow two flowery streams. These elements do not show us what Icxicoatl and Quetzaltehueyac saw when they arrived at Cholula, but rather serve as visual cues evoking several of Cholula's epithets.[4] The remainder of the painting is, in actuality, a concatenation of monikers: swirling water, a bird, a palace, and other signs distributed across the manuscript page present different names for Cholula.[5] The painting thus functions as a visual stage for verbal metaphors for the most sacred site in the annals. Kirchhoff et al. have suggested that the glyphs have spatial and political implications, serving to toponymically define the places where the Calmecatlaca (the Calmecac people) of Cholula resided (1976: 146, f7r, n.1). Little in the manuscript painting itself, however, hints at how, or even whether, these name signs might diagram Cholulan territory.

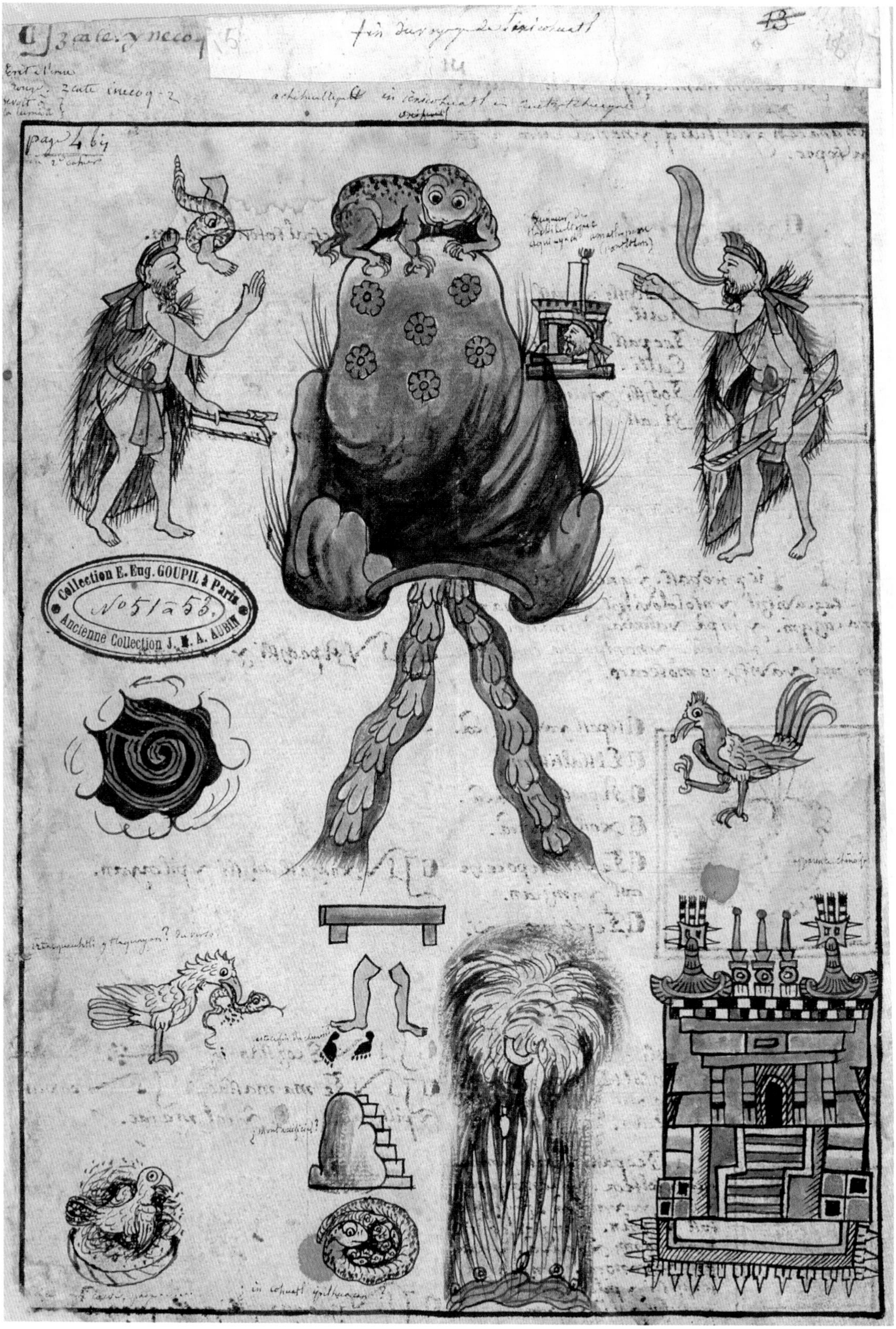
Collection E. Eug. GOUPIL à Paris
Ancienne Collection J. M. A. AUBIN

Style

As might be expected with an image of this sort, the painting exhibits many Pre-Hispanic–derived signs, from the glyph forms to their paratactic dispersal across the blank ground. Nevertheless, the imagery also indicates that European graphic techniques were neither anathema nor wholly foreign to the painter of this scene. The attempt to create an illusion of overlapping forms in the figures of Quetzaltehueyac and Icxicoatl, while not particularly convincing today, reveals an ambition to enlist new pictorial conventions (introduced via European images). So, too, do the shading effects in the primary toponym, the small bench below it, and the palace structure in the lower corner. This scene can also be analyzed for clues about its manufacture. For instance, the painter rendered the bodies of Quetzaltehueyac and Icxicoatl before superimposing arms and clothing; he also fashioned the small figure of the Aquiach Amapane, just below the raised arm of Quetzaltehueyac, before executing the main hill-sign for Cholula. In terms of the chronology of its production, then, the painting was concerned first with human actors, second with the stage for their deeds.

Narrative Implications

While heavily indebted to Pre-Hispanic iconography, this folio demonstrates a clear and resolute grasp of how opening sections of European books functioned. The writer and painter also understood how such manuscript pages define codicological boundaries. These points become apparent when we, as modern viewers, recognize that the painting and its text exhibit a composition reserved strictly for inaugurating new sections of the *Historia* narrative. In this case, the scene opens the portion of the annals that focuses on the first Tolteca-Chichimeca settlement in Cholula, setting the stage for their sovereignty over the site. Beyond this, as the first full-folio painting of Cholula, it foreshadows later manifestations of the site, which include similar glyphic forms and collections of signs, as well as the gesturing figures of important pre-conquest actors (see, for example, pl. 4).

Pl. 2 Arriving at Cholula, *Historia Tolteca-Chichimeca*.
Pigment on European paper, ca. 28.5 cm (height) × 19 cm
(width). Bibliothèque Nationale, Paris, f. 7v, ms. 51–53.
Photograph courtesy of the Bibliothèque Nationale, Paris.

PLATE 3

CHOLULA UNDER THE OLMECA XICALANCA

f. 9v–10r, ms. 54–58

This double-folio scene depicts Cholula as ruled by the Olmeca Xicalanca. It thus identifies not only the sacred site but also articulates its political arrangement when, according to the *Historia*, the Tolteca-Chichimeca first arrived.

Iconography and Composition

Offering a view of Cholula that will be repeated yet challenged elsewhere in the annals, this painting emphasizes the affinity between center and periphery. Three oversized toponyms dominate the central portions of the scene, evoking distinct appellations for Cholula. Each toponym refers to a different aspect of the site—the flowered hill and frog (Tlachiuhaltepetl, Place of the Built Pyramid), the stand of blue-green reeds sprouting from a pool of water (Iztactollin, Place of the White Reeds), and the willow tree (Iztacuexotl ycacan, Place Where the White Willow Stands). If the multiplication of signs calls Cholula into being through a litany of names, it also lends the site complexity, implying that a single moniker is insufficient to summon or even name the site. As is the case with all paintings of Cholula in the *Historia*, this one references Tollan. The prevalence of blues and greens, with their connotations of preciousness, surfaces only in pictures of these two sites. Moreover, the stand of reeds shown here parallels the reeds that form the toponym for Tollan on the first painted folio of the annals (fig. 7). While subtle, these painted elements perform the visual work of binding these two sacred sites together.

At the edges of the painting, ten rectangular boxes frame the Cholulan toponyms, each with an Olmeca Xicalanca lord sitting alongside, or atop, a glyphic representation of his particular place. Through this spatial arrangement, the painting adumbrates the distribution of Olmeca Xicalanca leadership.[6] Cholula therefore emerges as a place bounded by particular claims to rule. In keeping with most *Historia* images, no written text appears here. Cues to identity and place surface only in the name glyphs for each ruler and toponyms for each site conjoined within each rectangle, which frame the perimeter of the scene.[7]

Style

In its mix of elements of Pre-Hispanic and European origin, this painting resembles others in the annals, yet the technique and style of this image are unique. Not only are the combination of colors and their saturation unusual, this painting manipulates the scale of border images in a dramatic way. The proportions of each human figure strike the eye as familiar, yet the relationships between name glyphs—which traditionally appear as small affixes floating near or above the figure—and human bodies has been shifted so that the name glyphs are very large. Further, although outlines are firmly drawn, only two of the Cholulan toponyms (the hill and the reeds) have been shaded as have figures and objects elsewhere in the annals. The top of the willow tree, the Olmeca Xicalanca rulers, and their toponyms are, in contrast, stylistically quite distinct. This suggests that the painting was completed by at least two sets of hands of varying skill. Even though this painting appears less accomplished than many in the *Historia*, the tree in the upper left corner of the image sits firmly on the ground, indicating that the painters at work on this scene were well aware of European conventions for showing groundlines. This, along with the logical treatment of Pre-Hispanic-style forms, suggests these were not untutored hands.

Narrative Implications

Since scale is one strategy used by the *Historia* painters to convey importance, the relative size of the three Cholulan toponyms implies they are the principal elements of this scene. Examination of the painting's layers, however, indicates that the framing rectangles and Olmeca Xicalanca rulers were added before these central images. As is the case in many of the *Historia*'s paintings, the human components of the image preceded depiction of places. While not the first visual reference to Cholula in the annals, this painting is the first double-folio "map" of the site and so functions as a visual referent for later representations. This is critical because of the morality tale that emerges in the *Historia* narrative. According to the annals, Cholula achieves its true glory only under Tolteca rulership. Later, when the Tolteca defeat the Olmeca Xicalanca and come to rule Cholula themselves, the *Historia* painters render the site in lusher colors, more elaborate detail. The painting here seems to present a degraded version (or vision) of Cholula. This image thus participates in a larger visual narrative that unfolds across the annals, informing readers that this may well be Cholula, but it is not the site it should be—and will become.

21

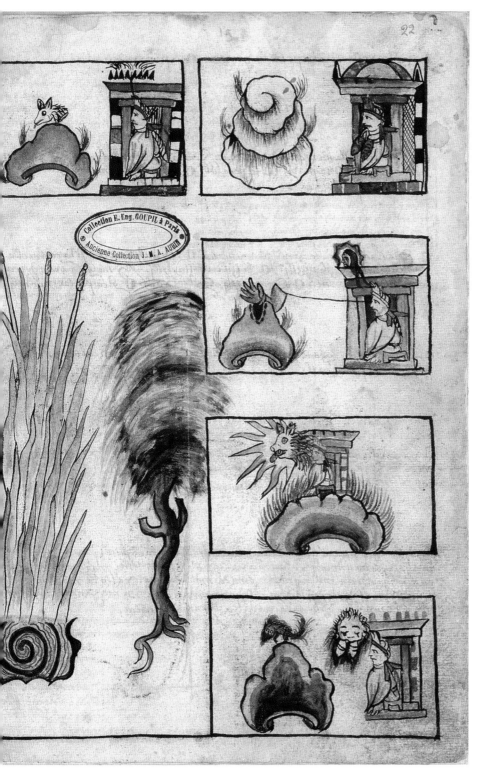

Pl. 3 Cholula under the Olmeca Xicalanca, *Historia Tolteca-Chichimeca*.
Pigment on European paper, ca. 27 cm (height) × 38.5 cm (width).
Bibliothèque Nationale, Paris, f. 9v–10r, ms. 54–58.
Photograph courtesy of the Bibliothèque Nationale, Paris.

PLATE 4

THE TOLTECA AT CHOLULA

f. 14r, ms. 54–58

This painting again treats the site of Cholula and the two ancestral heroes, Quetzaltehueyac and Icxicoatl, who initiated Tolteca rule there. The folio opens a new section of the narrative, and, as in opening pages elsewhere in the *Historia*, alphabetic text in red ink appears above the painted scene. This text does not describe the pictorial imagery but rather establishes the larger narrative context, noting that the story to follow concerns the Chichimeca who allied themselves with Tolteca and earned great fame for their marvelous deeds. The text reads:

> [h]ere is the story of the Chichimeca—the Cuauhtinchantlaca, the Moquihuixca, the Totomihuaque, the Acolchichimeca, the Tzauhcteca, the Zacateca, the Malpantlaca, the Texcaltlaca, the seven altepetl— when they left Chicomoztoc. [Here is the story of] the rulers who were the complement of Icxicoatl and Quetzaltehueyac. The deeds done at Colhuacatepec, and their fame were very marvelous.[8]

Although the text speaks of seven altepetl, it lists eight; this discrepancy betrays the partisan interest of the *Historia* in identifying the Moquihuixca, the ancestors of don Alonso de Castañeda's lineage, as a separate group on par with the others (Kirchhoff, Odena Güemes, and Reyes García 1976: 11; Leibsohn n.d.: 89–145).

Iconography and Composition

The graphic components on this folio all appear within a black outline that both frames the scene and sets it apart from the writing above. An immense hill glyph surmounted by an oversized frog appears at the center, and dominates the painting. This glyph, intense in its blue-green coloration, signs the site of Cholula.[9] To one side of the hill there appears a prominent stand of white reeds, and to the other a large willow tree; these are two glyphs that also reference the locale. Above both of these images, the painter placed a bannerlike scroll with the name of each object-glyph written alphabetically in capital letters: "IZTAC TORIN" and "IZTAC VEXOTR." This is one of the few instances in which the writer has substituted the letter "r" for "l," which was not uncommon in the mid-sixteenth century (Lockhart 1992: 294, 341); hence the banners "should read" Iztac Tolin (White Reed) and Iztac Huexotl (White Willow). Although the painter foregoes a groundline for these three glyphs, the hill, reeds, and tree all adhere to a single horizontal axis, coalescing to situate us, as image-readers, unambiguously in Cholula.

Pl. 4 The Tolteca at Cholula, *Historia Tolteca-Chichimeca*. Pigment on European paper, ca. 29 cm (height) × 20 cm (width). Bibliothèque Nationale, Paris, f. 14r, ms. 54–58. *Photograph courtesy of the Bibliothèque Nationale, Paris.*

IZTAC TORI

IZTAC VELOTR

Toward the bottom of the image the culture heroes, Icxicoatl and Quetzaltehueyac, stand facing an elaborate building—presumably a Cholulan palace or temple. Within the *Historia* narrative, this painting appears just after the Tolteca have overthrown their Olmeca Xicalanca enemies and become the rulers of their coveted Cholula; nevertheless the men still hold the bows and arrows of warriors, still wear the robes of Chichimeca. Later in the temporal flow of the annals, when they have fully secured their claims over Cholula, Quetzaltehueyac and Icxicoatl don the robes of rulers. In this painting, however, they appear in the process of transformation.

Style

The mix of elements here—from glyphs to painted scrolls—reveals how adeptly the *Historia* painters utilized models of diverse origin, purposely intermingling them. The hill glyph at the center of the scene provides an excellent example of this. The firm outlines and lower red lip derive from pre-conquest graphic conventions, but the shaded interior of blue, green, and tan owes much to European painting. Similarly, the lower sections of both the willow and stand of reeds evoke Pre-Hispanic conventions, while their upper sections betray an affinity for the shading familiar in European imagery. This engagement with different pictorial traditions pervades the entire image. The blank background, against which figures and elements float, reveals a painter well aware of Pre-Hispanic pictorial techniques. Yet the mirror reversal of the two figures, such that their poses, gestures, and accoutrements achieve a kind of heraldic symmetry, implies considerable awareness of European pattern books and concomitant modes of representation.

Narrative Implications

The function of this folio, to introduce a new section of the narrative (the third), firmly aligns the painting with codices of European origin. The painted scene should thus be understood as a hybrid invention, created expressly to address the requirements of this particular set of annals. Its relationship to the narrative remains both complex and intriguing. This scene opens a section about the Tolteca search for Chichimeca allies—allies who exercise military prowess, secure Tolteca sovereignty over Cholula, and then found their own altepetl. It is this last event, the founding of new altepetl, which drives the annals narrative. Yet the painted action per se signifies none of this. Instead, it evokes Cholula and presents the images of those who will rule there. In so doing it underscores a key narrative trope: no altepetl could have been founded, no story could have unfolded, had Tolteca rulership at Cholula not been secured. The painting thus turns on the order of affairs at the sacred site. Furthermore, the iconography, and to some extent composition, of this image parallels other portrayals of Cholula, especially those that emphasize the triad of glyphic signs: frog and hill, reeds, and willow.[10] Since each painting of the site stresses a distinct theme, through a play between similarity and difference this scene attempts to evoke key features of Cholula in readers' minds, yet eschews any consistent visual definition of the city and its leaders.

PLATE 5

LEAVING COLHUACATEPEC: THE SECOND EXODUS

f. 16r, ms. 51–53

This painting, perhaps the most elaborate and detailed of any in the *Historia*, shows Quetzaltehueyac and Icxicoatl at Colhuacatepec-Chicomoztoc in the midst of negotiations with the Chichimeca who live within the cave. According to the annals, the Tolteca came to the mountain cave expressly to enlist the Chichimeca warriors as allies in a battle to gain control of the holy site of Cholula. The transactions pictured here are therefore bathed in sacred as well as political connotations. From the perspective of people living in Cuauhtinchan in the sixteenth century, these negotiations were crucial. Had the Tolteca failed to convince the Chichimeca, Cuauhtinchan would never have been founded. Consequently, the painting, and the events it symbolizes, emerge as a pivot for the entire *Historia* narrative.

Iconography and Composition

In the lower right section of the image, Quetzaltehueyac and Icxicoatl appear in the guise of priests. With their skin blackened and their backs adorned with extraordinary ornaments and resplendent quetzal plumes, the figures face two Chichimeca warriors. The Chichimecan below, across from Icxicoatl, is Coatzin, the interpreter, and it is his footsteps that march into and out of the cave, leaving their trace as he negotiates between parties. The wispy speech scrolls linking the two figures clarify that the figures do, indeed, engage in conversation. Above the interpreter, the warrior Moquihuix, the ancestral hero most closely linked with don Alonso de Castañeda, raises his hand to greet Quetzaltehueyac. The doubled appearance of Moquihuix, both at the edge of the cave and crouched within its central space, underscores his importance to the story. Indeed, his role is far more prominent in this painting than in the *Historia*'s alphabetic text.

Splayed across the center of the folio, and dominating the scene, is a cross-sectional view of the sacred cavern. The painting offers multiple perspectives of the underground chamber, for viewers see both the inside and outside of the cave at once. In addition, the composition relates both a continuous narrative—replete with images of sequential events—and disparate moments in narrative time. The exterior of the cave has rocky edges studded with desert plants and cacti. The blue-green coloration implies preciousness, and toward the bottom of the cave floating glyphs refer to events that transpired at the cave as Icxicoatl and Quetzaltehueyac ritually prepared for contact with the Chichimeca. These events include feeling the heat of Chicomoztoc's exterior wall, listening for noises at the edge of the cave, and striking it (see discussion Chapter 2, Bernal-García 2006, and Leibsohn n.d.).

The interior of the cave is semidark, revealing the two central male figures, signs of their speech and transit, and kin sequestered in each of the caves' seven lobes. Small glyphs near the rear of every cavelet identify each Chichimeca group by name; the Cuauhtinchantlaca, for instance, live in the upper left, as indicated by a small eagle with the atl-tlachinolli (sacred warfare, burning water) sign spilling from its mouth. The only unnamed figures inside Colhuacatepec-Chicomoztoc are four women, whose heads surface at the right side of the cave, just behind Coatzin, the interpreter. These figures, the annals texts suggest, represent all the women who lived inside the cavern with the Chichimeca warriors.[11]

Style

The pictorial model for the Colhuacatepec-Chicomoztoc shown here is an unmistakable cousin of the one used in a painting of the mountain cave earlier in the annals (pl. 1). Comparing the two images, it is notable that the painter of this second scene placed several plant forms at different sites along the edges of the cave and added a few stock elements, such as the man drilling fire in the upper right. Nevertheless, these two images represent interpretations of a single source. The landscape here—the rocky perimeter of the mountain, the flowering cacti, and the shaded edges of the cave—owes much to European imagery. Although the postures of the negotiating figures also have ties to European prototypes, the modeling of form through mixed and shaded hues only surfaces in landscape elements. It is telling that the painter neither parses nor isolates Pre-Hispanic from European-derived techniques. As a result, European-inspired treatments do not merely limn the edges, nor do Pre-Hispanic–inspired features (e.g., the diagram of the cave, speech scrolls, or name glyphs) strictly dominate the compositional center. Rather, graphic conventions from both modes inextricably intertwine. This suggests that if the painter perceived any tension between the two methods of depiction, he did not signal this in any explicit manner within the painting itself.

Pl. 5 Leaving Colhuacatepec: the second exodus, *Historia Tolteca-Chichimeca*. Pigment on European paper, ca. 28 cm (height) × 20 cm (width). Bibliothèque Nationale, Paris, f. 16r, ms. 51–53. *Photograph courtesy of the Bibliothèque Nationale, Paris.*

Narrative Implications

As the second advent of Colhuacatepec-Chicomoztoc in the *Historia*, this painting both evokes the earlier version and develops a commentary upon it. Because this second cave is far more elaborate—in coloration, detail, and articulation of the interior—it symbolically enlivens the earlier scene. In bringing the cave scene to life, in repleteness both of color and detail, the painting deems this telling of the encounter at Colhuacatepec-Chicomoztoc as the more significant of the two. This painting also relates to the larger narrative along complex axes. For example, certain aspects illustrate the story in a forthright manner: speech scrolls symbolize negotiations between the Tolteca and Chichimeca, footsteps sign Coatzin's path as he enacts shuttle diplomacy, and the spear that Quetzaltehueyac thrusts into the cave portrays the one described in the alphabetic narrative. Other pictorial elements perform semiotic detours akin to Pre-Hispanic glyphs, pointing to Nahuatl words. These are the curling form atop the cave that evokes the name Colhuacatepec—part of the appellative for the mountain cave—and the floating hand, ear, and weapons at the cavern's lower edges, which evoke the shifting monikers of the Tolteca as they performed their sacred rites. Finally, there are features of the image that are neither descriptive nor linguistic, but rather metonyms for larger historical concepts. Here, the tiny flint knife and circle just above the first footprint within the cave and the man in a wolf skin drilling fire perform this kind of work. The knife is actually a date glyph signing the year 1 Flint Knife, the auspicious year of beginnings in many central Mexican histories.[12] The drilling of fire (*mamalli*) is associated with inaugural events—especially the founding of temples in Pre-Hispanic times. Together, these elements signal informed readers that the events depicted here do, indeed, initiate a new beginning.

A breach between alphabetic and pictorial modes of expression also opens around this image. Its visual doubling, and thus privileging of one figure—Moquihuix—has parallels later in the narrative (see Kirchhoff et al. 1976, and discussion, Chapter 2). Yet here the painting distinguishes and elevates this ancestor well in advance of the written components of the annals. Readers of the *Historia* could thus glean different lessons depending upon the expressive channel—painting or alphabetic writing—they most heavily focused on. And for those who attended equally to painting and writing, a stronger sense of nuance, particularly through pictorial foreshadowing, would likely result.

PLATE 6

BALL-GAME SCENE

f. 16v, ms. 51–53

This scene of a ritual ball game, which the narrative indicates took place shortly after the Chichimeca emerged from Colhuacatepec-Chicomoztoc, represents one of several sacred events experienced by the Tolteca and their Chichimeca allies as they prepared themselves to go to war against their enemies in Cholula. In conjunction with other rites, the game ultimately bestowed upon the leaders of each group the authority required to rule their own altepetl.

Iconography and Composition

This full-folio image is built of two registers: above, a pair of trees flanks a stand of lush reeds shooting up from a flowered enclosure that contains glyphic representations of water and a fiery liquid; below, in an I-shaped ball court, two Tolteca men face each other, as if locked in agonistic gamesmanship. In the written narrative of the *Historia*, only the ball game is mentioned and explained as an offering to the gods. The painting depicts two of the three men involved and the black rubber ball with which the game was played.[13] Dominating the painting, however, and setting its tone, are images of plants and liquids, which hover above the ball court, connoting preciousness and sacred warfare. The U-shaped enclosure at the center of the page sprouts blossoms; long, green blades of grass (or perhaps feathers); and a great stand of reeds. The interior of the rectangle contains both blue liquid, referring to water, and red liquid alluding to blood.[14] On either side of the enclosure stands a tree, dense with foliage. The physical relationships among the trees, enclosure, ball court, and ballplayers remain ambiguous. The plants suggest the setting for the ball game, yet they may also represent an apparition the ballplayers experience, or a metaphor for their deeds. In any case, one of the primary functions of the plants, water, and blood lies in offering pictorial explication of the scene's ritual associations.

Style

Compared to the scene of Chicomoztoc immediately preceding this painting (pl. 5), this image appears spare in detail. Yet the shading of colors—especially in the foliage of the trees and the stand of reeds—is the most sophisticated of any painting in the *Historia*. In particular, the use of different hues of green, along with gold, blue, and red, creates an impression of depth and lends the foliage visual variety. While the painter is not wholly successful in his application of white paint, his intention to brighten certain aspects of the leaves and reeds while leaving others dark reveals an ambition to create the illusion of three-dimensional objects mapped across a two-dimensional surface. This form of illusionistic painting would have been known in Cuauhtinchan in the sixteenth century through exposure to images of, and instruction in, European graphic traditions. Given the careful treatment of the feathered headdress of Apanecatl, the ballplayer on the lower right, it is clear that the painter of this scene is no novice. That he also executed, quite beautifully, the glyphic signs for water and blood as well as the Pre-Hispanic–style convention for ball courts, further reveals well-founded knowledge of Pre-Hispanic imagery. His mixing of these disparate iconographic elements, signs, and graphic techniques suggests something of his training; no less importantly, it also points up the porousness of graphic systems in mid-sixteenth-century altepetl.

Narrative Implications

This painting appears in the *Historia* several pages before the alphabetic text references the ball game. In fact, the pictorial cycle presents the ritual game as the first event in the Chichimeca preparation for war at Cholula. According to the narrative, however, the game transpires near the end of the warriors' preparations—after two other key events, a ritual fast and the Tolteca piercing of Chichimeca septa. Its placement thus creates two different accounts of the sacred events, one pictorial, the other alphabetic. Beyond this, the textual description of the ball game is succinct and receives no special attention. In rendering the scene so elaborately, however, the pictorial strand lends special emphasis to the event. This treatment of the game instantiates its importance: the image tells readers of the *Historia* that this particular ball game was a game with profound implications for the events that followed. In this, the painting does not so much contradict the alphabetic text as reprioritize, and thus alter, its implications.

Pl. 6 Ball-game scene, *Historia Tolteca-Chichimeca*.
Pigment on European paper, ca. 28.5 cm (height) × 19 cm
(width). Bibliothèque Nationale, Paris, f. 16v, ms. 51–53.
Photograph courtesy of the Bibliothèque Nationale, Paris.

PLATE 7

FASTING SCENE

f. 20r, ms. 54–58

This painting of a sacred fast continues the series of full-folio images that refers to ritual acts undertaken by the Tolteca and Chichimeca. In this image, it is the Chichimeca warriors who assume the main role in the ceremonial drama. The fasting rite readies the warriors for battle against the enemies of Cholula and augments each leader's authority to rule his own altepetl.

Iconography and Composition

Four Chichimeca leaders are shown resting in the branches of four trees: Teuhctlecozauhqui appears in the upper left, Aquiyahuatl in the upper right; below them, Tzontecomatl occupies the lower left, and Tecpatzin the lower right. According to the narrative, soon after their emergence from Chicomoztoc, these leaders began a four-day fast. Each Chichimeca is dressed in a striped costume and although the warriors appear otherwise physically identical, a bow and its arrows rest near the branches of just three trees, below the feet of each of three warriors. The warrior at odds with the others, who distinguishes himself by the priestly bag and flint knives at the base of his tree, is Teuhctlecozauhqui, who will become the primary founder of Cuauhtinchan. His name, like that of the other warriors, is indicated by a small glyph that appears at the crown of his head.

With their heads tipped skyward, the Chichimeca receive spiritual and physical nourishment from jaguars and eagles perching above them. These nurturing animals reference the Pre-Hispanic eagle and jaguar warrior societies of central Mexico and thus reinforce the military theme of the painting. To further underscore militaristic notions, the atl-tlachinolli, the pre-conquest metaphor and sign for sacred warfare, usually represented glyphically by a stream of water and fire symbols, spills from the mouths of the felines and raptors into those of the Chichimeca. Whether these animals—and their martial provisions—appeared to the warriors during the fast (i.e., as apparitions) or are visual cues strictly for the *Historia* readers remains unclear. One visual cue more likely intended to address readers of the annals rather than figures in the painted scene does surface. The shield, club, and arrows that float in midair near the top of the painting explicate the martial theme of the scene as a whole but do not refer to any specific event or moment in the narrative.

Compositionally, then, the painting rests upon a simple formula: four warriors, four animals, and four trees aligned both horizontally and vertically, forming a quadrilateral matrix. A thin, black line frames the scene and divides it in half along

Pl. 7 Fasting scene, *Historia Tolteca-Chichimeca.*
Pigment on European paper, ca. 29 cm (height) × 19.5 cm
(width). Bibliothèque Nationale, Paris, f. 20r, ms. 54–58.
Photograph courtesy of the Bibliothèque Nationale, Paris.

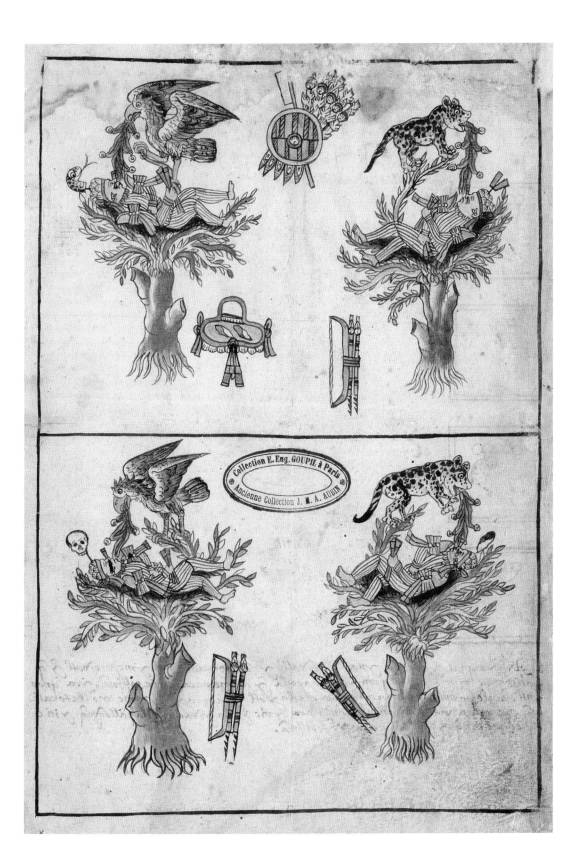

the horizontal axis. The image thus presents a foursome, yet is itself composed of two pairs. For those familiar with the story, the painting is prophetic in its dispersal of figures. The warriors at the top of the painting play the more significant roles in upcoming events: Teuhctlecozauhqui will guide the dominant group into Cuauhtinchan, while Aquiyahuatl will lead his kin to found Totomihuacan. In later images, both men will appear linked again, with their privileged roles made more explicit (see discussion below, pls. 11 and 12).

Style

If this painting seems to owe much to Pre-Hispanic sources for its iconography, stylistically it has both Pre-Hispanic and European roots. For example, the shading of the tree trunks, the eagles' breasts and wings, and the jaguars' bellies mimic illusionistic techniques unknown in Pre-Hispanic painting. This attempt to create gradations in hue, however, does not extend to the warriors or their implements; neither does it convincingly create the impression of light and shadow in the scene as a whole. Even so, it would be hard to say whether this painter did not fully "understand" his European models, or was, instead, unconcerned with replicating the conceptual nuances of their conventions. Equally important here, at least in terms of style, is the way that the trees and the weapons at their bases appear to float in space. No ground line exists, nor has the painter anchored the fasting warriors in any finite landscape. This reliance upon a blank ground has its origins in pre-conquest painting, and it strengthens the point that although many full-folio images in the *Historia* are inventions wrought from disparate models, the painters were not randomly plucking iconographic and stylistic elements from European sources. Instead, this scene demonstrates that certain traditions of painting were more acceptable, and seemingly more tenacious, than others. For in only one scene in the *Historia*, a scene of defeat for the Cuauhtinchantlaca (pls. 17/18), do figures appear situated within a landscape rather than superimposed against a blank ground.

Narrative Implications

Although the annals' text describes this fast as the first major event in the ritual cycle of preparations for battle, the painting occurs second in the series. Thus the pictorial and alphabetic components of the *Historia* conjure different versions of the events. This image does, however, share a repeated and insistent assertion with the alphabetic narrative: "local" or minute differences between similar competing groups and individuals are of profound import. It is the representation of four nearly, but not precisely, identical warriors that makes this point visible in pictorial form. For as any knowing reader would see, the two men on top come to play the more important roles in history, and of these, only one, the founder of Cuauhtinchan, both possesses the priest's bag and is nourished by an eagle—perhaps as a further cue to his destiny as founder of an altepetl called Cuauhtinchan (Home of the Eagle).

PLATE 8

RITUAL PIERCING AND FEEDING SCENE

f. 21r, ms. 46–50

This image is the third full-folio image in the *Historia* to depict the ritual acts of Chichimeca warriors as they prepare for battle and leadership of their own altepetl. After emerging from Chicomoztoc and undergoing a ritual fast, six warriors assemble before Quetzaltehueyac and Icxicoatl. One Tolteca leader pierces the noses of the Chichimeca so that they may adopt the jeweled nose ornaments of Central Mexican authority; the other feeds the warriors sacred corn so that they may speak a tongue intelligible to their allies, the Tolteca.

Iconography and Composition

A wide border of woven mats and branches frames the scene. Along each side of the enclosure, a small doorway segues through the painted border dividing it into four subsections and opening four pathways into the scene's interior.[15] The painting's central, vertical axis is traced by a trail of black footprints that enters through the topmost opening, descends the length of the manuscript page, and exits through the aperture at the lower edge. Near the top of the painting, interrupting the march of footprints, hover an eagle and jaguar—references to the two most elite warrior societies of the Mexica. Painted as a feline body overlaying that of a raptor, these beastly apparitions combine to form a heraldic emblem for the scene. Inside the image's frame stand eight human figures, arranged in double rows so that four occupy the upper portion of the painting, four below. The scene is thus organized along two counter thrusts—one vertical, one horizontal. At the far right are the Tolteca heroes, recognizable by their blackened skins, hairdos, and name glyphs. Quetzaltehueyac and Icxicoatl each face a cluster of three Chichimeca warriors who appear to queue up, and wait their turn for the culture heroes' attention. In the top row, reading from right to left, are Quetzaltehueyac, Aquiyahuatl, Teuhctlecozauhqui, and Moquihuix. Below them, again reading from right to left, stand Icxicoatl, Tecpatzin, Tzontecomatl, and Coatzin. In this lower register, Icxicoatl pierces the nose of one warrior, while above, Quetzaltehueyac offers another sacred corn. The grouping of Chichimeca men into dual rows underscores structural alliances, both among themselves and with the Tolteca culture heroes. At the same time, through color, gesture, and accoutrement, the image carefully maps cultural and ethnic differences, separating the Tolteca leaders from the Chichimeca warriors.

Style

Iconographically, the footprints, eagle, and jaguar, as well as the clothing and name glyph of each warrior and priest have roots in pre-conquest convention. In addition, the absence of ground lines—a graphic effect derived from Pre-Hispanic painting—seems to release the figures, so that they appear suspended in a temporal and spatial void. Nevertheless, the musculature and overlapping forms of the human bodies signal a painter conversant with European sources. And at the painting's edges, framing the scene, are two alternating patterns—one of woven mats set against blue, the other, intertwined branches silhouetted against brown. The mat pattern may symbolize rulership via the woven *icpalli* (a seat, often of authorities) that rulers occupied in pre-conquest times. More crucial for understanding the painted style of this image, however, is the fact that this kind of broad, framelike border often surfaces in European manuscripts and printed books of the fifteenth and sixteenth centuries. It would therefore seem the painter fashioned this scene so that it would (also) resonate with pages known from European books that reached New Spain in the first half of the sixteenth century. In this, the painting is atypical: no other *Historia* scene has been framed so elaborately, nor does any other border trade so conspicuously upon European manuscript and book illustrations.

Narrative Implications

In the *Historia*'s textual narrative the events pictured receive very little discussion; they are simply mentioned in passing, as preparatory acts that steel the Chichimeca for battle and rulership. Emblematically, however, the image is of considerable import. Had the Chichimeca not been readied, ritually and physically, they could not have vanquished their enemies at Cholula nor held the reigns of their own altepetl. Well in advance of the narrative, then, this painting offers *Historia* readers signs that the Chichimeca warriors were predestined for both martial victory (hence the eagle and jaguar above) and altepetl sovereignty. Also significant is the painter's insistent differentiation of the Tolteca and Chichimeca. Not only do the physical appearances of the two groups—from skin color to clothing— come through, the painter reinscribes a hierarchy of valued difference, for the Chichimeca are still learning to speak a language intelligible to the Tolteca (e.g., a "civilized" tongue). Over the next several pages, social and cultural distinctions between the Tolteca and Chichimeca wane, but not before the two groups wage their war against the foes of the Tolteca at Cholula.

Pl. 8 Ritual piercing and feeding scene, *Historia Tolteca-Chichimeca.* Pigment on European paper, ca. 27 cm (height) × 18.5 cm (width). Bibliothèque Nationale, Paris, f. 21r, ms. 46–50. *Photograph courtesy of the Bibliothèque Nationale, Paris.*

PLATE 9

SHOOTING CACTUS SCENE

f. 23r, ms. 46–50

According to the *Historia* narrative, four days after the exodus from Chicomoztoc two Chichimeca warriors, Micuexi and Macuexi, were prompted by their allies to sing a holy song and shoot arrows into blossoming *nopal* (cactus) and *malinalli* (twisted grass) plants. This painting—the fourth in the series of ritual preparations—both depicts their assault and makes visible the connection between sacred warfare and Chichimeca military prowess.

Iconography and Composition

This painting is explicit about the bellicosity of Micuexi and Macuexi, yet it also alludes to the sacral nature of the rites that prepared the Chichimeca for their migration to Cholula and their battle against its enemies. The scene has been composed in two parts. Placed diagonally at the center, and serving as an emblem for the whole image, an enormous arrow with downy balls points from the lower to the upper portion of the painting and links the two. Across the top of the scene extends a floating green hillock enclosed by woven panels studded with arrows. Five bearded men wearing only loincloths—and thus neither clearly Tolteca, nor Chichimeca—stand atop this hill, each with legs bent as if starting to genuflect (or perhaps run). Above them stretches a blue arc of sky and billowing clouds. Below, and forming the second part of the painting, the two Chichimec warriors—recognizable by their hairdos and skin cloaks—shoot arrows into two oversized burning plants, malinalli on the left and nopal on the right. The warriors' actions are both omens and metaphors: the plants dribble blood in this sacred piercing, just as human bodies will bleed when attacked on the battlefield. As if to reinforce this theme, large spermatic forms painted red and orange, presumably schematic drops of blood, cover much of the painted folio. Whether or not these forms emerge from the two punctured plants remains unclear, although they do seem to ascend the painted manuscript page to disappear into the heavens. As a result, they create a sense of "heat rising," animating the scene and connecting in yet another way the hilly enclosure with the military actions below.

Pl. 9 Shooting cactus scene, *Historia Tolteca-Chichimeca*. Pigment on European paper, ca. 27 cm (height) × 18 cm (width). Bibliothèque Nationale, Paris, f. 23r, ms. 46–50. *Photograph courtesy of the Bibliothèque Nationale, Paris.*

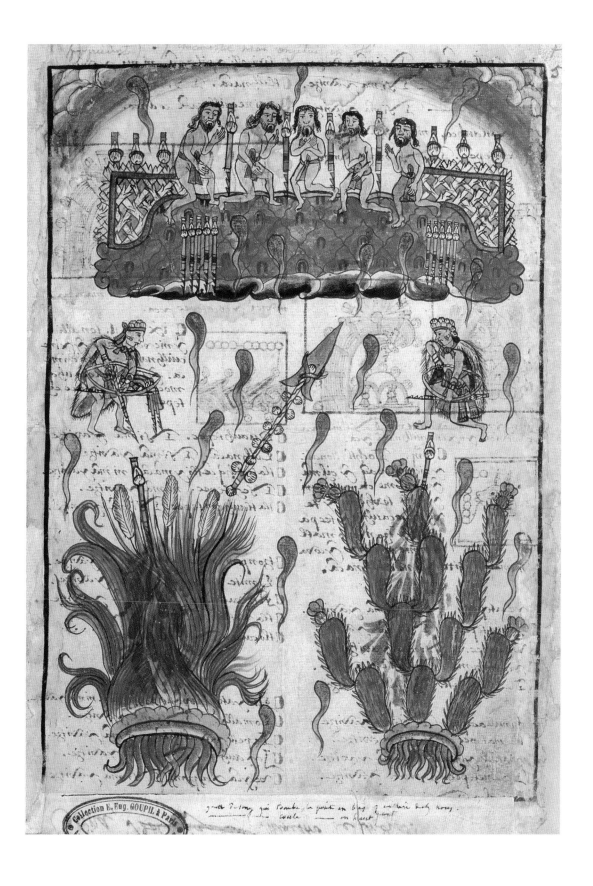

Style

Of all the paintings in the *Historia*, this one most clearly shows the freedom with which a Nahua painter could intertwine stylistic and iconographic elements of diverse origins. The celestial elements of the scene, as well as the warriors' poses and the modeling in yellow and green of the hillock, nopal, and malinalli all derive from European imagery. So, too, does the presence of a full-folio scene that illustrates a single, dramatic moment in the narrative. Yet the solid colors of the woven enclosure and warriors' clothing, along with the shape of the plant roots, netlike pattern of the hillock, and blank ground of the scene all have Pre-Hispanic roots. This visual complexity suggests that the painter interpolated several graphic sources to create this scene. And yet he worked from a limited number of models—at least in terms of the European imagery. The poses of the human figures make this apparent: except for differences in orientation and gesture, the bodies of the men in the woven enclosure are nearly identical, as are, mutatis mutandis, the bodies of the two archers. It is as if the painter traced two kinds of figures, flipping the prototype and making minor adjustments in gesture to create the composition. From this we grasp the skill of the painter as both translator and innovator of visual imagery.

Narrative Implications

Patently concerned with sacred warfare, this painting describes ritual preparations for sacrifice and military engagement. The picture also takes an event mentioned in passing and amplifies its importance by rendering the action in a full-folio scene. The *Historia* text mentions that a song was sung at the time of the ritual shooting, and even provides the words (some of which refer to the shooting of arrows into a nopal), yet the painting eschews any overt reference to singing.[16] Moreover, both acts—singing and shooting—surface in the narrative as merely two of many, equally significant, ritual events. This image is thus one more installment in the series of *Historia* paintings focused upon Tolteca-Chichimeca preparations for battle and rulership. What is notable about this set of images, which includes a ball game, a ritual fast, and a piercing of septa, is that each covers a full folio in the *Historia*. As a set, they represent the most prominent visual depiction of sacred events in the annals. In general, the *Historia* does not highlight Pre-Hispanic ritual or devotion to non-Christian deities; nonetheless, these paintings show that memories of sacred warfare and its associated rites had neither disappeared nor become unintelligible, at least within the context of ancestral hero tales.

PLATE 10

ANCESTRAL CHOLULA

f. 26v–27r, ms. 46–50

This double-folio painting of Cholula is the most elaborate representation of the site in the annals. It adumbrates the political leadership of the site under the Tolteca lords, Quetzaltehueyac and Icxicoatl, as well as the main buildings clustered in Cholula's center. An associated textual passage in the *Historia* refers explicitly to this painting, and vouches for its verisimilitude, its presentation of Cholula "as it really was," in days of old.[17]

Iconography and Composition

Compositionally, the picture signs the rapport, and distinction, between center and periphery. In this it alludes to another *Historia* painting of Cholula that shows the site under Olmeca-Xicalanca rulership (pl. 3). Seventeen rectangles form the perimeter of this scene; each contains at least one Tolteca or Chichimeca leader. In the upper left corner of the painting, Quetzaltehueyac and Icxicoatl appear as the Tlalchiach and Aquiach, the primary ritual leaders of the site. Across the top of the image, and along both sides, are other Tolteca leaders. Some flank small houses, which identify their *calpolli*. Perched upon stone seats at the bottom of the scene sit the six Chichimeca leaders who figured prominently in the exodus rites from Colhuacatepec-Chicomoztoc: Coatzin, Aquiyahuatl, Moquihuix, Teuhctlecoazauhqui, Tecpatzin, and Tzontecomatl. Each of these founding fathers will play significant roles in the future of the *Historia* narrative, although the first four of these men play more important roles as the narrative continues. Thus Coatzin and Aquiyahuatl will found Totomihuacan, while Teuhctlecozauhqui and Moquihuix will found Cuauhtinchan; in contrast, Tecpatzin and Tzontecomatl, as the leaders of the Texcalteca and Acolchichimeca, perform acts of bravery at Cholula but soon disappear from the annals.

At center left, a large temple with an elaborate roof fronted by a plaza enclosed with quetzal plumes dominates. This exquisite structure presumably represents the Temple of Quetzalcoatl. On the right stand a series of buildings and familiar toponymic signs for Cholula: the frog atop the mountain, the willow tree, and the "flowery stream." In contrast to other evocations of the site in the *Historia*, this image plays down the significance of the toponyms by reducing their scale relative to the built structures. This painting also differs from other depictions of Cholula in the trails of footprints tracing paths across the scene. These trails belong to the Chichimeca, who enter the central plaza from our left, advance from their enclosed space at the painting's perimeter to its central temple, and egress via two plaza exits along the upper and right edges of the painting. One of their trails passes an atl-tlachinolli, in the form of a looped shape of red-brown and blue, suggesting the Chichimeca headed in this direction were, indeed, heading into battle.

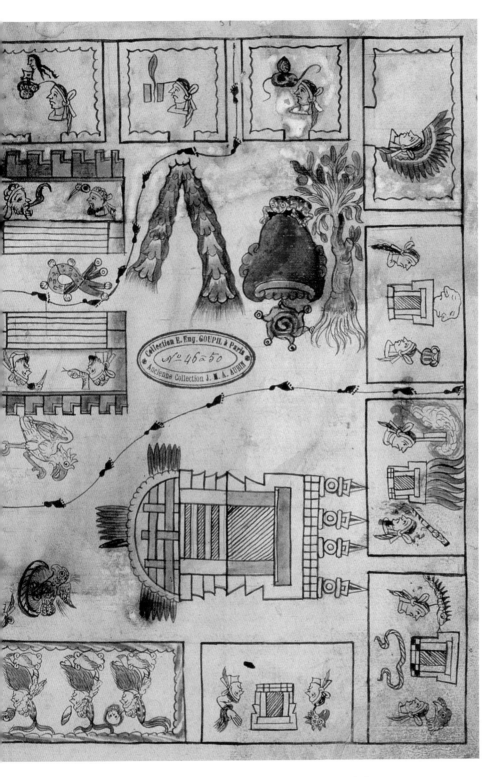

Pl. 10 Ancestral Cholula, *Historia Tolteca-Chichimeca*.
Pigment on European paper, ca. 27.5 cm (height) × 41.5 cm
(width). Bibliothèque Nationale, Paris, f. 26v–27r, ms. 46–50.
Photograph courtesy of the Bibliothèque Nationale, Paris.

Style

Most of the features of this image derive from well-known Pre-Hispanic graphic tropes: the glyphs, the blank ground, the treatment of water, and the "bird's-eye-view" footprints. A few stylistic elements of European origin are detectable, primarily in the blue-green shading of the Cholulan hillock at right, and in the arched doorways of the great temple. The painting's perspectival shifts anticipate viewers who recognize that key elements, such as the footprints, waterways, and temple plazas, are glimpsed from high above, while others, such as seated figures, toponymic labels for Cholula, and the buildings themselves, are depicted from the side or front. The image thus concatenates many schematic points of view. The painting also shows signs of reworking. Faint sketch lines beneath the Temple of Quetzalcoatl, for example, indicate an earlier image of the temple that opened in the opposite direction. Signs of correction appear, as does over-painting (especially in the six boxes along the painting's upper edge). Also evident, and seemingly related to the painted emendations, are images superimposed by a second hand.[18] The nature and character of these changes suggest that accuracy was not an incidental concern for the image-maker(s). Beyond this, the recasting of the scene makes it clear that the *Historia* painters did not always leave their images as first conceived.

Narrative Implications

This painting is similar to many in the *Historia* in its depiction of named figures and places that surface in the written text, and yet it does not exhaustively follow the textual narrative. There is no complete pictorial inventory of epithets for Cholula, nor does the image render all the calpolli leaders or Chichimeca warriors named alphabetically. This selectivity allows the painting to privilege both characters and places that the text does not. Perhaps most interesting is that this depiction of Cholula references an earlier, less glorious phase of the site's history (pl. 3). The composition and the iconography of the perimeter of the two paintings is similar; the grandeur of the later Cholula—the Cholula ruled by Quetzaltehueyac, Icxicoatl, and other Tolteca—however, is conveyed through elaborate and finely executed graphic detail. Enlisting the visual language of color, style, and detail, this painting persuades viewers that the Tolteca leadership of Cholula made the site far more splendid than before. In this the painting functions like the second image of Colhuacatepec-Chicomoztoc (pl. 5), which mimics and elaborates an earlier and less glorious image of the mountain cave to make a similar point about events that transpired earlier in time. There is, however, a particular temporal complexity in the Cholula scene. For the text of the *Historia* states explicitly that, at the time of the book's creation, the Cholula of the Toltecan era was a vestige of the past. This scene was thus understood, at least by the writer of the text, as a place alive in memory, yet, apart from the mediation of painting, invisible to sixteenth-century eyes.

PLATE 11

SCENE OF SACRIFICIAL VICTORY

f. 28r, ms. 46–50

This painting depicts the Tolteca and Chichimeca victory at Cholula. The *Historia* painters show none of the actual fighting, but rather concentrate on sacrificial events that took place in the wake of the conquest. This is a painting, then, about the triumph of the Tolteca and their Chichimeca allies and the rites that confirmed that achievement.

Iconography and Composition

Framing the scene is a thin, black outline and seven compartments, each containing a toponym and an unidentified leader pierced with an arrow. These boxes present the conquest of distinct ethnic groups or altepetl. Counterclockwise from the upper left, these are: Xochimilca, Ayapanca, Teciuhquemeque, Texallo, Tlilhua, Cuilocatl, and Auzolcatl. The central portion of the painting highlights another aspect of the Tolteca and Chichimeca victory: its celebration at Cholula. Toward the top, small busts representing Icxicoatl and Quetzaltehueyac frame diminutive glyphs for the site: a palace atop a hill glyph and the flowery canyon below. Directly beneath them, the tlatoani Quauhtzitzimitl appears stripped and strapped to a *quatzatzatli*, a wooden frame to which prisoners were bound for arrow sacrifices in Pre-Hispanic times. Two arrows puncture his body, drawing blood, as four Chichimeca warriors surround him, aiming to send more arrows his way. Below this sacrificial scene, two combatants take on another defeated leader, Tlazotli, who has been tied to a *quauhtemalacatl*, a circular stone with a hole in the center to which prisoners were tethered with rope and forced to defend themselves against attacks from fully armed warriors.[19] On either side of him stand battle-ready Chichimeca warriors: Teuhctlecozauhqui (who will soon lead the Cuauhtinchantlaca to found their own altepetl) wields a sharpened spear, while Aquiyahuatl (who will lead the Totomihuaque) wields a *macuahuitl* (an obsidian-studded club). That Tlazotli's own weapons are useless is made clear by his bloodied body.

This painting not only confirms the participation of specific individuals in events key to the *Historia* narrative, it also underscores alliances among these men. All of the warriors at the center of this scene, be they victors or losers, are glyphically labeled. Consequently, named individuals play all the main roles here. Moreover, the central vertical axis of the painting, composed of Cholula's glyphs and the two defeated warriors, divides the scene into halves. Although victorious warriors appear both to the left and right of this axis, subtle distinctions between the groups exist. For example, Moquihuix and Teuhctlecozauhqui, the soon-to-be founders of Cuauhtinchan, both appear on the left side of the painting, and are, throughout the narrative, bound together on numerous occasions. Similarly, Aquiyahuatl and Coatzin, who are linked at Chicomoztoc and go on to found Totomihuacan, both perform sacrificial deeds along the right side of the scene. The painter thus relies upon both iconographic and compositional effects in order to integrate the consanguinity of the Tolteca and Chichimeca with their bellicosity.

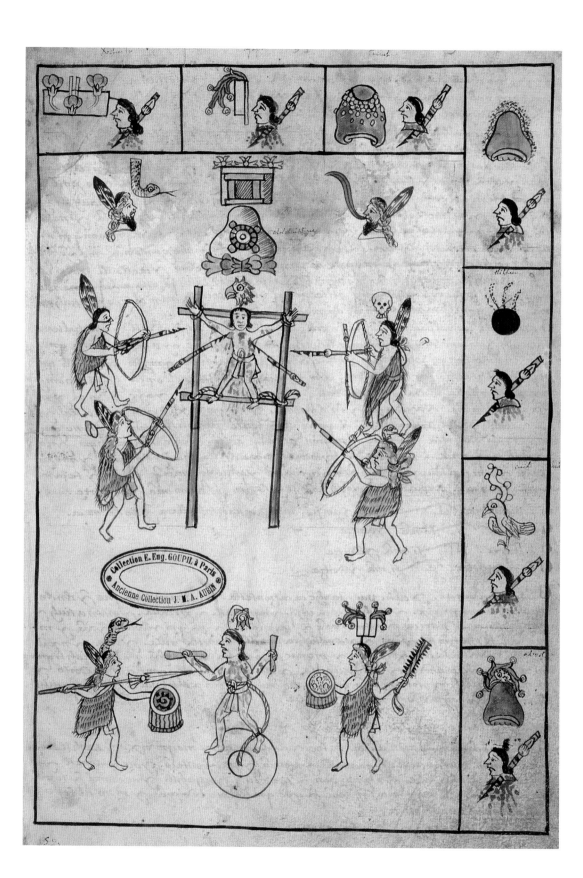

Style

While this painting exhibits knowledge of European imagery, it depends heavily upon pre-conquest concepts and conventions. The musculature of the warriors' legs, the poses of the standing figures, and the shadows cast onto the glyphs for Cholula are the primary elements that have no Pre-Hispanic precedent. The glyphs for names and places are consistent with known Pre-Hispanic examples and, except for Cholula (see discussion below), these mirror other glyphic representations in the *Historia*. Moreover, the disposition of figures against a blank ground corresponds with Pre-Hispanic representational practices, as does the application of color on the figures, objects, and glyphs depicted here. The use of boxes at the perimeter of the folio seems to be a compositional technique used throughout the *Historia* to depict the site of Cholula. Whether this is because a pre-conquest model survived and was used by painters is not known. What is certain: the style of the painting—which owes so much to Pre-Hispanic prototypes—enhances the antique affect and temporal displacement of the events portrayed.

Narrative Implications

This scene, which features the sacrifice of defeated enemies at Cholula, opens onto events that enable the ancestors of don Alonso de Castañeda, the patron and first owner of the *Historia*, to found Cuauhtinchan. Yet the pictorial arrangement is unusual in two regards. First, the painting not only depicts an arrow sacrifice, it centers this event on the folio and, in so doing, underscores its importance. Given that arrow sacrifice, as all forms of human sacrifice, was repressed under Spanish rule, its prominence here is striking. Only one other painting in the annals portrays arrow sacrifice, consequently this full-folio scene represents a significant break in the *Historia's* conventional repertoire.[20] Second, elsewhere in the *Historia*, Cholula appears fully elaborated as a site, either through accumulation of glyphs or through a double-folio pictorial image that combines glyphs, depictions of local leaders, and architectural landmarks. Here, in contrast, the site takes form as a miniature set of glyphs set off by images of Quetzaltehueyac and Icxicoatl and boxed rectangles along just two edges of the scene. While these features may appear subtle today, they represent notable interruptions in the visual rhetoric of the annals. What viewers come to understand is that nothing akin to these conquests ever transpired before or since. This painting thus implies that this victory and these sacrifices quite literally altered the course of history.

Pl. 11 Scene of sacrificial victory, *Historia Tolteca-Chichimeca*.
Pigment on European paper, ca. 27 cm (height) × 19 cm
(width). Bibliothèque Nationale, Paris, f. 28r, ms. 46–50.
Photograph courtesy of the Bibliothèque Nationale, Paris.

PLATE 12

FAREWELL SCENE: CROSSING THE RIVER

f. 29v, ms. 46–50

Bordered by a thin, black line, this painting depicts one of the migration stories recounted in the *Historia*. The key protagonists are the leaders of two groups, those that founded Totomihuacan and those that founded Cuauhtinchan. This painting concerns the route taken by Teuhctlecozauhqui and Aquiyahuatl, as they lead their people out of Cholula to the south and west to found their own altepetl.

Iconography and Composition

After their victory in Cholula, the annals describe how the Tolteca led their Chichimeca allies to the edge of their altepetl and bid them farewell, sending them into the world to settle and rule their own communities. Upon saying their goodbyes, the people led by Aquiyahuatl, the soon-to-be Totomihuaque, and the people led by Teuhctlecozauhqui, the soon-to-be Cuauhtinchantlaca, traveled through five sites (Cuitlaoztoc, Centepec, Teyahualolco, Xalticpac, and Teuhczacatzontetla) before splintering off to found their own altepetl.

This image, which depicts both the leave-taking and the migration, is sliced from top to bottom by a curving river, the Río Atoyac. On the left, the painted figures observe one orientation, on the right its mirror opposite. The river thus marks the passage, of both reader and Chichimeca travelers, from one coherent space into another. At the left, the Tolteca of Cholula wish their Chichimeca allies well. Quetzaltehueyac—who appears here in women's garb, perhaps in the guise of Cihuacoatl[21]—and Icxicoatl lead a group of musicians, fellow Tolteca who play drums, trumpets, and conch shells, to Xiuhtopolan, the site from whence the Chichimeca will depart. Across from the Tolteca, four Chichimeca leaders prepare to take their leave. In front are Teuhctlecozauhqui and Moquihuix, the figures most closely related to don Alonso de Castañeda; behind them stands Aquiyahuatl, the primary founder of Totomihuacan. To the right of Río Atoyac, the painting shifts orientation 180 degrees and presents four sites along the migration route. Just past the grassy knolls, Aquiyahuatl and Teuhctlecozauhqui converse. The two appear here newly dressed as rulers: they wear cloth mantles and perch atop stone seats. At the left of the painting, they wear animal skin robes; the shift in apparel thus affirms the symbolic importance of crossing the Río Atoyac, for it renders the men ready to rule. Black painted footsteps trace both the path Aquiyahuatl and Teuhctlecozauhqui shared on this migration and the routes they followed separately.

Pl. 12 Farewell scene: crossing the river, *Historia Tolteca-Chichimeca*. Pigment on European paper, ca. 26 cm (height) × 18 cm (width). Bibliothèque Nationale, Paris, f. 29v, ms. 46–50. *Photograph courtesy of the Bibliothèque Nationale, Paris.*

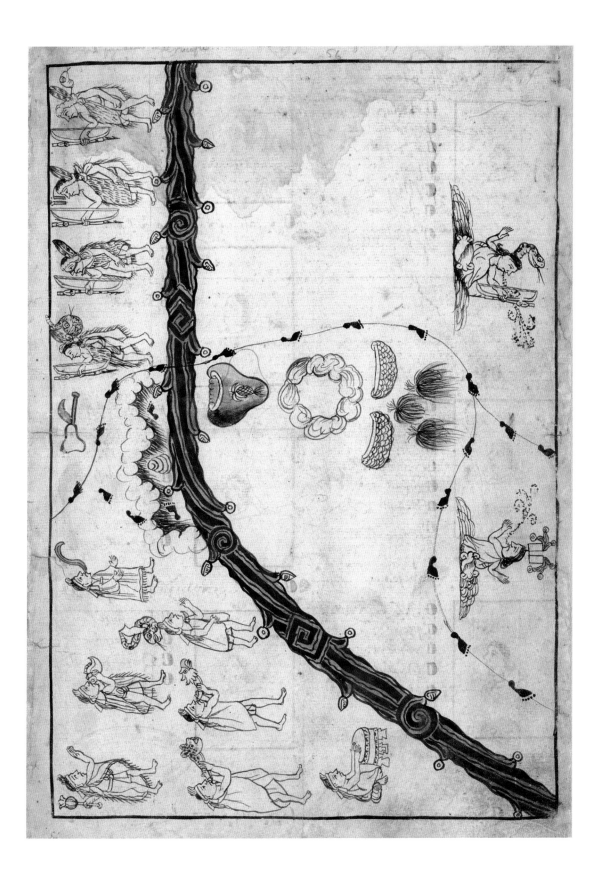

Style

Apart from the paintings of altepetl boundaries, no other image in the *Historia* relies so heavily upon glyphs and other Pre-Hispanic–style imagery. Closest in character to pre-conquest conventions are the river and footprints. The hill glyphs and other toponymic markers, as well as the representations of named individuals, exhibit a more mixed heritage. Iconographically, all of these features clearly derive from Pre-Hispanic rather than European models. In terms of style, however, the scene reveals a painter also familiar with imported, European imagery. This is evident in the gestures and musculature of the human figures, the shading of toponymic elements, and the depiction of the folds and draping of the clothing. The painter has attempted to adhere to the illusionistic tradition of figures occupying three-dimensional space, an enterprise most successful toward the bottom of the painting, in the treatment of the drummer's hands. As is the case with many sixteenth-century indigenous paintings, and certainly with all of those in the *Historia*, the footprints here were added last, after all of the other imagery was in place. Symbolically, their presence reveals that the painter moved through the scene, completing it by adding footsteps as signs of both his, and the painted figures', passage.

Narrative Implications

This painting demonstrates that the painter of the *Historia* continued to find pre-conquest–style glyphic conventions meaningful, and he expected his readers to do so as well. The image is iconographically rich—not only are the clothing and gestures of the figures laden with meaning, but the Tolteca instruments mingle pictorial and linguistic references: the text notes the playing of two wind instruments, *ocelotiquiquiztli* and *quauhquiquiztli*; the painting signs these with pictures of Tolteca playing ocelot-headed and eagle-headed trumpets. In fact, this painting parallels the narrative far more closely than many others in the annals, matching the text almost point for point. At each migration stop, the division between the Totomihuaque and Cuauhtinchantlaca, and the symbolic distinction between the land of the Tolteca and lands that belonged to "no-one" all receive attention. The only other paintings that are similarly meticulous are those that show the initial boundaries of Totomihuacan and Cuauhtinchan.

PLATE 13

FOUNDATION SCENE: TOTOMIHUACAN

f. 30v–31r, ms. 46–50

One of three paintings of altepetl foundation in the *Historia*, this double-folio scene draws upon an earlier image, the *Mapa Pintado* (fig. 17), to depict the territory of Totomihuacan and its boundaries. The annals' text explicitly indicates that Totomihuacan was neither settled all at once, nor by a single group of people. This scene, however, shows Aquiyahuatl, the Totomihuaque leader featured throughout the pictorial component of the *Historia*, as the sole founder of the altepetl.

Iconography and Composition

This painting, in keeping with all of the foundation scenes in the *Historia*, spans facing folios of the manuscript. At the center is the toponymic sign for Chiquiuhtepec (Place of Basket Hill), a mountain near the original settlement, an image of Aquiyahuatl, and a sacred bundle. The perimeter of the scene displays thirty-two boundary markers, all opening inward as if facing Chiquiuhtepec. Totomihuacan thus takes form in this scene as a site anchored in place by the communities, rivers, and mountains that define its limits. Although many of the boundaries cannot be identified on modern maps, their order was of considerable significance in the mid-sixteenth century.[22] On the back of this painting, the writer of the *Historia* listed the boundaries in alphabetic script, diligently following their sequence on the painted manuscript page (see fig. 18). The reading order prescribed by the list opens with Tepoxocho, just below the center of the left edge of the painting, and proceeds counterclockwise along the edge of the painting, ending with Centepetl, the toponym lying at the center of the painting's left edge. According to the alphabetic register, then, one both begins and ends the circuit of boundaries at the left edge of the scene. Image and text, however, stress different aspects of Totomihuacan's borders: the painting displays the whole circuit at once, whereas the alphabetic list, which marches down the manscript folio, implies a string of sites. Furthermore, the list groups the boundary names in units of five with two additions linked to those at the beginning. This may derive from a recitational pattern that is not visually inscribed in the painting. Although these differences do not affirm whether text or image is somehow "more authoritative," they do adumbrate how distinct kinds of knowledge were distributed across multiple channels of the *Historia*. To understand more than one mode of presentation would have required a reader or interpreter with multiple kinds of fluency.

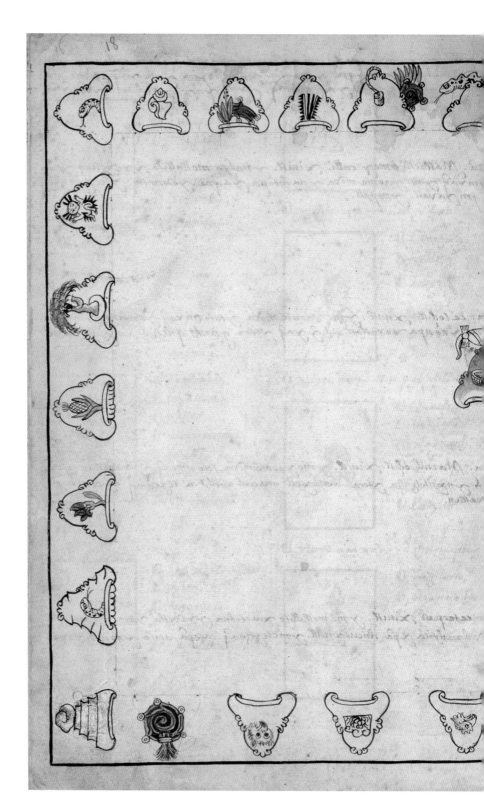

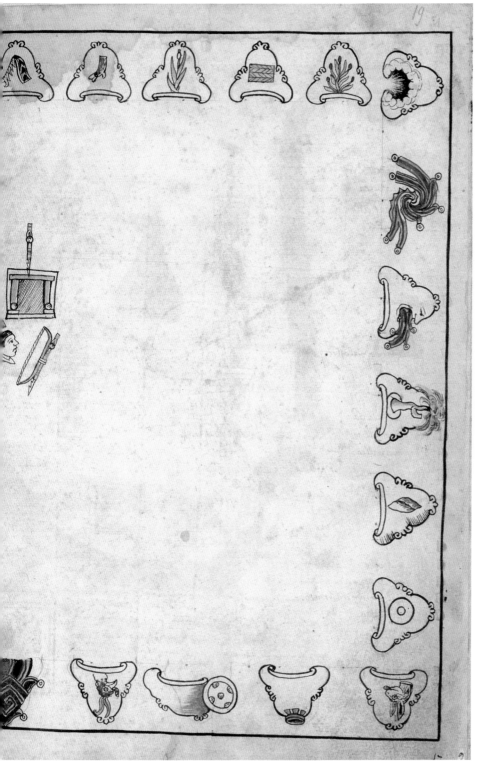

Pl. 13 Foundation scene: Totomihuacan, *Historia Tolteca-Chichimeca*.
Pigment on European paper, ca. 26.5 cm (height) × 39 cm (width).
Bibliothèque Nationale, Paris, f. 30v–31r, ms. 46–50.
Photograph courtesy of the Bibliothèque Nationale, Paris.

Style

As seen in other *Historia* boundary paintings, this image rests heavily upon Pre-Hispanic–style graphic conventions. In fact, apart from the elongated proportions of each toponym and the shading of a few hill glyphs, the painting reveals little interest in European techniques for rendering landscape or depicting three-dimensional objects on a flat surface. Interestingly, traces of the painter's working method can still be detected in the image. To maintain toponymic alignment, a slender ground line was sketched around all four sides of the paper creating a rectangular perimeter across both manuscript folios; small dots along this line defined the location of each hill glyph. These marks remain evident in the finished work, as do the initial sketch lines of several hill glyphs, many of which had their forms or proportions altered in the final painting. Given both the size of the paper and the fact that the toponyms all open inward (i.e., face four different directions), it seems likely that, as he worked, the painter would have turned the paper repeatedly to create this scene. The toponymic glyphs that most clearly reveal changes in proportion appear in the upper left corner of the painting (Tecciztitlan, Epazouac, Itzocan, and Tepipilolco), while those with sketch lines revealing a different initial form, such as Techimalli and the water of Atlpatlauacan, stretch across the bottom of the painted scene.

Narrative Implications

Comparison with an earlier rendition of Totomihuacan's boundaries, which can be traced on the *Mapa Pintado* (fig. 17), reveals that the order of boundaries and their glyphic signs remain consistent in both paintings. What distinguishes the two works are the style and disposition of images on the painted page. The later *Historia* painting, for example, is far more spare and open—in part because it registers less information in order to accommodate the narrative and structural requirements of the annals' codex format. Nevertheless, it is patently obvious, and I believe meaningful, that the "updated" image of Totomihuacan's boundaries cleave to an ancestral visual style. Since the *Historia*'s painters were both familiar with, and willing to fashion, more "Europeanized" landscapes (e.g., Cuauhtinchan's battle with Tlatelolco, pls. 17/18), the style here appears intentionally old-fashioned. This choice suggests that, even as he crafted new kinds of images for this European-style book, the painter deliberately sought to invest this scene of Totomihuacan's boundaries with authority, if not also authenticity, via an "old way" of rendering. This implies that sixteenth-century Nahua painters could, and did, enlist archaism to make moral, and perhaps political, claims about altepetl territory and its proper limits.

PLATE 14

MIGRATION SCENE

f. 32r, ms. 46–50

This painting, which fills three-quarters of a folio, is accompanied by written text in both black and red inks. The picture picks up the migration narrative begun several pages earlier, when Aquiyahuatl and Teuhctlecozauhqui were last seen exiting Cholula in search of their own altepetl. Whereas the first part of this tale (pl. 12) relies strictly upon these two leaders to represent all the Chichimeca in search of a homeland, the painting here elaborates upon the internal complexity of both the Totomihuaque and the Cuauhtinchantlaca.

Iconography and Composition

The branching headwater of the Río Atoyac organizes the scene: above and to the left of its confluence stands Totomihuacan. Here, the just-settled community is anchored by the toponym for Chiquiuhtepec, Place of Basket Hill, situated near the center of the folio. Surrounding it are six Totomihauque men, each associated with a small house. The houses represent distinct groups of settlers (identified by small glyphs atop the roof of these buildings), and the men, although not all named in the painting, are the primary leaders of each group who came to Totomihuacan.[23] Through this mode of depiction the painting is explicit that, from the outset, Totomihuacan had multiple founders and factions. So, too, the painting diagrams a hierarchy among groups. The two houses at the bottom of the scene, and the one to the right of the river without an image of a leader, represent the last arrivals in Totomihuacan and, presumably, the least prestigious. To the right of the river, two of Cuauhtinchan's founders, Teuhctlecozauhqui and Moquihuix, the ancestral heroes most closely linked with don Alonso de Castañeda, continue onward past Totomihuacan. The text and image concur that these leaders stopped first in a cave before heading into the lands that would become Cuauhtinchan. The small hill glyph with flowers at the right edge of the scene, a toponymic sign for Tepexocho, forms one of the boundaries that Cuauhtinchan will soon share with Totomihuacan. For informed readers, then, the presence of this toponym is both descriptive and prescriptive: it marks the edge of the just-settled Totomihuacan and the boundary of the soon-to-be-founded Cuauhtinchan.

Style

As with all boundary and migration paintings in the *Historia*, isolated elements—hill glyphs, a branching river, named individuals, and a trail of footprints—scatter against a blank ground and comprise the mise-en-scène. The iconographic roots of these images are pre-conquest. Yet both of the hill glyphs in this scene betray the painter's exposure to European conventions for shading; specifically, both exhibit an obscured side, suggesting a shadow enveloping one flank of each hillock. No source of light,

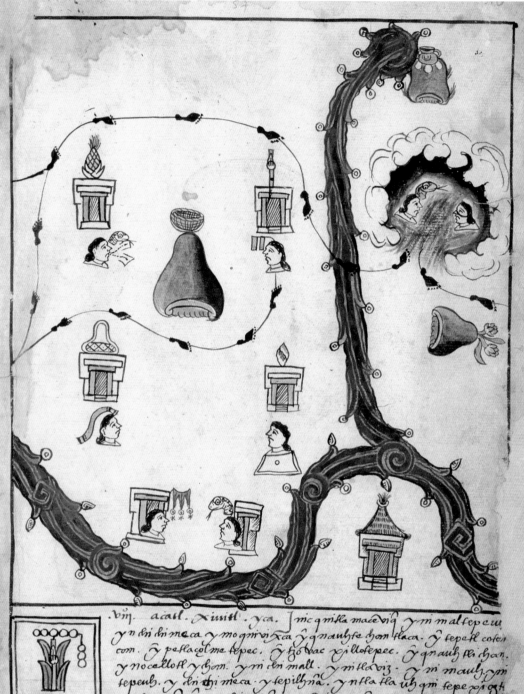

vij. acatl. xiuitl. yca. Jn qñ tla maceu̅q̄ y mi maltepeuh
yn dn chi me̅ca y mo g̅ñ vij̅ca. ỹ q̅nauhte chon tlaca. ỹ tepetl coten
com. ỹ petlaçol ma tepec. ỹ tzo vac xjllotepec. ỹ q̅nauh tli chan.
y nocalloll ỹ chom. ỹ mi dhi mall. y mi tla viz. ỹ mi mauh. ỹ mi
tepeuh. y dn chi me̅ca. y tepilhña. yn tla tla uh q̅mi tepe vij q̅t.
yn te yoca. ỹ ma dn yoca. y n̅ā vi̅ xco. ỹ tepe vij xco. auh m c̅a
mo ma dn yo͠tia y mi maltepeuh ỹ q̅mi maçeuhq̅ne.

⟨ Htoh yj a te q̅mi. y mi peuhca. ỹ tepan tli. ỹ q̅mi maceuh̅ꝗ̅
xon y mic tlal pollo ꝗ̅. ỹ dn dn me̅ca ...... maltepetl.

however, is indicated, nor does the painter carry this technique into his rendering of people or water. This stylistic disjunction appears elsewhere in the *Historia*. In scenes that most heavily emphasize glyphic components, toponymic hills reveal the greatest European stylistic influence. This is significant for our purchase on the conceptual and visual shifts that drove early colonial stylistic patterns. In Pre-Hispanic times, hill glyphs served a dual purpose: conceptually and functionally they were linguistic cues (i.e., they named places), and they were markers of sites in the world. In the *Historia* and many other sixteenth-century manuscripts, their latter role became more clearly defined. Indeed, these elements were the first, and often primary, forms to incorporate elements of European style, often becoming miniature landscape vignettes.

Narrative Implications

This painting and the writing beneath it differ in their thematic and temporal concerns. The painting treats events described several pages earlier in the alphabetic commentary, and so concerns the recent past. The text, in contrast, orients readers toward the immediate future by addressing the foundation of Cuauhtinchan, an event pictured on the next folio. The appearance on a single sheet of paper of text and image that evoke distinct temporal moments complicates the act of reading the annals. At one level, this arrangement should be understood as an attempt to privilege neither image-making nor alphabetic writing, but rather to allow both to do their proper work. That temporal unity would be confounded by this compromise must have been acceptable to the *Historia* writer and painters. This scene thus makes clear the commitment to both pictorial and alphabetic recordkeeping in this manuscript. Finally, it should be noted that this depiction of Totomihuacan's founding is the second in the *Historia*. Foundation scenes of just two altepetl, Totomihuacan and Cuauhtinchan, receive pictorial explication in the annals, and each is depicted through a pair of images. One stresses altepetl unity and external boundaries, the other explicates internal divisions. This doubling of images is one way the *Historia* links Cuauhtinchan and Totomihuacan as sister altepetl. Nevertheless, the foundation paintings of Cuauhtinchan are, in both instances, larger and more elaborate. This painting of Totomihuacan, then, contributes to the larger narrative in which the altepetl is represented as similar to, yet not nearly as grand as, Cuauhtinchan.

Pl. 14 Migration scene, *Historia Tolteca-Chichimeca*.
Pigment on European paper, ca. 28 cm (height) × 20 cm
(width). Bibliothèque Nationale, Paris, f. 32r, ms. 46–50.
Photograph courtesy of the Bibliothèque Nationale, Paris.

PLATE 15

CUAUHTINCHAN FOUNDATION SCENE: FIRST VIEW

f. 32v–33r, ms. 46–50

This double-folio painting is the first in the *Historia* to depict the foundation of Cuauhtinchan. Integral to the image are the altepetl's boundaries, first leaders, and early history—particularly its victorious battles over nearby enemies. This painting is one of three cartographic histories in the *Historia*, a genre of indigenous representation from New Spain wherein territorial and historical images were intertwined (see discussion, Chapter 3).

Iconography and Composition

Through both composition and scale the painter articulates a clear distinction between center and periphery. At the core of the painting stand the toponyms for Cuauhtinchan, surrounded by thirty-three place glyphs forming the altepetl's boundaries. The toponyms representing Cuauhtinchan are far larger than the boundary signs, and they are more detailed. In fact, the painter has enlisted multiple visual strategies, from placement and size to elaboration, to differentiate the signs for Cuauhtinchan from those of her neighbors. For example, the representation of Cuauhtinchan includes glyphic cues for multiple names: at the left, the eagle signs Cuauhtinchan; on the right, the maguey plant signs Metepec and the woody form sprouting corn signs the name Tzouac Xilotepec. In contrast, the boundary sites are identified by only one moniker and glyphic sign. Cuauhtinchan's glyphs are also unique in the extent to which they evoke the landscape of the altepetl, with its hills and canyon.

A single line of footprints enters the scene at the left, as if continuing a trek from the previous painted folio. Once this trail of footsteps passes the first hill glyph— a glyph that marks the boundary between Totomihuacan and Cuauhtinchan— the footprints diverge along several trails. Some continue toward the center of the scene and terminate with the seated men at, and near, the toponyms for Cuauhtinchan. These figures represent the initial five leaders who founded the altepetl.[24] Another set of footprints circumambulates the painted border, probably evincing the ritual inscription of boundaries at the time of the altepetl's founding.

Occupying the pictorial interstices between Cuauhtinchan's main toponyms and the altepetl's boundaries are signs that refer to local historical events of consequence to Cuauhtinchan's founding fathers. Next to several of these interstitial toponyms there appear human heads, each identified by name, pierced by arrows, and bleeding. These denote the key communities and leaders defeated by the Cuauhtinchantlaca in the first years after they settled the region. Two scenes of arrow sacrifice, which refer to similar events, are also portrayed. And in the upper right, just above the central toponym for Cuauhtinchan-Tzouac Xilotepec, the painter has fashioned an image of Moquihuix drilling fire.[25] Most unexpected, however, is the representation of Teuhctlecozauhqui, his palace, and his consort, Tepexoch ilama. All appear together, on the right side of the painting just below the drilling Moquihuix. Tepexoch ilama is the only named female figure to surface in any of the major paintings of the *Historia*, and she appears twice: here, and in the scene of Cuauhtinchan's defeat by the Tlaxcalans (pls. 17/18). Her presence is thus not incidental. Moreover, the palace she shares with Teuhctlecozauhqui has been pierced by arrows. This cluster of images thus signs two moments: the founding of Cuauhtinchan under Teuhctlecozauhqui and Tepexoch ilama, and the defeat of their lineage 224 years later (see discussion, Chapter 2).

Style

In keeping with *Historia* conventions, the painter isolates elements—toponymic glyphs, human figures, footprints—against an unarticulated ground. Consequently, the background landscape of the scene is, as in Pre-Hispanic painting, the unadorned manuscript page. Familiarity with European modes of image-making appears spottily: the small building with turrets near the bottom of the painting, just left of center, and the overlapping arms and legs of Moquihuix as he sits to drill fire offer two examples. More obvious, however, are the toponyms for Cuauhtinchan at the center of the scene. Here the cut-away hill glyph revealing an eagle inside (and thus translating the name of Cuauhtinchan, Home of the Eagle), along with the hill form across from it, are shaded and modeled with color in a manner derived from European imagery. Because only one boundary sign has been treated in a similar manner, an image depicting the verdant mountain of Matlacueye, in the upper left corner, the central toponyms are further distinguished from other sites in the scene through painterly style.

Narrative Implications

One of a pair of paintings derived from the *Mapa Pintado* (fig. 17) and showing Cuauhtinchan's foundation, this scene highlights the altepetl's early history and internal divisions. The image clearly depicts the establishment of Cuauhtinchan as an event involving several leaders, each settling in a distinct region. It also features military engagements and sacrificial acts that were necessary to preserve the autonomy of the altepetl. The temporal complexity of the scene—wherein events spanning two centuries transpire in the same pictorial field, and buildings of European prototype inhabit a twelfth-century locale—presumes two things. First, that the image-readers anticipated and interpolated by the painter would be well versed in the narrative history of Cuauhtinchan's founders and their demise; and second, that stylistic diversity did not undermine the authority of a pictorial scene, even one in which the history registered was of utmost importance.

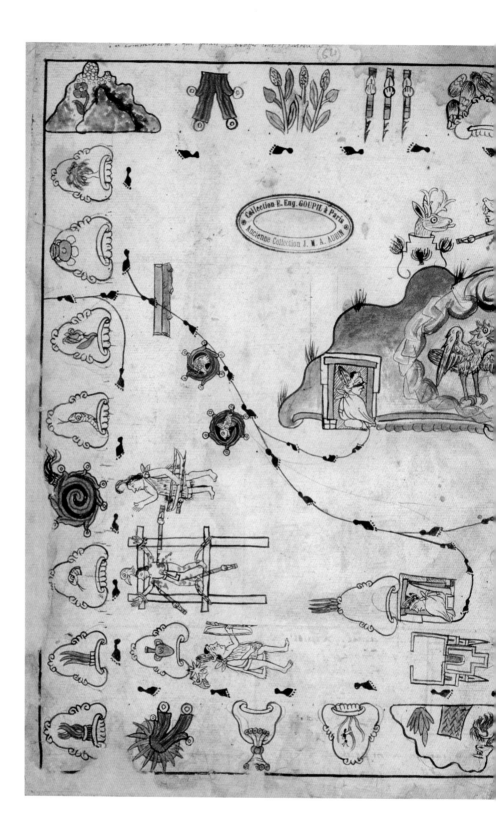

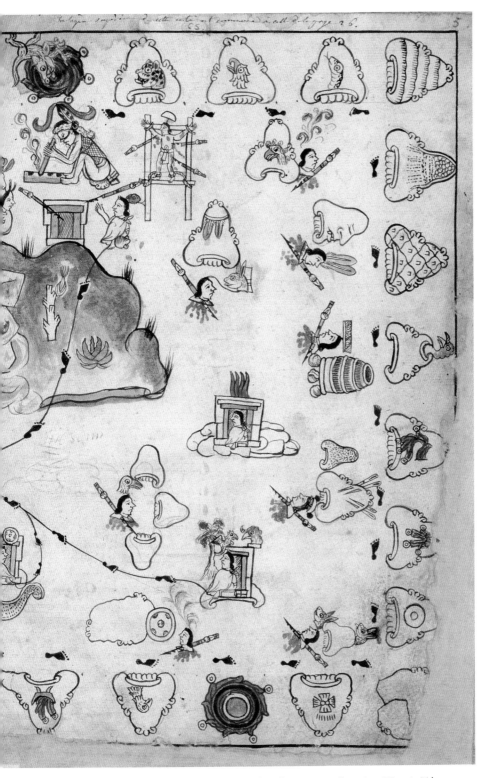

Pl. 15 Cuauhtinchan foundation scene: first view, *Historia Tolteca-Chichimeca*. Pigment on European paper, ca. 27.5 cm (height) × 40.5 cm (width). Bibliothèque Nationale, Paris, f. 32v–33r, ms. 46–50. *Photograph courtesy of the Bibliothèque Nationale, Paris.*

PLATE 16

CUAUHTINCHAN FOUNDATION SCENE: SECOND VIEW

f. 35v–36r, ms. 46–50

The second painting in the *Historia* to depict the founding of Cuauhtinchan, this double-folio spread also derives from the *Mapa Pintado* (fig. 17). In contrast to the earlier image, this painting has a narrower purview, yet its representational net is more inclusive, since the pictorial space was created by setting alphabetic Nahuatl amid toponymic signs, human forms, and name glyphs.

Iconography and Composition

As with other foundation scenes in the *Historia*, this painting locates the main altepetl (in this case, Cuauhtinchan) at the center of the compositional scene. Cuauhtinchan coalesces as two irregular-shaped hills suspended along the scene's central horizontal axis and encircled by diminutive glyphs that represent boundaries. Only two leaders bear primary responsibility for founding the altepetl in this scene. Moquihuix appears at the left, below one of Cuauhtinchan's toponyms; Teuhctlecozauhqui appears at the right, below the other. Between them hovers the date of their deed, the glyphic sign for the year 8 Reed. One trail of black footprints, which signs their migration into this region, enters the painted scene from the left and leads directly to the central glyphs for Cuauhtinchan.

Along the perimeter of the painting stand forty-nine toponyms. These represent the boundaries of both Cuauhtinchan and Totomihuacan. The painting implies that this territory was secured through a combination of negotiations and ritual circum-ambulations of these border sites. Indicating the latter are footprints that split into two paths at the left edge of the painting and rejoin at the right edge of the scene. At the fork where the footprints diverge, four men, represented by small busts in profile, engage in conversation. At the right, where the footprints unite, a similar convocation occurs. Present at each meeting are Quetzaltehueyac and Icxicoatl. Joining them are, at left, Teocon and Tonatiuh and, at right, Nopal and Aquiyahuatl—all Chichimeca leaders who assisted the Tolteca in their military struggle to gain control over Cholula and thus earned the right to lead sovereign altepetl.

Unique among the major *Historia* paintings is the Nahuatl inscription that surfaces amid, not above or below, the pictorial signs. This text unfurls from the glyph with two rocks, the toponym for Tetl ynepaniuhcan (Place Where Two Rocks Join), and continues down the length of the page, noting that these were the boundaries agreed upon in the year 8 Reed. The text reads:

> There at Tetl ynepaniuhcan, the Chichimeca, the Totomihuaque and the Cuauhtinchantlaca, the complement of the Tolteca Chichimeca Icxicoatl and Quetzaltehueyac, all met in order to raise the boundaries. In the year 8 Reed they agreed to even it out.[26]

Style

The style of this painting draws upon Pre-Hispanic models in its isolation of sign-elements against a blank ground. Also characteristic is the way that European-inspired modeling and shading encroach upon the central toponyms and a few hill glyphs, turning them into miniature landscape scenes. The most unusual feature of this work, its comingling of pictorial and alphabetic expressive forms, suggests something of the annals-makers' struggle to recast representations of historical events into new, yet meaningful forms. For this image is marked by extraordinary graphic tension. The writing interrupts the coherence of the painted space, and, at the same time, pictorial forms envelop and contradict the alphabetic inscription. Moreover, the pictorial imagery suggests that the ancestral leaders met and agreed upon the boundaries at Atlahuimolco (Place of Curling Water), whereas the written words claim the convocation occurred at Tetl ynepaniuhcan (Place Where Two Rocks Join).[27] Certainly, the *Historia* painter and writer intended their readers to understand the denotative sense of both image and text, yet what strikes viewers today is the sense that neither mode of recordkeeping was fully sufficient for representing ancient history in a European-style codex.

Narrative Implications

This painting of Cuauhtinchan's foundation highlights the date of the main event and ancestral negotiations over local boundaries. Although the scene presents two men, Moquihuix and Teuhctlecozauhqui, the two leaders with the closest genealogical ties to don Alonso de Castañeda, this version of the altepetl's settling focuses most intently on the relationships among different altepetl and their leaders, not internal divisions within Cuauhtinchan. The perspective onto history presented here thus resonates with, but differs from, the earlier depiction of the altepetl's settlement (pl. 15). Because the painting stages the founding of Cuauhtinchan under the auspices of the Tolteca, and because it depicts the initial boundaries as well as the processes of their negotiation and ritual inscription, this image also testifies to the "rightness" of Cuauhtinchan's first settlement.

In keeping with the other foundation scenes in the annals, the boundaries painted at the painting's perimeter are all recorded in alphabetic script on the reverse of this scene. While this list presents the boundary names in the same order as does the painting, it follows a different pattern than do the painted footprints.[28] At one level, then, the alphabetic text mirrors the pictorial image. Both create a ring of border signs. Yet ultimately the pictorial image rehearses a more telling tale, for it visually delineates both the ring of boundaries and the course traced by the ancestors as they first brought Cuauhtinchan into being.

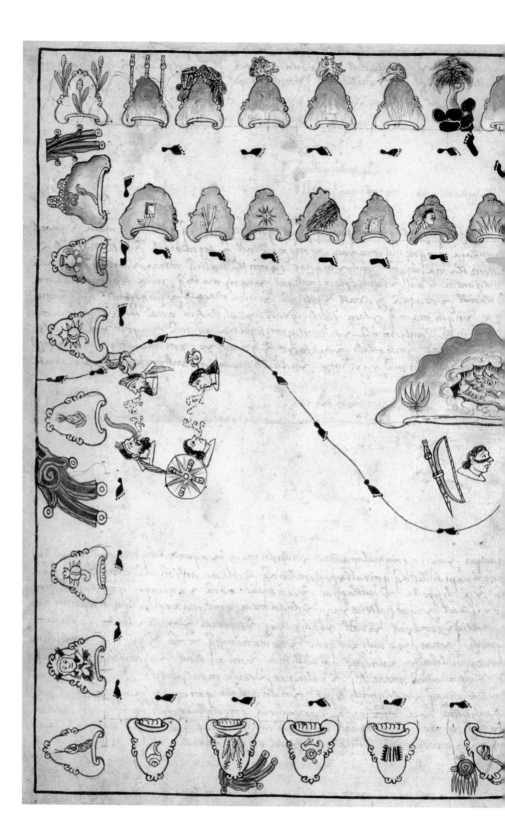

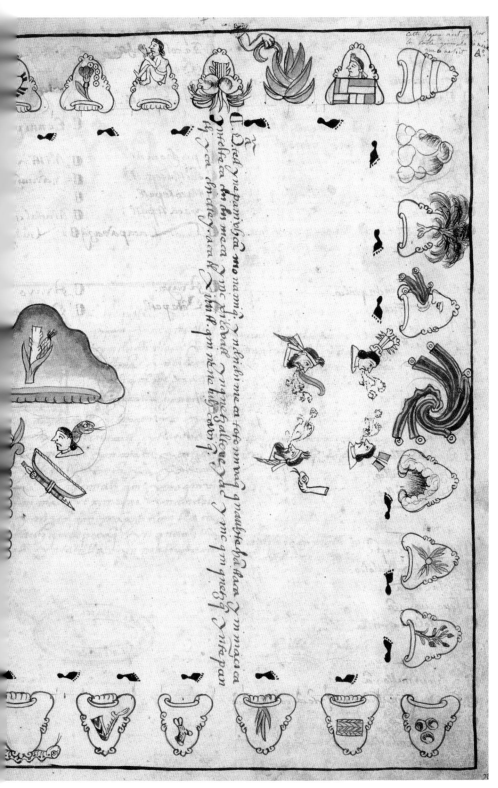

Pl. 16 Cuauhtinchan foundation scene: second view, *Historia Tolteca-Chichimeca*. Pigment on European paper, ca. 27 cm (height) × 39.5 cm (width). Bibliothèque Nationale, Paris, f. 35v–36r, ms. 46–50. *Photograph courtesy of the Bibliothèque Nationale, Paris.*

CUAUHTINCHAN BATTLE SCENE/ CUAUHTINCHAN'S DEFEAT

f. 42v, ms. 46–50 and f. 43r, ms. 54–58

This painting, which spans two facing folios of the *Historia*, depicts a battle between the forces of Cuauhtinchan and Tlatelolco.[29] According to the annals, it was in the year 10 Rabbit that the people of Cuauhtinchan endured conquest by their Mexica neighbors and were subjected to the rule of the Triple Alliance.

Iconography and Composition

Providing both landscape and setting for this scene is a large, terraced hill, irregular in form and covered with maguey plants. Two toponyms identify the battle site. At the left edge of the painting, an oversized eagle perches in a rocky cave, and at the center of this hill is a woody, cactuslike plant of considerable size. Together these elements secure the locale of this battle—it is in Cuauhtinchan (Home of the Eagle), Xilotepec (Hill of the Woody Corn Plant). The soon-to-be-overthrown ruler of the altepetl, Teuhctlecozauhqui, and his consort, Tepexoch ilama, appear atop the main hill, flanking a building that evokes both their palace and status as rulers. Neither he nor she joins the battle. Rather, Teuhctlecozauhqui sits on a small bench and Tepexoch ilama kneels before him. This compositional and iconographic detail is important, for at the right of the painting there appears a second hillock. It, too, is topped by a house flanked by a kneeling Tepexoch ilama and her consort, a male ruler seated on a bench. In this case, however, the man is no longer Teuhctlecozauhqui, but the victor in the battle, Quauhtlatoa. Without explicitly showing Teuhctlecozauhqui's defeat, the painting nevertheless underscores the outcome of this battle: the displacement of a local ruler by one from afar.

The battle between Cuauhtinchan's and Tlatelolco's warriors supplies the main visual drama here. And although the scene appears almost serene to modern eyes, within the context of the annals, it is unique for its depiction of sustained military engagement. Cuauhtinchan's forces rally near the top of the painting, defending their ruler from behind a rocky embankment atop the hill. Although they wear the same battle clothing as their adversaries, and deploy the same weapons— bows, arrows, shields, macuahuitl—only Cuauhtinchan's warriors don feathered headbands. The Tlatelolcan invaders range themselves along the lower band of the painting, attacking from below, as it were, with arrows and shields raised. No hand-to-hand combat is depicted, nor is actual killing or physical violence represented.

Rather, the painting creates a pronounced sense of suspended action: weapons are poised, but no blows are yet struck. Contributing to this sense are three warriors who appear to descend from the sky, akin to armed putti. Who these figures are, and whose side they will take, remains unclear. Perhaps they are militant angels arriving to aid Cuauhtinchan, or perhaps they are Tlatelolcan reinforcements, who descend upon the hill from all directions. In either case, their appearance reinforces the graphic impression that countless warriors engaged in this battle.

While the primary actors in this war are Cuauhtinchantlaca and Tlatelolcans, the scene clearly depicts the altepetl of Cuauhtinchan as a complex entity. Four small houses, each with a named ruler seated in front upon a small bench, dot the hilly landscape. Each of these represents a sector of the larger altepetl and its ruler. Thus, at the bottom of folio 42v, we see Xiuhtzon, and across from him, on folio 43r, appear Xochitzin, Tonatiuh, and Cuixin. In showing each ruler and his palace, the painting expresses two key points: first, all of Cuauhtinchan engaged in this battle and thus all of Cuauhtinchan was affected; second, because this situation is signified only through images of distinct altepetl rulers and locales, the totality "Cuauhtinchan" coalesces as the sum of its separate, named parts.

Style

This painting is the only one in the *Historia* to fashion an illusionistic landscape as a setting for the main action. All of the other annals paintings create a sense of place with Pre-Hispanic–style toponyms set against a blank ground. Beyond the landscape setting, the shading of the maguey plants and hilly terraces, as well as the poses of the warriors—both those whose feet rest firmly on the ground and those that descend from the sky—have their origins in European imagery. Yet many elements derive from Pre-Hispanic painting conventions, notably the footsteps, weapons, houses, representations of indigenous rulers, and use of toponyms and name glyphs. While most paintings in the *Historia* drew upon multiple sources, this scene is unique in its perspective. The painter has attempted to create the illusion of recession into three-dimensional space through the placement of human bodies, some of which face viewers of the scene, while others twist away revealing their backs. Yet, name glyphs, toponyms, and houses all appear flush against the paper ground and do not hint at depth effects. Consequently the painting both encourages a sense of three-dimensional space and routinely denies it. Further, the picture proffers many points of view onto this scene: to understand the angels and warriors one must observe the scene from outside and below, but to resolve the silhouetted footsteps one must observe the battle from above. Nowhere else in the annals are readers shown so many varied points of view.

Pl. 17 Cuauhtinchan battle scene, *Historia Tolteca-Chichimeca*. Pigment on European paper, ca. 27 cm (height) × 19.5 cm (width). Bibliothèque Nationale, Paris, f. 42v, ms. 46–50. *Photograph courtesy of the Bibliothèque Nationale, Paris.*

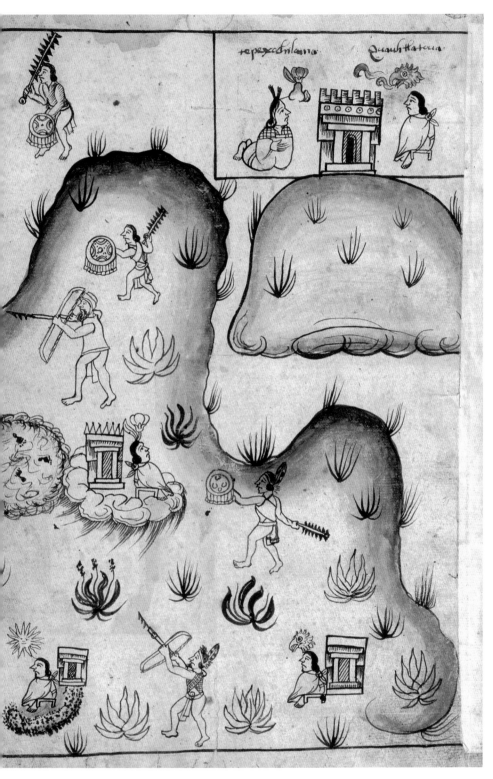

Pl. 18 Cuauhtinchan's defeat, *Historia Tolteca-Chichimeca*.
Pigment on European paper, ca. 27 cm (height) × 19.5 cm (width).
Bibliothèque Nationale, Paris, f. 43r, ms. 54–58. *Photograph
courtesy of the Bibliothèque Nationale, Paris.*

Narrative Implications

The *Historia* text describes the Tlatelolcan victory as the single most devastating loss suffered by the people of Cuauhtinchan: it led to the reorganization of political leadership within the altepetl, and to new relations of diminished power with nearby communities. Since the annals present a point of view sympathetic to don Alonso de Castañeda and his lineage, and his lineage was one of those displaced, the Tlatelolcan battle emerges in the *Historia* as a tragic event, far more tragic than the Spanish conquest. We sense this on three pictorial levels. First, the painter has corrected this scene in several places along its left edge; his commitment to accuracy and his attentiveness to detail suggest how important the image actually was. Second, this battle scene is the last, dual-folio painting in the *Historia*. Although space was left for subsequent full-folio images, these were never added for reasons no longer known. The battle scene thus becomes significant as the last event worthy of full pictorial implementation. Finally, this is the only painting in the annals to fashion an illusionistic landscape as a setting for the main action. Given the narrative and political implications of Cuauhtinchan's defeat by the Tlatelolcans, the visual qualities differentiating this scene from others are not incidental. Rather, these differences leave no doubt that the fall of Teuhctlecozauhqui's dynasty represented a major disruption in the proper order of things. Ultimately, then, this image reveals how the *Historia* painters were both able and willing to manipulate visual style in order to create ethical and moral commentaries on events in the past.

Notes

1. The Nahuatl reads "yzcatqui yn intlatollo yn tolteca chichimeca ynic ualleuaque yn colhuacatepec ynic acico yn tollan. yn imacica yn nonouallca. oncan yn mocauhque y moxeloque yn tollan yn imacica yn tolteca ynic ya yaui yn nonoualca. yn atlauimollco yn tepatzacapan yn quetzaltepec. quimocauhteuaque yn tolteca chichimeca."

2. The only exception is that of Quetzaltehueyac, whose mouth plume overlaps his weapon.

3. The Nahuatl reads "Yzcate in ecoque yn Tlachiuhaltepetl in icxicouatl in Quetzalteueyac."

4. One exception may be the small Pre-Hispanic–style house that floats just under Quetzaltehueyac's pointing finger; within this structure appears the head of the Aquiach Amapane, one of the primary Olmeca Xicalanca rulers at the time of the culture heroes' arrival in Cholula. Geoffrey McCafferty has suggested that this element signals a Tolteca/Chichimeca meeting at the palace of the Aquiach Amapane—a platform built on the northeast side of Cholula's Great Pyramid (2000: 352–353). The *Historia*, however, offers little to illuminate why the Aquiach appears in the painting. Kirchhoff et al. propose that his image may reference the very rulership to be overthrown by the Tolteca-Chichimeca heroes; alternatively, the image may represent the leadership role to be assumed by Quetzaltehueyac once the culture heroes take over Cholula (1976: 146, n. 1b). In terms of the larger narrative, the image foreshadows upcoming events, for no mention of the Aquiach Amapane appears in the written portion of the annals until several pages later.

5. The names, in the order given by the alphabetic text of the *Historia* are: Tlachiuhaltepec (Place of the Built Pyramid), Atlyayauhcan (Place of Dark Water), Quetzaltototl yycacan (Place Where the Quetzal Bird Stands), Iztaczollin ynemoxohuayan (Place Where the White Quail [ynemoxohuayan] Is), Apechtli yyonocan (Place Where the [apechtli] Is), Xochatlauhtli ypilcayan (Place Where the Flowery Stream Comes Down), Iztaquauhtli ytlaquayan (Place Where the White Eagle Eats), and Temamatlac (At the Stone Steps). In a separate column on the same folio, the alphabetic text reiterates and spatially differentiates several of these names, adding Ecoztlan (At Ecoztlan), Couatl ypilhuacan (Place Where the Snake Children Are), and Calmecac (Calmecac). On the painting, however, the doubling of names is not mirrored in any obvious way by the pictorial cues; moreover, the black glosses for each glyph were added well after the sixteenth century.

6. According to the *Historia*, the Aquiach Amapane was one of two primary Olmeca Xicalanca leaders to rule Cholula, the other being the Tlalchiach Tizacozoque. Only Amapane appears twice: once next to the large hill glyph at the center of the painting, and once in a rectangular box at the lower left of the scene. A solid black line connects the two images. Apart from the hierarchy implied by this reiteration, relationships between Amapane and the other rulers shown here remain unclear. Kirchhoff, Odena Güemes, and Reyes García argue that the painting represents the ten most important Olmeca Xicalanca rulers and sites near, but not in, Cholula. Further, because several of the toponyms can be located on modern maps, but in a spatial arrangement different from that of the *Historia* painting, they suggest that this scene may portray rulers and sites in their order of importance (1976: 150, n. 3).

7. The previous folio of the *Historia* identifies the Olmeca Xicalanca groups shown here pictorially. The text also lists a greater number of names—of both individuals and places—than are rendered. For instance, the painting depicts Cuetlachtonac at Tenanticpac, whereas the written text links this leader with six places. Also associated with Cuetlachtonac are four women, none of whom appear in the painting. In the *Historia* this is not uncommon: women are infrequently mentioned, and even more rarely represented in painted imagery (see discussion, Chapter 2). Following the text, and reading clockwise from the lower left corner to the lower right, the rulers and their "homes" depicted are: Tlalchiyach Tizacozque at Tecaxpan Tlatzintlan, Aquiach Amapane at Tlachiuhaltepetl, Mixtoma at Axocotitlan, Chichiyaua at Ce Ocotl ycacan, Tzontecomatl yzomoca at Xaltepec, Itztlitzon at Tlaquaquelloc, Telcoyolle at Tizatepetitlan, Naualle tlamacazqui at Olman, Cuetlachtonac at Tenanticpac, and Tecciztlitlan at Tozatepec.

8. The Nahuatl reads "Izcatqui In Intratoro. In Chichimeca. yn quauhtinchantlaca. yn moquiuixca yn totomiuaque yn acollchichimeca yn tzauhcteca yn zacateca yn malpantlaca yn texcalteca yn chicome altepetl ynic ualquizque yn chicomoztoc yn tlatoque yn cenca mauizauhqui yn intenyo in intlatolo yn quichiuhque yn colhuacatepec yn nimacica yn icxicouatl yn quatzalteueyac."

9. This hill, representing Tlachiuhaltepetl, is consistently connected—especially via coloring and the frog at its summit—with lushness nourished by rains and springs, and thus with preciousness and fertility. Yet its iconographic details vary across the *Historia* (e.g., the frog faces to the reader's left in some images, in others, it faces right; in some scenes the hillock has six flowers, in others seven, in yet others, none). Given the density of symbolic meanings attached to Cholula in these annals, and across Central Mexico in the sixteenth century, the connotative range of this image would have been both deep and broad. The visual language of the *Historia*, however, consistently lends this glyph richness of meaning strictly through chains of association with other images in the annals, and not as a stand-alone element. A number of modern interpretations have nevertheless sought to secure the meaning of this particular glyphic emblem. For a range of perspectives, see Bernal-García (1997, 2006), Kirchhoff et al. (1976), Lind (n.d.), and McCafferty (2000, 2001).

10. The closest parallels in terms of the glyphic signs for Cholula appear in plates 2 and 3 (f. 7v, ms. 51–53 and fs. 9v–10r, ms. 54–58). The gestures and position of the two Tolteca-Chichimeca figures (facing each other, yet flanking a central glyph) also appear on the first page of the annals, in a depiction of Tollan. Through pictorial composition, then, the *Historia* creates a symbolic connection between events that transpired at the two sacred sites.

11. Reading clockwise from the reader's upper left, where the Cuauhtinchantlaca dwell, are the Totomihuaque and their leader Aquiyahuatl, the Acolchichimeca and their leader Tzontecomatl, the Tzauhcteca, the Zacateca, the Malpantlaca, and the Texcalteca. The women neither bear personal names, nor are they affiliated with any named group of Chichimeca. They appear here simply as "Chichimeca women"; given the attention to the identity of specific male leaders, their anonymity is all the more striking.

12. On the associative concepts of the year 1 Flint Knife, see Boone (2000: 42), Nicholson (1963), and Umberger (1981). According to the *Historia*, 1 Flint Knife is neither the year of the Tolteca trek to Chicomoztoc, nor the date upon which their negotiations with the Chichimeca took place. These events transpired in the year 6 Calli. The presence of the year 1 Flint Knife within the cave refers to Central Mexican concepts about migration history well known to Nahuas in the late fifteenth and early sixteenth centuries.

13. Kirchhoff et al. identify the two players as Quauhtiliztac (at the reader's left) and Apanecatl (at the right). The Tolteca mentioned in the annals' written text, but not shown, is Cuitliz. Although the scholars do not comment upon why only two of the three ballplayers appear, they note that the description, and depiction, of these men reveals that members of the *calmecactlaca* and the *calpolleque* participated in the trek to Chicomoztoc and the bringing to Cholula of Chichimeca warriors (1976: 172, n. 2). Several other interpretations of this scene have also been posited. Linda Manzanilla implies that it represents a Mesoamerican cave–spring–ball-court complex and thus has parallels to the foundation site of Tenochtitlan (2000: 103–104); see also Bernal-García (2006). While the interpretation I offer here adheres closely to the *Historia* narrative, for annals' readers of the sixteenth century the painting likely resonated with other significant sites in history and their pictorial depiction.

14. This gold-red fluid appears nowhere else in the annals, although in a later image red and gold droplets, representing blood, spill from sacred cacti and grasses during another preparatory event in the larger ritual cycle (pl. 9). Moreover, the combination of blue water and red liquid resonates with the notion of *atl-tlachinolli*, a Pre-Hispanic metaphor for warfare—usually represented glyphically by intertwining symbols for water and fire; but see Heyden (2000). And on the associative relationships among things that blossom, flame, and come to life, see Burkhart (1992).

15. Michael Lind (n.d.) suggests that this enclosure represents an actual building at Cholula. Yet according to the *Historia*'s alphabetic and pictorial narratives, the Chichimeca warriors have yet to make their way from Chicomoztoc to Cholula. Because the manuscript traces their journey in great detail, I think it unlikely that this painting "skips ahead" to show events taking place in the sacred city. It is possible, however, that the painting was fashioned so that the events shown here—which *Historia* readers are led to believe occur in the wilderness near Chicomoztoc— would resonate with those that transpired on other occasions in Cholula.

16. The song seems to concern both divination and the offering of food to the gods. It is set forth in the *Historia*: "Queni uiztzin. Queni uiztzin notzin moxcapi yn quamaxoxauali alimanita qua uetzin uaya tomi uaya niuetzin uaya tomi uaya." (f. 22v, ms. 54–58; see Kirchhoff et al. [1976: 174] for commentary). As a whole, the *Historia* paintings imply rather than explicitly render singing, battle cries, and speech-making. The primary instances of oral exchange depicted in imagery, and signaled by speech scrolls, involve negotiations between leaders of different communities (see, for example, pls. 5, 12, and 16). In depicting silent rather than singing figures this image adheres to the annals' conventions.

17. See *Historia*, f. 26r, ms. 46–50. Here the text also refers to the image as one that depicts Cholula for those of the sixteenth century, so that they can know the site as it was known, long ago, by their ancestors.

18. These images are visible in the name glyphs of the figures at the top of the painting and in the faces and name glyphs of the Tolteca leaders who appear on the two stepped structures near the center of the painting's right side.

19. On these forms of battle and sacrifice, see Clendinnen (1982, 1995).

20. The only other depictions of an arrow sacrifice appear on plate 15, f. 32v–33r, ms. 46–50. In the lower left corner of a scene of Cuauhtinchan's founding two Chichimeca (Tzoncolli and Quauhcitlal) witness the sacrifice of Tototzintli at Tzotzocollecan, and in the upper right corner of the same painting another sacrifice is portrayed. In these instances, however, the sacrifices are small in scale and set at the edges of the scene.

21. While the scholarship on male gender identity in Pre-Hispanic Central Mexico, and particularly its performative aspects and connotations, is not yet extensive, see Cecelia Klein's essay on the Cihuacoatl, particularly for its discussion of political iconography and clothing (1988). For a broader, and more provocative approach to male sexualities in the early colonial period, see Sigal (2003, 2007); several of the essays collected in Klein (2001) also address the visual, linguistic, and material representation of maleness.

22. According to Kirchhoff et al. the boundaries depicted here are those established in the fifteenth century by the Mexica, not the altepetl's original limits (1976: 192, n. 1). If they are correct, then the painting presents a mid-sixteenth-century plea for a Mexica assignment of territory—the last, official pre-colonial assignment—to be viewed as the binding one. Based on the few toponymic signs that can be located on modern maps, this scene is oriented such that the top row of boundary markers sits to the southwest of Totomihuacan; yet, compared to modern maps, the painting also presents a mirror reversal of sites. Kirchhoff et al. propose a more "correct" ordering of the boundary map. I prefer to read the painting as the *Historia* painters created it, viewing their decisions about the placement of glyphs as significant. See discussion, Chapter 3.

23. According to the text and image, the groups settled so that they first encircled Chiquiuhtepec, and then extended outward. Following clockwise around the glyph for Basket Hill, and in their order of appearance in the text, are Aquiyahuatl and the Tlaxichca (reader's upper right), Teuhctzintli and the Itzmahuaque (lower right), Maxtlauilan and the Xauetochca, and Coatzin the interpreter and the Xilotzinca. Below this group are Coatzin of Axomolco and Quauhtzin of Atepantlacpac. Finally, off to the right, are the people of Acaxouayan whose leader does not appear.

24. Moquihuix appears to have settled first, as his path leads him to the foot of the central toponym and is the shortest of all. The other leaders include Teuhctlecozauhqui, who settles above, and to the right, of Cuauhtinchan's main glyphs, and Xiuhtzon, Tonatiuh, and Tochtepeua, all of whom settle beneath the main toponym. See Reyes García (1977).

25. The role of this figure becomes clear only from reading the alphabetic text. In the year after Cuauhtinchan's founding, Moquihuix defeated and sacrificed the Citeca ruler at Tziuhqueme. He commemorated his victory by founding a deer-reed *tetelli (mazazacatzontetelli)*, or type of pyramid, at the site. While the structure is not shown in the *Historia*, the act of drilling fire always signs inaugural events, especially of temples. Moquihuix's action here likely references not only the general foundation theme of the scene, but also this event. See *Historia* (f. 37r, ms. 46–40) and Kirchhoff et al. (1976: 203, n. 2).

26. The Nahuatl reads "Oncan tetl ynepaniuhcan monamique yn chichimeca totomihuaque quauhtechantlaca yn imacica yn tolteca chichimeca yn icxicouatl yn quetzalteueyac ynic quiquetzque yn tepantli yca chicuey acatl xihuitl quineneuhcauique."

27. According to the *Mapa Pintado*, the source for this scene, the rulers' meeting did occur at Tetl ynepaniuhcan, but this site was located at the central, right edge of the painting, where Atlahuimolco now sits and the leaders now appear to meet. Thus, both the pictorial imagery and the written text tell the "proper" story. See discussion, Chapter 3.

28. The alphabetic list opens at the reader's left, near the center of the page at Centepetl, just above the bust of Quetzaltehueyac; it then proceeds counterclockwise around both pages to end where it began, at the left, near the center of the page, at the glyph for Centepetl. The footprints, in contrast, enter near Centepetl and immediately diverge into three paths—one passes by the upper rows of boundary markers, one proceeds into the center of the painting toward the toponym for Cuauhtinchan, and the third travels past the lower set of boundary signs. The upper and lower paths of painted footprints then meet at the right of the scene, near the sign of Atlahuimolco.

29. The arrangement of *Historia* folios in the facsimile edited by Kirchhoff et al.—as well as in the original manuscript housed in the Bibliothèque Nationale in Paris—is incorrect. At some point after the *Historia* was created, the folio now numbered 43 was reversed. Thus folio 42v (ms. 46–50), which shows part of the battle, should directly face folio 43r (ms. 54–58), which depicts the rest of the confrontation. At present, battle scenes are interrupted by folio 43v (ms. 54–58), whose alphabetic text describes the events following Cuauhtinchan's defeat. This was certainly not the original intention of the *Historia's* painters and writer.

SIXTEENTH-CENTURY DOCUMENTS FROM CUAUHTINCHAN

THE MANUSCRIPTS AND PAINTINGS described here represent the primary sixteenth-century histories to survive from Cuauhtinchan. Emphasis has been placed on pictorial manuscripts. For an inventory and transcriptions of other colonial documents from Cuauhtinchan, see Luis Reyes García (1977, 1988).

Historia Tolteca-Chichimeca

Location

Bibliothèque Nationale, Paris, France, Manuscript Mexicain nos. 46–50, 51–53, and 54–58. Other names: Anales de Cuauhtinchan (Quauhtinchan), Annales Tolteco-Chichimèques.

Description

A set of illustrated annals written in Nahuatl on European paper measuring ca. 30 × 22 cm, the *Historia* takes the form of a codex with folios bound on the left. Following European conventions, the writing reads across each page from top to bottom, and left to right. Today, fifty folios are extant, although evidence suggests the *Historia* was originally comprised of fifty-two folios (Kirchhoff et al. 1976: 10). The text of the *Historia* was set down—in black ink, with red highlights for paragraph markers, dates, and important passages—by a single person well trained in European scribal conventions.

In contrast to the alphabetic text, several hands crafted the visual images. The paintings are mixed in heritage, drawing upon Pre-Hispanic and European graphic conventions. In general, narrative paintings rely more heavily upon European stylistic traditions than do images focused on geographical sites. Throughout the manuscript, the painters used black, blue, yellow, green, red, pink, orange, brown, gold, and tan pigments. Most paintings, however, exhibit only three or four of these hues. Sketch lines are common and layout lines for the text remain visible on most pages. The paintings have been distributed unevenly throughout the annals, with images concentrated toward the middle of the manuscript, where the narrative describes Tolteca sovereignty at Cholula and the founding of Cuauhtinchan. Indeed, there are no pictorial scenes associated with the Spanish conquest or any post-conquest events.[1]

History

On the basis of watermarks and paleography, the manuscript can be dated to circa 1545–1563. No sixteenth-century text from Cuauhtinchan refers to the *Historia*, but a reference to the manuscript surfaces in the 1652 testament of doña María Ruiz de Castañeda, the granddaughter of don Alonso de Castañeda, a tlatoani identified in the *Historia* (Reyes García 1988: 172–74). This suggests that the *Historia* was held as a family, or lineage, possession for at least one hundred years. After the seventeenth century, mention of the *Historia* appears in an inventory of community papers made in 1718 in Cuauhtinchan. By the early 1740s, Lorenzo Boturini had collected the *Historia*; he briefly describes it in his 1746 catalogue. Along with much of Boturini's collection, the *Historia* became the property of J. M. A. Aubin between 1830 and 1840 and was transported to France. Toward the end of the nineteenth century, the *Historia* was owned by Eugène Goupil, and, in 1898, it entered the Bibliothèque Nationale collections in Paris.

When catalogued at the Bibliothèque Nationale, the order of the pages was confused and copies of the manuscript were interspersed with the original. This ensemble of documents was assigned three separate inventory numbers. In addition to the original, the Bibliothèque Nationale holds two partial copies of the *Historia*. The library of the Instituto Nacional de Antropología e Historia in Mexico City also possesses a partial copy dating from the nineteenth century (Glass 1975: 221).

Bibliography

Boturini (1746); Boban (1891: 2, 51–101); Preuss and Mengin (1937, 1938); Mengin (1942); Berlin and Rendón (1947); Glass (1975: 220–222); Kirchhoff et al. (1976); Reyes García (1977: 6–11); Leibsohn (n.d.).

Mapa Pintado en Papel Europeo y Aforrado en el Indiano

Location

Bibliothèque Nationale, Paris, France, Manuscript Mexicain nos. 54–58. Other names: Mapa de los linderos de Cuauhtinchan y Totomihuacan.

Description

The *Mapa Pintado* was executed on European paper, later attached to a piece of native-made paper (now measuring ca. 30 × 44 cm). At some point, the painting was trimmed across the top and left side, slicing through several toponyms and a few footprints. At least two hands worked on the painting, and original sketch marks remain visible in several places. Black, gray, green, red, yellow, and orange comprise the palette, yet the range of colors is more restricted than that of the *Historia* or the *Mapas de Cuauhtinchan*. Before the *Mapa Pintado* was removed from Cuauhtinchan in the eighteenth century, it was emended in several places. Examination of the original indicates reworking, especially in the central portions of the painting. Some images were painted over, for example, and elaborated (e.g., a few human heads had new hair styles or eyebrows added; some had their eyes reshaped and pupils darkened). In other places more formal "corrections" appear—sections were painted with white to obscure (if not "erase") the initial imagery, then reworked with additional color.

Using footprints as a guide, the primary narrative cued by the *Mapa Pintado* unfolds, generally, from left to right. This story concerns the foundation of Cuauhtinchan and Totomihuacan under the guidance of the Tolteca culture heroes Quetzaltehueyac and Icxicoatl. Although the painting emphasizes the foundation and boundaries of Cuauhtinchan, the painting is not about Cuauhtinchan per se. Rather, the *Mapa Pintado* chronicles several narratives which, taken together, establish relations of dominance and subordination between Cuauhtinchan and its neighbors.[2]

History

To date, no explicit reference to the *Mapa Pintado* has appeared in the colonial documents known from Cuauhtinchan. Paul Kirchhoff, Lina Odena Güemes, and Luis Reyes García suggest it may have been created in 1532 for a land dispute (1976: 8–9). The first textual reference to the painting I have found is Lorenzo Boturini's catalog of 1746, suggesting he collected the document with the *Historia*. The *Mapa Pintado* then passed to J. M. A. Aubin between 1830 and 1840, and to Eugène Goupil in 1889. It entered the Bibliothèque Nationale in Paris in 1898, where it was catalogued with the *Historia*.

Bibliography

Boturini (1746); Robertson (1959: 179–180); Kirchhoff et al. (1976: 8–9); Reyes García (1977: 12–13); Yoneda (1981); Leibsohn (1996); Prem (1997: 488–496); Boone (2000: 179–182).

Mapa de Cuauhtinchan No. 1

Location

Bibliothèque Nationale, Paris, France, Manuscript Mexicain no. 375. Other names: Mapa de las Conquistas Chichimecas, Mapa Baur-Goupil.

Description

Executed on native-made paper and currently stitched to cloth, the painted portion of *Mapa* 1 measures 1.14 × 1.68 m. The imagery was painted by at least two hands, using pink, red, gold, white, yellow, blue, black, green, and gray. No alphabetic writing appears on the painting and, of all the *Mapas de Cuauhtinchan*, the scenes on *Mapa* 1 seem the most restricted temporally and thematically. The painting focuses on Chichimeca conquests and alliances—events that Reyes García suggests all transpired in the twelfth century CE (1977: 14)—in a region defined by Cholula and Tlaxcala on the west, and Pico de Orizaba and the Pacific on the east. Martial motifs predominate; many of the sites and individuals appear pierced by arrows, and arrows placed end-to-end define paths of war. The presence of two kinds of paths, one defined by footprints and one by arrows, seems to align *Mapa* 1 with both Central Mexican and Mixtec graphic traditions. The double paths also distinguish *Mapa* 1 from its contemporaries, for no other *Mapa de Cuauhtinchan* enlists arrows to mark military routes. Warfare is further evoked near the center of *Mapa* 1, where thirty-six Chichimeca warriors meet at Tollan Calmecahuacan, just above an atl-tlachinolli emblem and a *tzompantli* (skull rack) with three skewered heads. The altepetl of Cuauhtinchan takes a prominent position just above the center of the painting, yet no footprints lead directly to the site. This, and the fact that many places and people on *Mapa* 1 surface in neither the *Historia* nor the other *Mapas de Cuauhtinchan*, has led Reyes García to suggest that this painting presents a factional perspective on the settlement of the altepetl (1977: 13–14).[3]

Although *Mapa* 1 seems to show a series of related events, examination of the original indicates that the painting was not completed all at once. Differences in the proportions of figures and their features indicate that several figures on *Mapa* 1 were added at a later date. Ultimately this implies that, over the colonial period, *Mapa* 1 was used to record a number of histories and enlisted for a variety of purposes in Cuauhtinchan.

History

The original painting dates to the mid-sixteenth century, and receives mention in an inventory of the Cuauhtinchan municipal archive dated 1877 (Yoneda 1981: 21). *Mapa* 1 apparently remained in Cuauhtinchan until 1891. In the following year, Eduardo Bello copied the painting for the Exposición Histórico-Americana held in Madrid. The original was brought to Paris in 1893 by Charles Baur, while the Bello copy has remained in the Museo Nacional de Antropología in Mexico City.

Bibliography

Orozco (1892: 28); Mateos Higuera (1946a: 175–177); Simons (1968: 87–92); Glass (1964: 76–77, pl. 34, 1975: 118–119); Reyes García (1977: 13–14); Yoneda (1981).

Mapa de Cuauhtinchan No. 2

Location

Collection of Ángeles Espinosa Yglesias, Mexico. Other names: Mapa de la ruta Chicomoztoc-Cuauhtinchan, Peregrinación de los Totomihuacas.

Description

Mapa 2 measures about 1.10 × 2.03 m, and is the largest of the *Mapas de Cuauhtinchan*. The painting has black, white, tan, blue, green, orange, yellow, pink, and gray color applied to native-made paper.[4] Two primary narrative themes organize the map. The left side highlights the migration of Chichimeca from the mountain cave of Chicomoztoc to Cholula. The right focuses on Cuauhtinchan's boundaries and foundation.

Mapa 2 also registers the largest number of sites of all the *Mapas de Cuauhtinchan*. Prominent places include Popocatepetl and Iztaccihuatl, La Malinche, Pico de Orizaba, Cholula, Cuauhtinchan, and Tepeaca. Unlike the other paintings, which generally read from left to right (with digressive paths along the way), the narrative on *Mapa* 2 begins at the center of the painting, at Cholula. A trail of footprints leads toward the left, linking Cholula to Chicomoztoc in the upper left-hand corner. From the cave, a road twists across the left side of the painting. It passes through sites in the Valley of Mexico and winds its way back to the temples of Cholula. This migration account parallels, but does not replicate, the account set down in the *Historia*.[5] Along the road, *Mapa* 2 supplies the dates for key events in the migration. Using the indigenous calendar, year-dates are most common but day-dates also appear.[6]

    Mapa 2 and the *Historia* are the only sixteenth-century sources from Cuauhtinchan to describe the migration from Chicomoztoc to Cholula. *Mapa* 2, however, is not solely a migration history. Because of the boundary markers and the scenes of altepetl foundation on its right side, this painting cues at least four types of narratives—those of peregrination, settlement, transformation, and territorial possession (Boone 2000; Carrasco and Sessions 2007a). Indeed, the geographical scope of *Mapa* 2 includes both Cuauhtinchan's immediate surroundings and more distant sites. For example, close to the altepetl, the Sierra of Tepeaca and the mountains Totolquetzale and Tlenamacone are shown. At a greater distance, Acatlan, Chila, and Coixtlahuaca can be seen.[7] Scenes of conquest and sacrifice also appear, as do revisions to iconographic elements and boundaries—defined by red and black lines that demarcate claims to territory surrounding Cuauhtinchan.[8]

History

The original painting is usually dated to the mid-sixteenth century, although Eleanor Wake has recently suggested that the original paintings may have been created in the 1530s (2007). An 1877 inventory of the Cuauhtinchan municipal archive mentions it along with *Mapas de Cuauhtinchan* 1 and 3. Until 1891/92, *Mapa* 2 was housed in Cuauhtinchan, where Eduardo Bello copied it for the Exposición Histórico-Americana held in Madrid in 1892. This copy is currently housed in the Museo Nacional de Antropología in Mexico City. The original was reportedly deposited in the Museo Regional de Puebla in the 1930s and declared a historic monument by the Instituto Nacional de Antropología e Historia in the 1960s. At some point before 1990, *Mapa* 2 entered a private collection in Mexico. Currently *Mapa* 2 remains in Mexico, in the collection of the family of Ángeles Espinosa Yglesias.

Bibliography

Miyar (1928: 201–207); Mateos Higuera (1946b: 177–179); Martínez Marin (1963); Glass (1964: 66, pl. 25, 1975: 118–119); Simons (1968: 25–80); Reyes García (1977: 14–15); Dávila Zaragoza (1977); Boone (2000: 173–178); Yoneda (1981, 2000, 2001, 2003, 2005), Carrasco and Sessions (2007b).

Mapa de Cuauhtinchan No. 3

Location

Museo Nacional de Antropología, Mexico City, Mexico. Other names: Mapa de las migraciones Huexotzinco-Tepeaca.

Description

Mapa 3 focuses on migrations into the region surrounding Cuauhtinchan, the altepetl's foundation, and the foundation of Tepeaca. Executed on native-made paper—probably by two or three different hands—the painting measures .92 × 1.12 m. Similar in palette to the other two *Mapas de Cuauhtinchan*, the colors include blue, green, tan, gray, black, red, orange, and gold.

As with the other cartographic histories from Cuauhtinchan, the painting represents a series of conquests, although it devotes most of its attention to the foundation of altepetl around Cuauhtinchan, and especially that of Tepeaca. While *Mapa* 3 resembles the other *Mapas de Cuauhtinchan* in the kind of narrative it cues, landmarks familiar from the other paintings, but some distance from Cuauhtinchan—La Malinche and Pico de Orizaba—are absent here. Sites that are indicated include Tlaxcala, Huejotzingo, Cholula, Tepeaca, Totomihuacan, Acatzingo, Tecali, Amozoc, the Río Atoyac, and the Sierra of Tepeaca. The map thus depicts a smaller geographical realm than do several other *Mapas de Cuauhtinchan*.

History

This painting was mentioned in the 1877 inventory of the municipal archive of Cuauhtinchan. *Mapa* 3 remained in Cuauhtinchan until 1891/92, where it was copied by Eduardo Bello for the Exposición Histórico-Americana held in Madrid in 1892. This copy has since been lost. The original was acquired by Arístides Martel in Puebla; circa 1919 it was expropriated by Mexico's Inspección General de Monumentos Artísticos e Históricos. Since 1939, *Mapa* 3 has been housed in the Museo Nacional de Antropología e Historia in Mexico City.

Bibliography

Boban (1891); Orozco (1892: 27–37); Mateos Higuera (1947a: 255–256); Glass (1964: 123, pl. 73, 1975: 119); Simons (1968: 81–86); Reyes García (1977: 15–16); Galarza and Yoneda (1979); Yoneda (1981, 1989: 29–39, 1996).

Mapa de Cuauhtinchan No. 4

Location

Museo Nacional de Antropología, Mexico City, Mexico. Other names: Mapa colonial de los linderos de Cuauhtinchan (1563).

Description

Executed on native-made paper, this painting measures approximately 1.13 × 1.58 m, and dates to the mid-sixteenth century. *Mapa* 4 is now in poor condition, although many of the colors originally used—black, red, green, blue, and tan—can still be seen. Of all the images known from sixteenth-century Cuauhtinchan, this painting most closely parallels European-style cartographic maps. *Mapa* 4 depicts the mountains, rivers, roads, and communities around Cuauhtinchan. La Malinche, Citlaltepetl, and the Río Atoyac all appear, as do the communities of Tlaxcala, Puebla, Tepeaca, Tecali, and Totomihuacan. Mountains, hills, and rivers are treated with naturalistic detail. Each town, however, takes the same conventionalized form: a church and open plaza centered within a grid. In contrast to the depictions of mountains and rivers, which are not glossed, written labels identify each settlement shown. In addition to the names of towns, two short alphabetic texts were set down on the painting.[9]

Mapa 4 may have initially documented claims to boundaries, as two sets of lines—one red and one black—outline distinct portions of territory. Reyes García suggests that the document may have been created to establish the boundaries between Cuauhtinchan and Puebla, with each line demarcating a border of a different historical moment (1977: 19).[10] Similar lines also appear on the right side of *Mapa* 2, suggesting that this was a conventional way to indicate shifting boundaries (Simons 1968: 22–23, 80).

History

This painting was apparently collected by Lorenzo Boturini in the early 1740s, since *Mapa* 4 is described in his 1746 catalogue. In contrast to the other Cuauhtinchan documents he collected—which passed to J. M. A. Aubin and were sent to France—this painting remained in Mexico. Toward 1919, *Mapa* 4 was relocated from the Biblioteca Nacional to the Museo Nacional de Antropología e Historia in Mexico City, along with other painted documents previously claimed by Boturini.

Bibliography

Boturini (1746: 41); Gómez de Orosco (n.d.); Mateos Higuera (1947b: 256–257); Simons (1968: 5–24); Glass (1964: 75, pls. 32–33, 1975: 119–120); Reyes García (1977: 18–19); Yoneda (1981, 1994).

Prose Documents

In addition to pictorial records, several prose documents from sixteenth-century Cuauhtinchan still exist. While integral to the altepetl's colonial history, only a few of these works explicitly address Pre-Hispanic events or concerns. Most prominent among these writings are the *Libro de los Guardianes*—a set of historical annals written in Nahuatl and Spanish, and covering the years 1519–1640—and two manuscripts, that of 1546–1547, and that of 1553, which register the testimony offered in conflicts over territory and tribute obligations by indigenous people from Cuauhtinchan and nearby altepetl. The *Libro* has one pictorial page—a scene of the Spanish conquest of Tenochtitlan.[11] The other two manuscripts are strictly alphabetic. As of this writing, the *Libro* was housed in the Biblioteca del Instituto de Investigaciones Jurídicas, Universidad Nacional Autónoma de México, Mexico City, and the two manuscripts in the municipal archive of Cuauhtinchan.

Other works of significance, especially for understanding the transition from Pre-Hispanic to Novohispanic society are the *Ordenanzas de Cuauhtinchan*, the *Memoriales de Tierras de los Principales de Cuauhtinchan*, and the late-sixteenth-century testaments of several Cuauhtinchan tlatoque. More detailed information on these and later works, including transcriptions of selected examples, appears in Medina Lima (1995) and Reyes García (1974, 1988).

Notes

1. This may reflect the existence of more elaborate or complete pictorial models for Pre-Hispanic times, although several pages toward the end of the manuscript have blank spaces, originally intended for date glyphs, and a few blank pages display faint sketch lines marking the placement of images intended but not executed. The distribution of images is nevertheless quite uneven: many more painted scenes of far greater richness appear in the midsections of the manuscript than at either the beginning or end. This suggests that the *Historia* painters and writer were making intentional decisions about which events in the narrative were most worthy of pictorial elaboration.

2. Elizabeth Hill Boone presents an excellent analysis of the narrative threads cued by the *Mapa Pintado*, describing the three toponymic circuits of the image, as well as the primary community-foundation events (2000: 180–181); see also Prem (1997: 488–496) for a reading that compares the *Mapa Pintado* with related images in the *Historia* and revises the earlier readings offered by Paul Kirchhoff.

3. For other assessments of this image, see Yoneda (1981: 41–43) and Wake (2007), who views this painting, along with *Mapas* 2 and 3, as the craftsmanship of Pinome painters in Cuauhtinchan, who claim Mixtec-Nahua, rather than wholly Nahua descent (on this point, see also, Kirchhoff et al. 1976: 7).

4. Marina Straulino's conservation reports represent the most current analyses of the material supports and method of construction of *Mapa* 2 (2007). For a wide-ranging selection of perspectives on *Mapa* 2—all representing recent research—see especially Yoneda (2005) and Carrasco and Sessions (2007b).

5. For discussion of the migration narratives depicted in the *Historia* as compared to *Mapa* 2, see Simons (1968: 27), Reyes García (1977: 14), Boone (2000: 175–77), Yoneda (2005), and Wake (2007).

6. Approximately fifty calendrical dates are given on *Mapa* 2. Most are clustered around the sites of Cholula, Cuauhtinchan, and Tepeaca. Boone argues that several of these dates bear symbolic meaning; in particular, she sees the sequence of day-count dates marking the migration from Chicomoztoc to Cholula as references to notions of beginning and completion (2000: 177). For other interpretive positions on the dates, see Aveni (2007) and Wake (2007). A diagram of the distribution of date glyphs on *Mapa* 2 appears in Yoneda (1981: 233).

7. Yet other locations depicted on this side of *Mapa* 2 include Teopantlan, Tehuitzingo, Totoltepec, Huehuetlan, Pico de Orizaba, Cofre de Perote, Maltrata, Huamantla, La Malinche, Citlaltepec, Capulac, Chachapa, Amalucan, Tepoxuchil, and Totomihuacan. Further discussion of the sites indicated on the right-hand section of *Mapa* 2 appears in Simons (1968), Dávila Zaragoza (n.d.), Reyes García (1977), Boone (2000), and Carrasco and Sessions (2007a, 2007b).

8. A similar set of lines also appears on *Mapa de Cuauhtinchan* No. 4; see Simons (1968) and Yoneda (1994, 2000, 2005) on both sets of boundaries. Many specific emendations to *Mapa* 2 are described in Wake (2007).

9. One text appeared near the town of Amozoc, the other below La Malinche. Today neither text can be read in its entirety. As was the case on many indigenous maps painted in the sixteenth century, the writing may have verified the scene depicted by the map. For a partial transcription of both texts, see Simons (1968: 6–7). In addition to alphabetic writing and European-derived imagery, *Mapa* 4 exhibits knowledge of graphic practices that predate the conquest. The painter used Pre-Hispanic–style place glyphs to mark sites, and included a few date glyphs (although the events to which these dates refer are not specified).

10. In support of this position, a document in the Archivo Municipal de Cuauhtinchan refers to a *pintura* created in 1550 to define the boundary between Cuauhtinchan and Puebla, in which a black line was used to make the demarcation (transcribed in Reyes García 1988: 107). See also Simons (1968) and Yoneda (1994) for slightly different positions on this.

11. For a description of this image, see Barlow (1946); for a color reproduction, see Medina Lima (1995).

BIBLIOGRAPHY

Primary Documents: Annals, Codices, Document Compilations

Anales de Cuauhtitlan
1975 *Códice Chimalpopoca* (Primo Feliciano Velázquez, trans.), 3–118. Universidad Nacional Autónoma de México, México, D.F.

Anales de Tecamachalco
1981 *Anales de Tecamachalco: Crónica local y colonial en idioma nahautl, 1398–1590* (Antonio Peñafiel, ed.). Editorial Innovación, México, D.F.

Anales de Tlatelolco
1948 *Anales de Tlatelolco: Unos anales históricos de la nación mexicana y Códice de Tlatelolco* (Heinrich Berlin and Robert Barlow, eds). Antigua librería Robredo de José Porrúa e hijos, México, D.F.

Anales de Tula
1949 Anales de Tula, Hidalgo, 1361–1521 (Robert Barlow, commentator). *Tlalocan* 3: 2–13.

Berlin, Heinrich, and Silvia Rendón (trans.)
1947 *Historia Tolteca-Chichimeca: Anales de Quauhtinchan.* Antigua librería Robredo de José Porrúa e hijos, México, D.F.

Boturini, Lorenzo
1746 Catálogo del museo histórico del cavallero Lorenzo Boturini. In *En idea de una nueva historia general de la América septentrional.* Les Editions Genet, Paris.

Codex Aubin
1963 *Historia de la nación mexicana: Reproducción a todo color del Códice de 1576* (Códice Aubin) (Charles Dibble, trans. and ed.). José Porrúa Turanzas, Madrid.

Codex Mendoza
1992 *Codex Mendoza* (Frances Berdan and Patricia Anawalt, eds.). University of California Press, Berkeley and Los Angeles.

Códice Boturini
1975 *Códice Boturini: Tira de la peregrinación.* Colección de documentos conmemorativos del DCL aniversario de la fundación de Tenochtitlan 1. SEP, México, D.F.

Códice Franciscano
1941 *Códice Franciscano, siglo XVI: Informe de la provincia del Santo Evangelio al Visitador Lic. Juan de Ovando.* Editorial Salvador Chávez Hayhoe, México, D.F.

Códice Xolotl
1951 *Códice Xolotl* (Charles Dibble, ed.). Universidad Nacional Autónoma de México, México, D.F.

Dorantes de Carranza, Baltasar
1970 *Summaria relación de las cosas de la Nueva España.* Jesús Medina, México, D.F.

Durán, Diego
1993 *The History of the Indies of New Spain* (Doris Heyden, trans.). University of Oklahoma Press, Norman.

García Icazbalceta, Joaquín (ed.)
1941 *Nueva colección de documentos para la historia de México: Cartas de religiosos de Nueva España 1539–1594.* Editorial Salvador Chávez Hayhoe, México, D.F.

1981 *Bibliografía mexicana del siglo XVI: Catálogo razonado de libros impresos en México de 1539 a 1600.* Fondo de Cultura Económica, México, D.F.

Historia de los Mexicanos por sus pinturas
1941 *Nueva colección de documentos para la historia de México* (Joaquín García Icazbalceta, ed.), 3: 209–240. Editorial Salvador Chávez Hayhoe, México, D.F.

Historia Tolteca-Chichimeca
See Berlin and Rendón (1947); Kirchhoff, Odena Güemes, and Reyes García (1976); Mengin (1942); and Preuss and Mengin (1937, 1938).

Histoyre du Mechique
1905 *Histoyre du Mechique* (Edouard de Jonghe, ed.). *Journal de la Société des Américanistes de Paris* 2: 1–41.

Horcasitas, Fernando, and Bente Bittmann Simons, eds.
1974 Anales jeroglíficos e históricos de Tepeaca. *Anales de Antropología* 11: 225–293.

Kirchhoff, Paul, with Lina Odena Güemes and Luis Reyes García (trans. and eds.)
1976 *Historia Tolteca-Chichimeca.* CIS-INAH, SEP. México, D.F.

Libro de las tasaciones de pueblos de la Nueva España, siglo XVI.
1952 Prólogo by Francisco González de Cossío. Archivo General de la Nación, México, D.F.

Manuscript of 1546 and *Manuscript of 1553*
See Reyes García (1988)

Medina Lima, Constantino (trans.)
1995 *Libro de los guardianes y gobernadores de Cuauhtinchan (1519–1640).* Centro de Investigaciones y Estudios Superiores en Antropología Social, México, D.F.

Mendieta, fray Geronimo de
1945 *Vidas franciscanas.* Universidad Nacional Autónoma de México, México, D.F.

1971 *Historia eclesiástica Indiana: Obra escrita a fines del siglo XVI.* Editorial Porrúa, México, D.F.

Mengin, Ernst (ed.)
1942 *Historia Tolteca-Chichimeca: Liber in lingua Nahuatl manuscriptus picturisque ornatus, ut est conservatus in Bibliotheca Nationis Gallicae Parisiensi sub numeris XLVI–LVIII bis.* Corpus codicum Americanorum medii aevi I. E. Munksgaard, Copenhagen.

Molina, fray Alonso de
1977 [1571] *Vocabulario en lengua castellana y mexicana y mexicana y castellana.* Antigua librería Robredo de Porrúa e hijos, México, D.F.

Motolinia (Benavente), fray Toribio de
1971 *Memoriales; O Libro de las cosas de la Nueva España y de los naturales de ella* (Edmundo O'Gorman, ed.). Serie de historiadores y cronistas de Indias 2. Universidad Nacional Autónoma de México, México, D.F.

1988 *Historia de los indios de la Nueva España.* Alianza Editorial, Madrid.

Paso y Troncoso, Francisco del (ed.)
1905–48 *Papeles de Nueva España.* Sucesores de Rivadeneyra, Madrid.

1939–42 *Epistolario de Nueva España, 1505–1818.* Antigua librería Robedo de José Porrúa e hijos, México, D.F.

Preuss, Konrad, and Ernst Mengin (trans.)
1937 Die Mexicanische Bilderhandschrift Historia Tolteca-Chichimeca, Die Manuskripte 46–58 bis der Nationalbibliothek in Paris. *Baessler-Archiv*: supplement 9, part I.

1938 Die Mexikanische Bilderhandschrift Historia Tolteca-Chichimeca, die Manuskripte 46–58 bis der Nationalbibliothek in Paris: Der Komentar. *Baessler-Archiv* 21: 1–66.

Quiñones Keber, Eloise
1995 *Codex Telleriano-Remensis: Ritual, Divination and History in a Pictorial Aztec Manuscript.* University of Texas Press, Austin.

Sahagún, Bernardino de
1950–1982 *General History of the Things of New Spain: Florentine Codex* (Arthur J. O. Anderson and Charles Dibble, trans.). School of American Research and University of Utah, Santa Fe and Salt Lake City.

1982 *Historia general de las cosas de Nueva España* (facsimile ed., Alfredo López Austín and Josefina García Quintana, eds.). Banamex, México, D.F.

1993 *Primeros memoriales* (facsimile ed., Ferdinand Anders, photographer). University of Oklahoma Press, Norman.

Scholes, France, and Eleanor Adams
1958 *Sobre el modo de tributar los indios de Nueva España a Su Majestad 1561–1564.* Documentos para la historia del México colonial 5. José Porrúa e Hijos, México, D.F.

Siméon, Rémi
1981 *Diccionario de la lengua Náhuatl o Mexicana.* Siglo Veintiuno, México, D.F.

Zorita, Alonso de
1941 *Breve y sumaria relación de los señores ... de la Nueva España.* In *Nueva colección de documentos para la historia de México* (Joaquín García Icazbalceta, ed.). Editorial Salvador Chávez Hayhoe, México, D.F.

Secondary Sources

Adorno, Rolena
2000 [1986] *Guaman Poma: Writing and Resistance in Colonial Peru.* University of Texas Press, Austin.

Aguilar Moreno, Manuel
2002 *Indio Ladino as a Cultural Mediator in the Colonial Society. Estudios de Cultura Nahuatl* 33: 149–184.

2006 *Handbook to Life in the Aztec World.* Facts on File, New York.

Anderson, Arthur, and Susan Schroeder (eds. and trans.)
1997 *Codex Chimalpahin: Society and Politics in Mexico Tenochtitlan, Tlatelolco, Texcoco, Culhuacan, and other Nahua Altepetl in Central Mexico.* University of Oklahoma Press, Norman.

Arnold, Philip
1998 *Eating Landscape: Aztec and European Occupation of Tlalocan.* University Press of Colorado, Niwot.

Asselbergs, Florine
2004 *Conquered Conquistadors: The Lienzo de Quauhquechollan; A Nahua Vision of the Conquest of Guatemala.* CNWS, Leiden, The Netherlands.

Aveni, Anthony
2007 Calendar, Chronology and Cosmology in the *Mapa de Cuauhtinchan No. 2.* In *Cave, City, and Eagle's Nest: An Interpretive Journey Through the Mapa de Cuauhtinchan No. 2* (David Carrasco and Scott Sessions, eds.), 147–160. University of New Mexico Press, Albuquerque.

Baird, Ellen
1993 *The Drawings of Sahagún's* Primeros Memoriales: *Structure and Style.* University of Oklahoma Press, Norman.

Barlow, Robert
1946 The Codex of the derrumbe del Templo Mayor. *Notes on Middle American Archaeology and Ethnology* 72: 75–78.

Basso, Keith
1996 *Wisdom Sites in Places: Landscape and Language among the Western Apache.* University of New Mexico Press, Albuquerque.

Behar, Ruth
1986 *Santa María del Monte: The Presence of the Past in a Spanish Village.* Princeton University Press, Princeton.

Berdan, Frances
2006 The Role of Provincial Elites in the Aztec Empire. In *Intermediate Elites in Pre-Columbian States* (Christina Elson and R. Alan Covey, eds.), 154–165. University of Arizona Press, Tucson.

Bernal-García, María Elena

1997 From Mountain to Toponym in the *Historia Tolteca-Chichimeca*. In *Latin American Indian Literatures: Messages and Meanings* (Mary Preuss, ed.), 85–102. Labyrinthos Press, Los Angeles.

2006 Tu agua, tu cerro, tu flor: Orígenes y metamorfosis conceptuales del altepetl de Cholula, siglos XVII y XVI. In *Territorialidad y paisaje en el altepetl del siglo XVI* (Federico Fernández Christlieb and Ángel Julián García Zambrano, eds.), 231–338. Fondo de Cultura Económica and Instituto de Geográfia de la Universidad Nacional Autónoma de México, México, D.F.

2007 The Dance of Time, the Procession of Space at Mexico-Tenochtitlan's Desert Garden. In *Sacred Gardens and Landscapes: Ritual and Agency* (Michel Conan, ed.), 69–112. Dumbarton Oaks Research Library and Collection, Washington, D.C.

Bhabha, Homi

1984 Of Mimicry and Man: The Ambivalence of Colonial Discourse. *October* 28: 125–133.

Boban, Eugène

1891 *Documents pour servir à l'Histoire du Mexique: Catalogue raisonné de la collection de M. E. Eugène Goupil (Ancienne Collection J. M. A. Aubin)*. Ernest Leroux, Paris.

Boone, Elizabeth Hill

1991 Migration Histories as Ritual Performance. In *To Change Place: Aztec Ceremonial Landscapes* (David Carrasco, ed.), 121–151. University Press of Colorado, Niwot.

1992 Glorious Imperium: Understanding Land and Community in Moctezuma's Mexico. In *Moctezuma's Mexico* (David Carrasco and Eduardo Matos Moctezuma, eds., with essays by Anthony Aveni and Elizabeth Hill Boone), 159–176. University Press of Colorado, Niwot.

1994 *The Aztec World*. St. Remy Press, Montreal.

1996 Manuscript Painting in Service of Imperial Ideology. In *Aztec Imperial Strategies* (Frances Berdan et al.), 181–208. Dumbarton Oaks Research Library and Collection, Washington, D.C.

1998 Pictorial Documents and Visual Thinking in Postconquest Mexico. In *Native Traditions in the Postconquest World* (Elizabeth Hill Boone and Tom Cummins, eds.), 149–200. Dumbarton Oaks Research Library and Collection, Washington, D.C.

2000 *Stories in Red and Black: Pictorial Histories of the Aztecs and Mixtecs*. University of Texas Press, Austin.

2006 The Defining Sample: How We Pursue the Pre-Columbian Past. In *A Pre-Columbian World* (Jeffrey Quilter and Mary Miller, eds.), 21–53. Dumbarton Oaks Research Library and Collection, Washington, D.C.

Boone, Elizabeth Hill (ed.)

2005 *Painted Books and Indigenous Knowledge in Mesoamerica: Manuscript Studies in Honor of Mary Elizabeth Smith*. Middle American Research Institute, New Orleans.

Boone, Elizabeth Hill, and Tom Cummins (eds.)

1998 *Native Traditions in the Postconquest World*. Dumbarton Oaks Research Library and Collection, Washington, D.C.

Brady, James, and Keith Prufer (eds.)

2005 *In The Maw of the Earth Monster: Mesoamerican Ritual Cave Use*. University of Texas Press, Austin.

Brotherston, Gordon

1992 *Book of the Fourth World: Reading the Native Americas Through Their Literature*. University of Cambridge Press, Cambridge.

Brown, Betty Ann

1983 Seen But Not Heard: Women in Aztec Ritual—The Sahagún Texts. In *Text and Image in Pre-Columbian Art* (Janet C. Berlo, ed.), 119–138. BAR, Oxford.

Brumfiel, Elizabeth
2006 Provincial Elites and the Limits of Dominant Ideology in the Aztec Empire. In *Intermediate Elites in Pre-Columbian States* (Christina Elson and R. Alan Covey, eds.), 166–174. University of Arizona Press, Tucson.

Bruner, Jerome
1994 The "Remembered" Self. In *The Remembering Self: Construction and Accuracy in the Self-Narrative* (Ulric Neisser and Robyn Fivush, eds.), 41–54. Cambridge University Press, Cambridge.

Burkhart, Louise
1989 *The Slippery Earth: Nahua-Christian Moral Dialogue in Sixteenth-Century Mexico.* University of Arizona Press, Tucson.

1992 Flowery Heaven: The Aesthetic of Paradise in Nahuatl Devotional Literature. *Res* 21: 88–109.

1998 Pious Performances: Christian Pageantry and Native Identity in Early Colonial Mexico. In *Native Traditions in the Postconquest World* (Elizabeth Hill Boone and Tom Cummins, eds.), 361–381. Dumbarton Oaks Research Library and Collection, Washington, D.C.

Byland, Bruce, and John M. D. Pohl
1994 *In the Realm of 8 Deer: The Archaeology of the Mixtec Codices.* University of Oklahoma Press, Norman.

Camelo Arredondo, Rosa, Jorge Gurría LaCroix, and Constantino Reyes-Valerio
1964 *Juan Gerson, Tlacuilo de Tecamachalco.* Instituto Nacional de Antropología e Historia, México, D.F.

Carrasco, David, and Scott Sessions
2007a Middle Place, Labyrinth and Circumambulation: Cholula's Peripatetic Role in *Mapa de Cuauhtinchan No. 2.* In *Cave, City, and Eagle's Nest: An Interpretive Journey Through the Mapa de Cuauhtinchan No. 2* (David Carrasco and Scott Sessions, eds.), 427–454. University of New Mexico Press, Albuquerque.

Carrasco, David, and Scott Sessions (eds.)
2007b *Cave, City, and Eagle's Nest: An Interpretive Journey Through the Mapa de Cuauhtinchan No. 2.* University of New Mexico Press, Albuquerque.

Carrasco, Pedro
1963 Las tierras de dos indios nobles de Tepeaca en el siglo XVI. *Tlalocan* 4: 97–119.

1984 Royal Marriages in Ancient Mexico. In *Explorations in Ethnohistory: Indians of Central Mexico in the Sixteenth Century* (H. R. Harvey and Hanns Prem, eds.), 41–82. University of New Mexico Press, Albuquerque.

Caruth, Cathy (ed.)
1995 *Trauma: Explorations in Memory.* Johns Hopkins University Press, Baltimore.

Casey, Edward
2002 *Representing Place: Landscape Painting and Maps.* University of Minnesota Press, Minneapolis.

Certeau, Michel de
1984 *The Practice of Everyday Life* (Steven Rendall, trans.). University of California Press, Berkeley and Los Angeles.

Chakrabarty, Dipesh
2000 *Provincializing Europe: Postcolonial Thought and Historical Difference.* Princeton University Press, Princeton.

Clanchy, Michael T.
1979 *From Memory to Written Record: England 1066–1307.* Harvard University Press, Cambridge.

Clendinnen, Inga
1982 The Cost of Courage in Aztec Society. *Past and Present* 94: 44–89.

1995 *Aztecs: An Interpretation.* Canto ed. Cambridge University Press, Cambridge and New York.

Clifford, James
1997 *Routes: Travel and Translation in the Late Twentieth Century.* Harvard University Press, Cambridge.

Cline, S. L.

1986 *Colonial Culhuacan, 1580–1600: A Social History of an Aztec Town.* University of New Mexico Press, Albuquerque.

1993 *The Book of Tributes: Early Sixteenth-Century Nahuatl Censuses from Morelos.* University of California Press, Los Angeles.

Cohen, David William

1994 *The Combing of History.* Chicago University Press, Chicago.

Conkey, Margaret

2001 Epilogue: Thinking About Gender with Theory and Method. In *Gender in Pre-Hispanic America* (Cecelia Klein, ed.), 341–362. Dumbarton Oaks Research Library and Collection, Washington D.C.

Conley, Tom

1996 *The Self-Made Map: Cartographic Writing in Early Modern France.* University of Minnesota, Minneapolis.

Connerton, Paul

1989 *How Societies Remember.* Cambridge University Press, Cambridge.

Cummins, Tom, and Joanne Rappaport

1998 The Reconfiguration of Civic and Sacred Space: Architecture, Image, and Writing in the Colonial Northern Andes. *Latin American Literary Review* 52: 174–201.

Davies, Nigel

1980 *The Toltec Heritage: From the Fall of Tula to the Rise of Tenochtitlan.* University of Oklahoma Press, Norman.

1987 *The Aztec Empire: The Toltec Resurgence.* University of Oklahoma, Norman.

Dávila, Patricio

n.d. Cuauhtinchan: Estudio arqueológico de un área. Master's thesis, Universidad Nacional Autónoma de México, México, D.F, 1974.

Dávila Zaragoza, Diana

n.d. Procesos de desarrollo en el área de Cuauhtinchan-Tepeaca: Constatación arqueológica de algunos rasgos del Mapa de la Ruta Chicomoztoc-Quauhtinchan. Master's thesis, Universidad Nacional Autónoma de México, México, D.F, 1977.

Diel, Lori Boornazian

2005 The Inclusion and Exclusion of Noblewomen in Aztec Pictorial Histories. *Res* 47 (Spring): 83–106.

Douglas, Eduardo

2003 Figures of Speech: Pictorial History in the "Quinaztin Map" of about 1542. *Art Bulletin* 85 (2): 281–309.

Edgerton, Samuel

2001 *Theaters of Conversion: Religious Architecture and Indian Artisans.* University of New Mexico Press, Albuquerque.

Escalante Gonzalbo, Pablo

1997 El patrocinio del arte indocristiano en el siglo XVI. La iniciative de las autoridades indígenas en Tlaxcala y Cuauhtinchan. In *Patrocinio, colección, y circulación de las artes* (Gustavo Curiel, ed.), 215–235. Universidad Nacional Autónoma de México, Instituto de Investigaciones Estéticas, México, D.F.

Félix Bolaños, Alvaro, and Gustavo Verdesio (eds.)

2002 *Colonialism Past and Present: Reading and Writing about Colonial Latin America Today.* State University Press of New York, Albany.

Fentress, James, and Chris Wickham

1992 *Social Memory.* Blackwell, Oxford.

Fields, Virgina, and Victor Zamudio-Taylor (eds.)

2001 *The Road to Aztlan: Art from a Mythic Homeland.* Los Angeles County Museum of Art, Los Angeles.

Fiering, Norman, and M. Mathes (eds.)
1990 *The Book in the Americas: The Role of Books and Printing in the Development of Culture and Society in Colonial Latin America.* Americas Society Art Gallery, New York.

Florescano, Enrique
1985 La reconstrucción histórica elaborada por la nobleza indígena y sus descendientes mestizos. In *La memoria y el olvido,* 11–20. Instituto Nacional de Antropología e Historia, México, D.F.

1994 *Myth, Memory, and Time in Mexico: From the Aztecs to Independence* (Albert and Kathryn Bork, trans.). University of Texas Press, Austin.

Galarza, Joaquín
1980 *Estudios de escritura indígena tradicional (Azteca-Nahuatl).* Archivo General de la Nación: México, D.F.

Galarza, Joaquín, and Keiko Yoneda (eds.)
1979 *Mapa de Cuauhtinchan No. 3.* Colección manuscritos indigenas tradicionales 3. Archivo General de la Nación, México, D.F.

Gerhard, Peter
1972 *A Guide to the Historical Geography of New Spain.* Cambridge University Press, Cambridge.

Gibson, Charles
1964 *The Aztecs Under Spanish Rule.* Stanford University Press, Stanford.

Gillespie, Susan
1989 *The Aztec Kings: The Construction of Rulership in Mexica History.* University of Arizona Press, Tucson.

1998 The Aztec Triple Alliance: A Postconquest Tradition. In *Native Traditions in the Postconquest World* (Elizabeth Hill Boone and Tom Cummins, eds.), 233–264. Dumbarton Oaks Research Library and Collection, Washington, D.C.

Glass, John
1964 *Catálogo de la colección códices.* Museo Nacional de Antropología, Instituto Nacional de Antropólogía e Historia, México, D.F.

1975 Survey of Native Middle American Pictorial Manuscripts. In *Handbook of Middle American Indians* (Robert Wauchope, gen. ed. and Howard F. Cline, vol. ed.), 14: 3–81. University of Texas Press, Austin.

Gómez de Orosco, Federico
n.d. Mapa de Cuauhtinchan No. 4. Manuscript on file, Museo Nacional de Antropología. México, D.F.

Graulich, Michel
1997 *Myths of Ancient Mexico* (Bernard Ortiz de Montellano and Thelma Ortiz de Montellano, trans.). University of Oklahoma Press, Norman.

Gruzinski, Serge
1992 *Painting the Conquest: The Mexican Indians and the European Renaissance* (Deke Dusinberre, trans.). Flammarion, Paris.

1993 *The Conquest of Mexico: The Incorporation of Indian Societies into the Western World, 16th–18th Centuries* (Eileen Corrigan, trans.). Polity Press, Cambridge, England.

1994 *L'Aigle et la sibylle: Fresques indiennes du Mexique.* Imprimerie nationale, Paris.

1998 Mutilated Memory: Reconstruction of the Past and Mechanisms of Memory among Seventeenth-Century Otomís. In *Colonial Spanish America: A Documentary History* (Ken Mills and William Taylor, eds.), 214–226. Scholarly Resources, Wilmington, DE.

2002 *The Mestizo Mind: The Intellectual Dynamics of Colonization and Globalization* (Deke Dusinberre, trans.). Routledge, New York.

Haskett, Robert

1991 *Indigenous Rulers: An Ethnohistory of Town Government in Colonial Cuernavaca.* University of New Mexico Press, Albuquerque.

2005 *Visions of Paradise: Primordial Titles and Mesoamerican History in Cuernavaca.* University of Oklahoma Press, Norman.

Hellbom, Anna-Britta

1967 *La participación cultural de las mujeres: Indias y mestizas en el México precortesiano y postrevolucionario.* Ethnographical Museum, Stockholm.

Heyden, Doris

1981 Caves, Gods, and Myths: World-View and Planning in Teotihuacan. In *Mesoamerican Sites and World-Views* (Elizabeth Benson, ed.), 1–40. Dumbarton Oaks Research Library and Collection, Washington, D.C.

2000 From Teotihuacan to Tenochtitlan: City Planning, Caves, and Streams of Red and Blue Waters. In *Mesoamerica's Classic Heritage: From Teotihuacan to the Aztecs* (David Carrasco, Lindsay Jones, and Scott Sessions, eds.), 165–184. University Press of Colorado, Boulder.

2005 Rites of Passage and Other Ceremonies in Caves. In *The Maw of the Earth Monster: Mesoamerican Ritual Cave Use* (James Brady and Keith Prufer, eds.), 21–34. University of Texas Press, Austin.

Himmerich y Valencia, Robert

1992 *The Encomenderos of New Spain 1521–1555.* University of Texas Press, Austin.

Hirschberg, Julia

n.d. A Social History of Puebla de los Angeles 1531–1560. Ph.D. dissertation, Department of History, University of Michigan, Ann Arbor, 1976.

Horn, Rebecca

1997 *Postconquest Coyoacan: Nahua-Spanish Relations in Central Mexico, 1519–1650.* Stanford University Press, Stanford, CA.

Ingold, Tim

1993 The Temporality of the Landscape. *World Archaeology* 25 (2): 152–174.

Kagan, Richard

2000 *Urban Images of the Hispanic World, 1493–1793.* Yale University Press, New Haven and London.

Karttunen, Frances

1983 *An Analytical Dictionary of Nahuatl.* University of Texas Press, Austin.

Karttunen, Frances, and James Lockhart

1987 *The Art of Nahuatl Speech: The Bancroft Dialogues.* Latin American Center Publications, University of California, Los Angeles.

Kellogg, Susan, and Matthew Restall (eds.)

1998 *Dead Giveaways: Indigenous Testaments of Colonial Mesoamerica and the Andes.* University of Utah Press, Salt Lake City.

Kirchhoff, Paul

1947 La Historia Tolteca-Chichimeca: Un estudio histórico-sociológico. In *Historia Tolteca-Chichimeca: Anales de Quauhtinchan* (Heinrich Berlin and Silvia Rendón, trans.), xix–lxiv. Antigua librería Robredo de José Porrúa e hijos, México, D.F.

1958 La ruta de los Tolteca-Chichimeca entre Tula y Cholula. *Miscellanea Paul Rivet, octogenario dicata*, 485–494. Universidad Nacional Autónoma de México, México, D.F.

1961 Das Toltekenreich und sein Untergang. *Saeculum* 12: 248–265.

Klein, Cecelia F.

1988 Rethinking Cihuacoatl: Aztec Political Imagery of the Conquered Woman. In *Smoke and Mist: Mesoamerican Studies in Memory of Thelma D. Sullivan* (J. K. Josserand and Karen Dakin, eds.): 237–277. BAR, Oxford.

1995 Wild Woman in Colonial Mexico: An Encounter of European and Aztec Concepts of the Other. In *Reframing the Renaissance: Visual Culture in Europe and Latin America, 1450–1650* (Claire Farago, ed.), 245–265. Yale University Press, New Haven.

2002 Not Like Us and All the Same: Pre-Columbian Art History and the Construction of the Nonwest. *Res 42*: 131–138.

Klein, Cecelia F. (ed.)

2001 *Gender in Pre-Hispanic America.* Dumbarton Oaks Research Library and Collection, Washington, D.C.

Klor de Alva, Jorge

1989 Language, Politics and Translation: Colonial Discourse and Classical Nahuatl in New Spain. In *The Art of Translation: Voices from the Field* (Roseanna Warren, ed.), 143–162. Northeastern University Press, Boston.

Klor de Alva, Jorge, H. B. Nicholson, and Eloise Quiñones Keber (eds.)

1988 *The Work of Bernardino de Sahagún: Pioneer Ethnographer of Sixteenth-Century Aztec Mexico.* Institute for Mesoamerican Studies at University of Albany, State University of New York and University of Texas Press, Albany and Austin.

Kubler, George

1948 *Mexican Architecture of the Sixteenth Century.* Yale University Press, New Haven.

1964 On the Colonial Extinction of the Motifs of Pre-Columbian Art. In *Essays in Pre-Columbian Art and Archaeology* (Samuel K. Lothrop, ed.), 14–34. Harvard University Press, Cambridge.

Kuhn, Annette

2000 A Journey Through Memory. In *Memory and Methodology* (Susannah Radstone, ed.), 179–196. Berg, Oxford and New York.

LaCapra, Dominick

1998 *History and Memory after Auschwitz.* Cornell University Press, Ithaca.

Lavrin, Asunción (ed.)

1989 *Sexuality and Marriage in Colonial Latin America.* University of Nebraska Press, Lincoln.

Leibsohn, Dana

1992 Nahua Writing After the Conquest: Pictures, Texts and Translations in the *Historia Tolteca-Chichimeca.* In *Five Centuries of Mexican History/Cinco Siglos de Historia de México* (Virginia Güeda and Jaime Rodríguez O., eds.), 64–76. Dr. José María Luis Mora, México, D.F.

1994 Primers for Memory: Cartographic Histories and Nahua Identity. In *Writing Without Words: Alternative Literacies in Mesoamerica and the Andes* (Elizabeth Hill Boone and Walter Mignolo, eds.), 161–188. Duke University Press, Durham.

1996 Mapping Metaphors: Conquest, Territory and Legal Arenas in New Spain. *Journal of Medieval and Early Modern Studies* 26: 499–523.

2000 Mapping after the Letter: Graphology and Indigenous Cartography in New Spain. In *The Language Encounter in the Americas, 1492–1800* (Edward Gray and Norman Fiering, eds.), 119–152. Berghan Books, Providence, RI.

n.d. The *Historia Tolteca-Chichimeca:* Recollecting Identity in a Nahua Manuscript. Ph.D. dissertation, Department of Art History, University of California, Los Angeles, 1993.

León-Portilla, Miguel

1963 *Aztec Thought and Culture: A Study of the Ancient Nahuatl Mind* (Jack Emory Davis, trans.). University of Oklahoma Press, Norman.

1980 *Toltecáyotl: Aspectos de la cultura náhuatl.* Fondo de Cultura Económica, México, D.F.

Lind, Michael

n.d. La gran cuadra de la ciudad: El gobierno Prehispánico de Cholula. A paper presented at the Mesa Redonda of the Sociedad Mexicana de Antropología, Mexico, 2007.

Lockhart, James

1982 Views of Corporate Self and History in Some Valley of Mexico Towns: Late Seventeenth and Eighteenth Centuries. In *The Inca and Aztec States 1400–1800* (George Collier, Renato Rosaldo, and John Wirth, eds.), 367–393. Academic Press, New York.

1991 *Nahuas and Spaniards: Postconquest Central Mexican History and Philology.* Stanford University Press and UCLA Latin American Center, Stanford and Los Angeles.

1992 *The Nahuas after the Conquest: A Social and Cultural History of the Indians of Central Mexico, Sixteenth through Eighteenth Centuries.* Stanford University Press, Stanford, CA.

1994 Sightings: Initial Nahua Reactions to Spanish Culture. In *Implicit Understandings: Observing, Reporting, and Reflecting on the Encounters Between Europeans and Other Peoples in the Early Modern Era* (Stuart B. Schwartz, ed.), 218–248. Cambridge University Press, Cambridge.

Lockhart, James (trans. and ed.)

1993 *We People Here: Nahuatl Accounts of the Conquest of Mexico.* University of California Press, Berkeley and Los Angeles.

Lockhart, James, Susan Schroeder, and Doris Namala

2006 *Annals of His Time: Don Domingo de San Antón Muñón Chimalpahin Quauhtlehuanitzin.* Stanford University Press, Stanford, CA.

López-Austín, Alfredo

1985 La construcción de la memoria. In *La memoria y el olvido,* 75–79. Instituto Nacional de Antropología e Historia, México, D.F.

Magaloni Kerpel, Diana

2003 Imagenes de la conquista de México en los codices del siglo XVI. Una lectura de su contenido simbólico. *Anales del Instituto de Investigaciones Estéticas* 25 (82): 5–45.

Manzanilla, Linda

2000 The Construction of the Underworld in Central Mexico. In *Mesoamerica's Classic Heritage: From Teotihuacan to the Aztecs* (David Carrasco, Lindsay Jones, and Scott Sessions, eds.), 87–116. University Press of Colorado, Boulder.

Marcus, Joyce

1992 *Mesoamerican Writing Systems: Propaganda, Myth, and History in Four Ancient Civilizations.* Princeton University Press, Princeton.

2003 Review of *Stories in Red and Black: Pictorial Histories of the Aztec and Mixtec* by Elizabeth Hill Boone. *Latin American Antiquity* 14 (3): 356–357.

Marin, Louis

1990 *Utopics: The Semiological Play of Textual Spaces* (Robert A. Vollarth, trans.) Humanities Press International, Atlantic Highlands, NJ.

Martínez, Hildeberto

1984 *Tepeaca en el siglo XVI: Tenencia de la tierra y organización de un señorío.* Casa Chata, México, D.F.

Martínez Marin, Carlos
1963 El Códice No. 2 de Cuauhtinchan. *Boletín del Instituto Nacional de Antropología e Historia* 13: 1–3.

Mateos Higuera, Salvador
1946a Lienzo de Cuauhtinchan No. 1. *Tlalocan* 2: 175–177.

1946b Lienzo de Cuauhtinchan No. 2. *Tlalocan* 2: 177–179.

1947a Mapa de Cuauhtinchan No. 3. *Tlalocan* 2: 255–256.

1947b Mapa de Cuauhtinchan No. 4. *Tlalocan* 2: 256–257.

McCafferty, Geoffrey
2000 Tollan Cholollan and the Legacy of Legitimacy During the Classic-Postclassic Transition. In *Mesoamerica's Classic Heritage: From Teotihuacan to the Aztecs* (David Carrasco, Lindsay Jones, and Scott Sessions, eds.), 341–67. University Press of Colorado, Boulder.

2001 Mountain of Heaven, Mountain of Earth: The Great Pyramid of Cholula as Sacred Landscape. In *Landscape and Power in Ancient Mesoamerica* (Rex Koontz, Kathryn Reese-Taylor, and Annabeth Headrick, eds.), 279–316. Westview Press, Boulder.

Merwick, Donna
1997 The Suicide of a Notary: Language, Personal Identity, and Conquest in Colonial New York. In *Through a Glass Darkly: Reflections on Personal Identity in Early America* (Ronald Hoffman, Mechal Sobel and Fredrika Teute, eds.), 122–153. University of North Carolina Press, Chapel Hill.

1999 *Death of a Notary: Conquest and Change in Colonial New York.* Cornell University Press, Ithaca.

Messick, Brinkley
1993 *The Calligraphic State.* University of California Press, Berkeley and Los Angeles.

Mignolo, Walter
1989 Literacy and Colonization: The New World Experience. In *1492–1992: Re/Discovering Colonial Writing* (René Jara and Nicholas Spadaccini, eds.), 51–96. University of Minnesota Press, Minneapolis.

1992 On the Colonization of Amerindian Languages and Memories: Renaissance Theories of Writing and the Discontinuity of the Classical Tradition. *Comparative Studies in Society and History* 34: 301–330.

Mignolo, Walter
1994 Signs and Their Transmission: The Question of the Book in the New World. In *Writing Without Words: Alternative Literacies in Mesoamerica and the Andes* (Elizabeth Hill Boone and Walter Mignolo, eds.), 220–270. Duke University Press, Durham.

1995 *The Darker Side of the Renaissance: Literacy, Territoriality, and Colonization.* University of Michigan Press, Ann Arbor.

2000 *Local Histories/Global Designs: Coloniality, Subaltern Knowledges, and Border Thinking.* Princeton University Press, Princeton.

Miller, Arthur G.
1991 Transformations of Time and Space: Oaxaca, Mexico, Circa 1500–1700. In *Images of Memory: On Remembering and Representation* (Susanne Küchler and Walter Melion, eds.), 141–175. Smithsonian Institution Press, Washington, D.C.

Mitchell, W. J. T.
1996 What Do Pictures Really Want? *October* 77: 711–782.

Miyar, Carlos Alonso
1928 La Pirámide de Tepalcayo. *Memoriales de la Sociedad Científica "Antonio Alzate"* 49: 201–207.

Monaghan, John
1990 Performance and the Structure of the Mixtec Codices. *Ancient Mesoamerica* 1: 133–140.

Mundy, Barbara

1996 *The Mapping of New Spain: Indigenous Cartography and the Maps of the Relaciones Geográficas*. University of Chicago Press, Chicago.

Navarrete, Federico

1999 Las fuentes indígenas más allá de la dicotomía entre historia y mito. *Estudios de Cultura Nahuatl* 30: 231–256.

2000 The Path from Aztlan to Mexico: On Visual Narration in Mesoamerican Codices. *Res* 37: 31–48.

Neisser, Ulric, and Robyn Fivush (eds.)

1994 *The Remembering Self: Construction and Accuracy in the Self-Narrative*. Cambridge University Press, Cambridge.

Nicholson, Henry B.

1963 The Concept of History in Prehispanic Mesoamerica. In *VIe Congrés International des Sciences Anthropologiques et Ethnologiques, Paris, 30 Juillot–6 Août, 1960*, 2: 455. Musée de l'Homme, Paris.

1971 Prehispanic Central Mexican Historiography. In *Investigaciones contemporáneas sobre historia de México: Memorias de la tercer reunión de historiadores mexicanos y norteamericanos*, 38–81. Universidad Nacional Autónoma de México, El Colegio de México, and University of Texas Press, México, D.F. and Austin.

Oettinger, Marion

1983 *Lienzos coloniales: Una exposición de pinturas de terrenos comunales de México (siglos XVII–XIX)*. Universidad Nacional Autónoma de México, México, D.F.

Olivera, Mercedes

1976 El despotismo tributario en la región de Cuauhtinchan-Tepeaca. In *Estratificación social en la Mesoamérica prehispánica* (Pedro Carrasco and Johanna Broda, eds.), 181–206. CISINAH, México, D.F.

1978 *Pillis y macehuales: Las formaciones sociales y los modos de producción de Tecali del siglo XII al XVI*. Casa Chata, México, D.F.

Orozco, Enrique

1892 Fragmentos de un manuscrito inédito existente en Cuauhtinchan (E. de Puebla) communicados por el Sr. socio correspondiente. *Revista Científica y Bibliográfica de la Sociedad Científica Antonio Alzate* 5: 27–37.

Parmenter, Ross

1982 *Four Lienzos of the Coixtlahuaca Valley*. Studies in Pre-Columbian Art and Archaeology 26. Dumbarton Oaks Research Library and Collection, Washington, D.C.

Passerini, Luisa

1987 *Fascism and Popular Memory: The Cultural Experience of the Turin Working Class*. Cambridge University Press, Cambridge.

2007 *Memory and Utopia: The Primacy of Intersubjectivity*. Equinox, London.

Pasztory, Esther

1983 *Aztec Art*. Abrams, New York.

Peterson, Jeanette

1988 The *Florentine Codex* Imagery and the Colonial *Tlacuilo*. In *The Work of Bernardino de Sahagún: Pioneer Ethnographer of Sixteenth-Century Aztec Mexico* (Jorge Klor de Alva, H. B. Nicholson, and Eloise Quiñones Keber, eds.), 273–293. Institute for Mesoamerican Studies at University of Albany, State University of New York and University of Texas Press, Albany and Austin.

1993 *Paradise Garden Murals of Malinalco: Utopia and Empire in Sixteenth-Century Mexico*. University of Texas Press, Austin.

2003 Identity and Mimetic Tradition in the Florentine Codex. In *Sahagún at 500: Essays on the Quincentenary of the Birth of Fr. Bernardino de Sahagún* (John Schwaller, ed.), 223–254. Academy of American Franciscan History, Berkeley, CA.

Pohl, John
1994 Mexican Codices, Maps, and Lienzos as Social Contracts. In *Writing Without Words: Alternative Literacies in Mesoamerica and the Andes* (Elizabeth Hill Boone and Walter Mignolo, eds.), 137–160. Duke University Press, Durham.

2003 Royal Marriage and Confederacy Building among the Eastern Nahuas, Mixtecs and Zapotecs. In *The Post Classic Mesoamerican World* (Michael E. Smith and Frances Berdan, eds.), 243–248. University of Utah Press, Salt Lake City.

Pratt, Mary Louise
1994 Transculturation and Autoethnography: Peru 1615/1980. In *Colonial Discourse, Postcolonial Theory* (Francis Barker, Peter Hulme, and Margaret Iverson, eds.), 24–46. Manchester University Press, Manchester.

Prem, Hanns
1978 *Milpa y hacienda: Tenencia de la tierra indígena y española en la cuenca del Alto Atoyac, Puebla, México (1520–1560).* Franz Steiner Verlag, Wiesbaden.

1997 Límites de reinos mexicanos tempranos: Qué forma de realidad representan? In *Códices y documentos sobre México: Segundo Simposio* (Salvador Rueda Smithers, Constanza Vega Sosa, and Rodrigo Martínez Baracs, eds.), I: 475–504. Instituto Nacional de Antropología e Historia, México, D.F.

Quilter, Jeffrey
2001 Review of *Stories in Red and Black, Maya Art and Architecture, Pre-Columbian Art,* and *Teotihuacan: An Experiment in Living.* In *Art Bulletin* 83 (4): 762–65.

2006 Introduction. In *A Pre-Columbian World* (Jeffrey Quilter and Mary Miller, eds.), 7–19. Dumbarton Oaks Research Library and Collection, Washington, D.C.

Rabasa, José
2000 *Writing Violence on the Northern Frontier: The Historiography of Sixteenth-century New Mexico and Florida and the Legacy of Conquest.* Duke University Press, Durham.

Rappaport, Joanne
1990 *The Politics of Memory: Native Historical Interpretation in the Colombian Andes.* Cambridge University Press, Cambridge.

1994 Object and Alphabet: Andean Indians and Documents in the Colonial Period. In *Writing Without Words: Alternative Literacies in Mesoamerica and the Andes* (Elizabeth Hill Boone and Walter Mignolo, eds.), 271–292. Duke University Press, Durham.

2002 Imagining Andean Colonial Culture. *Ethnohistory* 49 (3): 687–701.

Restall, Matthew
2003 A History of the New Philology and the New Philology in History. *Latin American Research Review* 38 (1): 113–134.

Restall, Matthew, Lisa Sousa, and Kevin Terraciano (eds.)
2005 *Mesoamerican Voices: Native-Language Writings from Colonial Mexico, Oaxaca, Yucatan and Guatemala.* Cambridge University Press, Cambridge and New York.

Reyes García, Luis
1972 Ordenanzas para el gobierno de Cuauhtinchan, año 1559. *Estudios de Cultura Nahuatl* 10: 245–313.

1974 Catálogo de documentos sobre Cuauhtinchan, Puebla. *Comunicaciones: Proyecto Puebla Tlaxcala Deutsche Forschungsgemeinschaft* 10: 31–51.

1977 *Cuauhtinchan del siglo XII al XVI: Formación y desarrollo histórico de un señorío prehispánico.* Franz Steiner Verlag, Wiesbaden.

1988 *Documentos sobre tierras y señoríos de Cuauhtinchan.* Fondo de Cultura Económica, México, D.F.

Reyes Valerio, Constantino
1976 Una pintura indígena en Cuauhtinchan. *Boletín del Instituto Nacional de Antropología e Historia* 29: 1–6.

1989 *El pintor de conventos: Los murales del siglo XVI en la Nueva España.* Instituto Nacional de Antropología e Historia, México, D.F.

Robertson, Donald
1959 *Mexican Manuscript Painting of the Early Colonial Period.* Yale University Press, New Haven.

Roman Castellon Huerta, Blas
2001 Chicomoztoc. In *Oxford Encyclopedia of Mesoamerican Cultures* (David Carrasco, ed.), 1: 189–190. Oxford University Press, Oxford and New York.

Ruiz Medrano, Ethelia
2007 The Historical Context of the *Mapa de Cuauhtinchan No. 2.* In *Cave, City, and Eagle's Nest: An Interpretive Journey Through the Mapa de Cuauhtinchan No. 2* (David Carrasco and Scott Sessions, eds.), 91–120. University of New Mexico Press, Albuquerque.

Russo, Alessandra
2005 *El realismo circular: Tierras, espacios y paisajes de la cartografía indígena novo-hispana, siglos XVI y XVII.* Instituto de Investigaciones Estéticas, Universidad Nacional Autónoma de México, México, D.F.

Salomon, Frank
1982 Chronicles of the Impossible: Notes on Three Peruvian Indigenous Historians. In *From Oral to Written Expression: Native Andean Chronicles of the Early Colonial Period* (Rolena Adorno, ed.), 9–40. Foreign and Comparative Studies, Latin American Series 4. Maxwell School of Citizenship and Public Affairs, Syracuse University, Syracuse, NY.

1998 Collquiri's Dam: The Colonial Re-Voicing of an Appeal to the Archaic. In *Native Traditions in the Postconquest World* (Elizabeth Hill Boone and Tom Cummins, eds.), 265–294. Dumbarton Oaks Research Library and Collection, Washington, D.C.

Sandstrom, Alan
1991 *Corn is Our Blood: Culture and Ethnic Identity in a Contemporary Aztec Indian Village.* University of Oklahoma Press, Norman.

Scharlau, Birgit
1986 Altindianische Oralkultur zwischen Bilderschrift und Alphabet. In *Qellqay: Mündliche Kultur und Schrifttradition bei Indianern Lateinamerikas* (Birgit Scharlau and Mark Münzel, eds.), 13–154. Campus Verlag, Frankfurt.

Schroeder, Susan
1991 *Chimalpahin and the Kingdoms of Chalco.* University of Arizona Press, Tucson.

Schroeder, Susan, Stephanie Wood, and Robert Haskett (eds.)
1997 *Indian Women of Colonial Mexico.* University of Oklahoma Press, Norman.

Schwaller, John (ed.)
2003 *Sahagún at 500: Essays on the Quincentenary of the Birth of Fr. Bernardino de Sahagún.* Academy of American Franciscan History, Berkeley, CA.

Sigal, Peter
2007 Queer Nahuatl: Sahagún's Faggots and Sodomites, Lesbians and Hermaphrodies. *Ethnohistory* 54 (1): 9–34.

Sigal, Peter (ed.)
2003 *Infamous Desire: Male Homosexuality in Colonial Latin America.* Chicago University Press, Chicago.

Simons, Bente Bittmann
1968 *Los mapas de Cuauhtinchan y la Historia Tolteca-Chichimeca.* Instituto Nacional de Antropología e Historia, México, D.F.

Smail, Daniel Lord
1999 *Imaginary Cartographies: Possession and Identity in Late Medieval Marseille.* Cornell University Press, Ithaca.

Smith, Mary Elizabeth
1973 *Picture Writing from Ancient Southern Mexico.* University of Oklahoma Press, Norman.

1994 Why the Second Codex Selden was Painted. In *Caciques and their People: A Volume in Honor of Ronald Spores* (Joyce Marcus and Judith Zeitlin, eds.), 111–142. University of Michigan Press, Ann Arbor.

Solís, Felipe (ed.)
2004 *The Aztec Empire.* Guggenheim Museum Publications, New York.

Sousa, Lisa
2007 Tying the Knot: Nahua Nuptials in Colonial Mexico. In *Religion in New Spain* (Susan Schroeder and Stafford Poole, eds.), 33–45. University of New Mexico Press, Albuquerque.

n.d. Women in Native Societies and Cultures of Colonial Mexico. Ph.D. dissertation, Department of History, University of California, Los Angeles, 1998.

Spiegel, Gabrielle
2002 Memory and History: Liturgical Time and Historical Time. *History and Theory* 41: 149–162.

Stock, Brian
1984 *The Implications of Literacy: Written Language and Models of Interpretation in the Eleventh and Twelfth Centuries.* Princeton University Press, Princeton.

Stone, Cynthia
2004 *In Place of Gods and Kings: Authorship and Identity in the Relación de Michoacán.* University of Oklahoma Press, Norman.

Strathern, Marilyn
1999 The Aesthetics of Substance. In *Property, Substance and Effect: Anthropological Essays on Persons and Things,* 45–63. Athlone Press, London.

Straulino, Marina
2007 The Conservation and Digital Restoration of the *Mapa de Cuauhtinchan No. 2.* In *Cave, City, and Eagle's Nest: An Interpretive Journey Through the Mapa de Cuauhtinchan No. 2* (David Carrasco and Scott Sessions, eds.), 49–80. University of New Mexico Press, Albuquerque.

Swanton, Michael
2001 El texto popoloca de la *Historia Tolteca-Chichimeca. Relaciones* 22 (86): 115–140.

Taussig, Michael
1993 *Mimesis and Alterity: A Particular History of the Senses.* Routledge, New York.

2003 Miasma. In *Culture and Waste: The Creation and Destruction of Value* (Gay Hawkins and Stephen Muecke, eds.), 9–23. Rowman and Littlefield, Lanham, MD.

Terraciano, Kevin
2001 *The Mixtecs of Colonial Oaxaca: Ñudzahui History, Sixteenth through Eighteenth Centuries.* Stanford University Press, Stanford, CA.

Thurner, Mark, and Andrés Guerrero (eds.)
2003 *After Spanish Rule: Postcolonial Predicaments of the Americas.* Duke University Press, Durham.

Tomasch, Sylvia, and Sealy Gilles (eds.)
1998 *Text and Territory: Geographical Imagination in the European Middle Ages.* University of Pennsylvania Press, Philadelphia.

Tomlinson, Gary
1996 Unlearning the Aztec Cantares
(Preliminaries to a Postcolonial History).
In *Subject and Object in Renaissance
Culture* (Margreta de Grazia, Peter
Stallybrass, and Maureen Quilligan, eds.),
260–286. Cambridge University Press,
Cambridge.

Townsend, Richard
1992a *The Aztecs.* Thames and Hudson,
London.

Townsend, Richard (ed.)
1992b *The Ancient Americas: Art from
Sacred Landscapes.* Prestel Verlag and
the Art Institute of Chicago, Munich
and Chicago.

Umberger, Emily
1981 The Structure of Aztec History.
Archaeoastronomy 4: 10–17.

Urton, Gary
1990 *The History of a Myth:
Pacariqtambo and the Origin of the Inkas.*
University of Texas Press, Austin.

Wake, Eleanor
2007 The Serpent Road: Iconic
Encodings and the Historical Narrative
of *Mapa de Cuauhtinchan No. 2.*
In *Cave, City, and Eagle's Nest: An
Interpretive Journey through the Mapa de
Cuauhtinchan No. 2* (David Carrasco and
Scott Sessions, eds.), 205–254. University
of New Mexico Press, Albuquerque.

White, Hayden
1978 *Tropics of Discourse.* Johns Hopkins
University Press, Baltimore, MD.

1981 The Value of Narrativity in the
Representation of Reality. In *On
Narrative* (W. J. T. Mitchell, ed.), 1–24.
University of Chicago Press, Chicago.

White, Luise
2000 Telling More: Lies, Secrets, and
History. *History and Theory* 39 (4): 11–22.

White, Richard
1991 *The Middle Ground: Indians, Empires
and Republics in the Great Lakes Region,
1650–1815.* Cambridge University Press,
Cambridge and New York.

Yoneda, Keiko
1981 *Los mapas de Cuauhtinchan y la
historia cartográfica prehispánica.* Archivo
General de la Nación, México, D.F.

1989 Lectura del Mapa de Cuauhtinchan
no. 3 y el contexto histórico en que se
produjo. In *Primer coloquio de documentos
pictográficos de tradición Nahuatl.*
(Carlos Martínez Marin, ed.), 29–39.
Universidad Nacional Autónoma de
México, México, D.F.

1994 *Cartografía y linderos en el mapa de
Cuauhtinchan no. 4: Estudio preliminar.*
Instituto Nacional de Antropología e
Historia, México, D.F.

1996 *Migraciones y conquistas: Descifre
global del Mapa de Cuauhtinchan no. 3.*
Instituto Nacional de Antropología
e Historia, México, D.F.

2000 Reflexiones sobre la organización
socio-política y la religión de los
Chichimecas (siglo XII). *Journal of
Intercultural Studies* 27: 184–193.

2001 La migración Chichimeca y su
cosmovisión (siglo XVII): Un estudio
acerca de Ehecatl, el dios del viento.
Journal of Intercultural Studies 28: 68–79.
2003 Los caminos de Chicomoztoc a
Chollan: Una migración Chichimeca
(siglo XII) [Segunda parte]. *Journal of
Intercultural Studies* 30: 178–227.

2005 *Mapa de Cuauhtinchan núm. 2.*
Miguel Angel Porrúa, CIESAS, México,
D.F.

Page numbers in italics refer to figures and plates.

jaguar. *See* warrior societies

land
  claims and disputes, 17, 19–20, 22, 27,
    36n2, 37n17, 62, 98, 171, 176
  documents, *63, 64, 67*
  indigenous holdings, 1, 20–21, 35, 36n5,
    37n7, 61n14
  perceptions of, 66–67, 79, 97–98, 104n1
  See also boundaries *and see under*
    writing, as mapping
landscape images, European-inspired,
  49, 84–85, *107, 108, 120, 121, 128,* 148,
  152–53, 154–55, 157, 158–59, 160–61,
  162–63
language
  and identity, 34, 45, 131
  visual representation of, 43, 50, *72–73,*
    89, 109, 110, 119–22 passim, *121, 143,*
    158–59, 167n16
  See also oral recitation
Libro de los Guardianes, 6, 26, 36n1, 37n13,
  100, 176, 177n11

macuahuitl, *37, 139, 140, 162–63*
Malinche, La (interpreter), 37n13
Malinche, La (Matlalcueye, mountain),
  49, 154–55, 173, 174, 175, 177n7, 177n9
malinalli, *132, 133, 134*
manuscripts
  Anales de Tepeaca, 100
  Annals of Tecamachalco, 26
  Codex Azcatitlan, 59n1
  Codex Borgia, 70
  Codex Mendoza, 5, 13, 59n2
  Codex Mexicanus, 59n1
  Codex Selden, 8, 100
  Codex Telleriano Remensis, 23
  Codex Vienna, 81
  Codex Xolotl, 13, 100
  Comentarios Reales de los Incas, 100
  Florentine Codex, 5, 23, 37n12, 52, 59n2,
    96
  Manuscript of 1546 and *Manuscript of*
    1553, 27, 36n2, 36n4–5, 37n17, 98, 176

  Manuscript of Huarochiri, 100
  Nueva corónica y buen gobierno, 5, 100,
    102
  Primeros Memoriales, 52
  Relación de Michoacan, 102
  See also maps, mapas
manuscript painting
  emendations
    in the *Historia, 82, 88–90, 89,* 109,
      136–37, 138, *158–59, 162, 164*
    and *Mapa Pintado, 72–73,* 170–71
    and *Mapas de Cuauhtinchan,* 172, 173,
      177n8
  scholarly interpretations of, 4–5, 6,
    12n5, 23–24. *See also under* history,
    modern interpretations
  style and technique
    in the *Historia,* 2, 25–26, 38, 44, 45,
      86–90, *108,* 111, 113, 118, 120,
      123–24, *128,* 131, 134, 138, 141, 144,
      148, *149–51, 153, 157, 161, 169*
    in other Cuauhtinchan paintings,
      170–71, 172, 173
Mapa Pintado en papel Europeo y aforrado
  en el Indiano, 6, 68, 70, *72–73,* 100,
  177n2
  collection history, 92n7, 100, 171
  as model for *Historia* paintings, 61n15,
    85–88, 145, 148, 153, 156, 168n27
  physical description, 170–71
Mapas de Cuauhtinchan, 6, 68, 92n2, 99,
  100, 102
  No. 1, 171–72, 177n3
  No. 2, 59n1, 172–73, 177n4–8
  No. 3, 174
  No. 4, 175, 177n9–10
Maps, mapas, 37n8, 67, 70, 86, 92n8
  Lienzo de Quauhquechollan, 13
  lienzos from Coixtlahuaca, 59n1
  Mapa de Sigüenza, 59n1, 100
  merced maps, *63, 64*
  Relaciones Geográficas, 67
  See also boundaries *and under* writing,
    as mapping
Mendieta, fray Geronimo de, 17, 36n3,
  59n1